Praise for *Tinderbox*

"I LOVED this book! It's a story that c [...]
Lynn brilliantly captures two decades of her adoption j[...]
With openness and grace, she shares her spiritual journey and hard-won wisdom. I recommend this book to families and mental health professionals struggling with children's extreme behaviors."

— Julia D. Rivera, Esquire, board director of Learning Disabilities Association Texas and cofounder of North TX FASD Network

"*Tinderbox* is a sacred gift: honest, vulnerable, humble, and hopeful. Whether your journey has included similar experiences to Lynn and her family or not, *Tinderbox* is a timely reminder of our shared humanity and our need to care for one another through both the challenges and celebrations of life. Lynn's writing is compelling, authentic, and inviting—I couldn't put it down once I started. I highly recommend that you create space for this book to become a part of your journey; you will be inspired, challenged, informed, and uplifted."

— Rev. Sharon Seyfarth Garner, United Methodist pastor, spiritual director, author, and founder of Belly of the Whale Spiritual Direction & Retreat

"Lynn Alsup is a gifted teacher and writer. She converts parenting challenges into soul wisdom and love, for herself and her girls. In *Tinderbox* she shares an inspiring story of family resiliency and equips the reader (through vital encouragement and resourcing) to surrender any illusion of how family life is 'supposed' to go and instead open to the breathtaking beauty of each child or family's unique path to wholeness."

— Courtney Pinkerton, MDiv, MPP, certified coach, Enneagram mentor, and author of *The Flourish Formula: An Overachiever's Guide to Slowing Down & Accomplishing More*

Tinderbox

One Family's Story of Adoption,
Neurodiversity, and Fierce Love

Lynn Alsup

SHE WRITES PRESS

Published 2023
Printed in the United States of America
Print ISBN: 978-1-64742-541-8
E-ISBN: 978-1-64742-542-5
Library of Congress Control Number: 2023904193

For information, address:
She Writes Press
1569 Solano Ave #546
Berkeley, CA 94707

Interior Design by Kiran Spees

She Writes Press is a division of SparkPoint Studio, LLC.

All company and/or product names may be trade names, logos, trademarks, and/or registered trademarks and are the property of their respective owners.

Names and identifying characteristics have been changed to protect the privacy of certain individuals.

Selections from the On Being with Krista Tippett episode "Lawrence Kushner: Kabbalah and Everyday Mysticism", first aired May 15, 2014, onbeing.org are reprinted here with permission from The Onbeing Project.

For Clare, Anna, and Lucy
—who light the path.

And always Jeff
—you and me at each day's end.

Telling our stories,
first to ourselves
and then to one another
and the world,
is a
revolutionary act.

Janet Mock

Contents

Author's Note

My beloved writing teachers, Sean Murphy and Tania Casselle, taught me that memoir is the study of memory. That maxim proved itself to me in the writing of this book. While I stayed true to my memory of the almost twenty years of my life recorded here, I realize we each have our own version of the past created by the complexity of our brains and emotions. The neuroscience of memory is fascinating. The scenes within these pages are recounted to the best of my memory or recreated as faithfully as possible to reflect each person's voice and experience at the time; I checked in along the way with the people who appear here to assure fidelity. I changed several names and created composites of just a few characters and experiences for the sake of privacy and the narrative itself. My journey of writing this story down has been one of profound insight and healing. My hope is the reader will find it so as well.

Gateway to Transformation

At almost thirteen, Clare stood with her shoulders nearly level with mine. She had surprising new curves at hip and breast. We walked our neighborhood hand in hand, her slim mahogany fingers entwined with my pale ones. Her long, dark braids swung in rhythm with our steps under the canopy of pecan trees as she described to me in detail her plan to kill herself one week later.

She'd just said with calm determination, "Life is too hard, Mom. I'm confused, embarrassed, and lonely all the time. This is the answer."

∼

After school that day, she had beelined to her attic bedroom with a book in hand. I'd been grateful. Space from her storms for a while. Anna and Lucy, Clare's little sisters, had sat with me at our long pine table pushing peanut butter into banana boats for a snack and telling me interesting bits of their second-grade and kindergarten days. Lucy had wiped sticky peanut butter from her lips with the back of her hand, smeared it across her tan cheek, and then pushed a tight, dark ringlet of hair out of her eyes. I smiled and shook my head; peanut butter was everywhere. Warm sun streamed in the west window beside us.

A few minutes later, the pounding of Clare descending the steps made me brace myself. I expected unhappy demands, dark shadows. But the door opened to out-of-control, heaving sobs.

I jumped up. "What's wrong? Are you hurt?"

"I can't. I can't. I can't," I heard, staccato between gasps.

I raised my voice. "I need to know if you're hurt, Clare."

Anna and Lucy came to my side. Lucy's small, brown hand clutched her blankie and my pant leg. Anna stood one step behind and peered out with wide, blue eyes. I looked Clare over: no blood, no bones askew, a routine meltdown. My mind pivoted to getting Anna and Lucy away to protect them from Clare's hurricane.

Taking Clare and Lucy's hands, I asked Anna to follow me to Lucy's bedroom. As the little girls sat on the floor, I pushed play on the *Free to Be You and Me* CD to drown out Clare's sobs. Pulled down coloring books and promised them Clare would be okay. Anna sat up tall, tucked loose strands of her dirty blond hair behind her ear, and handed crayons to Lucy as Clare and I walked onto the front porch and sat on our wicker love seat. Tears and snot poured down Clare's dark cheeks, her book still clutched in her hand. When she didn't calm after a short while, I pulled my phone from my pocket and called Jeff—my husband, Clare's dad—to come home.

Then I faced Clare, trying to summon my exhausted compassion. "What is it, babe?"

"I can't do it anymore. It's too hard," she stammered. Her seventh-grade year had been a return to the familiar chaos and confusion she spun at school and home. We'd gotten a diagnosis of anxiety disorder and ADHD that spring, but clearly something else was desperately wrong.

I put my arm around Clare, and she leaned her head on my shoulder. Heat radiated from her. And the Texas swelter was already building, though it was just the very beginning of May. I felt sweat beading up at the small of my back. The flurry of different shades of green on the trees along our street accosted me. Clare's heaving sobs continued. I thought of the day six years before when we'd brought baby Lucy home to Clare and Anna sitting on this love seat on our porch: our last adoption. Three daughters collected into our family with the hopes and joy that were the best of family beginnings.

Jeff pulled up in his green Explorer. His shoulders slumped as he emerged, shrinking him from his almost six-foot height. He looked like he'd been carrying a giant sack of feed on his family's farm. Weariness and furrows showed on his usually open, peaceful face. His green eyes locked with mine in alliance.

"I'm here," he said.

"Anna and Lucy are inside. Clare and I are going to take a walk."

"How many times, Clare?" Jeff looked at our daughter with that mix of sadness and frustration that had become too familiar. "How many times do I have to come home this way?"

Clare glared at him, and her tears dried up. His obvious anger shut her down. She'd turned away from me to Jeff's calm acceptance for support as she entered adolescence. That day she got a battlefield. *What was happening inside us all? Could we survive?* My hand reached for Clare's, and we stood up as Jeff walked through the front door. She tossed her book, *Thirteen Reasons Why,* onto the khaki cushion and walked with me. Cars whizzed past us at the corner, bass thumping out their windows. At a break in traffic, we crossed into a neighborhood of Tudor-style houses and huge pecan trees.

As we passed her best friend's house, I asked, "What's happening, Clare?"

"It's too hard, Mom. I can't do it anymore."

"Do what?"

"Get up every day. Go to school."

"But you like being with your friends. And writing stories and theater." I tried to remind her, convince her.

"Everyone is mean. They make fun of me." Clare had started to struggle in elementary school. We'd gotten accommodations and supports in place at yet another new school over the last year, but it wasn't enough. I tried to just listen and not say things I'd said a hundred times before. She talked about boys and her math teacher, with whom she fought daily.

She stopped and her deep-brown eyes peered into me. "I'm done, Mom."

A chill went through me. "What do you mean?"

"I want to die."

I was speechless, sucker-punched. Through all our years of struggle, she'd never said that before. My professional social-worker self woke up and kept her talking. I asked if she had a plan. She said she'd use a knife, in her room, in one week, after bedtime. Fire burned in my belly, and my chest tightened.

"What about us, your family?" I fought to stay calm, but my voice quickened. "Can you imagine what that would do to us? To Anna and Lucy?"

As Clare started walking again, she assured me, "Life would be so much better for you all without me."

I followed her around a corner as she turned back toward our home. Purple irises stood tall, and the creek murmured a block away. Clare had shifted to serene, entered the eye of the storm. My heartbeat hammered in the eerie calm. No matter what I said, she didn't falter. Suicide was her best option. We made our way back up the steps to our house, and Clare picked up her book. She said reading it had broken her open and given her a solution. In the book, Hannah Baker had the courage to end it. Now she did, too. Clare walked inside and ambled back up to her room.

"Mommy?" Anna came out to check on us, eyes questioning, her cheeks their perpetual pink. "Is Clare okay now?"

"She's okay," I lied. "She's going to rest in her room for a while."

I looked over at Jeff who was picking up the detritus of our banana boat snack and tried to convey desperation without the girls noticing. Then I switched to autopilot. I knew Clare would stay calm for a while. We'd get the littles fed and to bed. And then face our terror.

Manman Clare

Twelve years earlier, Clare had embedded her tiny, one-year-old body in her second mother's lap. Nanotte was first; Karen was second; I was third. I sat behind Clare and Karen. I imagined Clare's first mother as a grown-up version of her: Haitian with dark-brown, velvet skin, almond eyes, tight russet curls, and a blazing smile whenever it appeared. Don, Karen's husband, Clare's dad for the last year, had just said goodbye to her on the tarmac in Cap-Haïtien, Haiti. His six-five, hardworking frame had engulfed her twenty-pound self. He'd kissed her, told her he loved her, and brushed tears off his cheeks with big, rough hands as a stream of sweat flowed from his temples to his chin in the July Caribbean heat.

Clare stared from Karen's lap out the plane window at Don. He shrank, diminished by the goodbye, and we taxied away. Clare's face morphed from blank seriousness as she gauged the situation through wrinkled confusion and curiosity to wide-eyed panic and O-mouth screams as the plane lifted off the ground.

I reached over to her. "It's okay, babe. Want your octopus?" The toy octopus's arms crinkled as I tried to hand him to her. As I tried to act like her mother.

"Clare, you hush now," Karen said and pushed her pacifier into her mouth. It fell right back out, sliming Karen's blue blouse with slobber. I rubbed Clare's arm and tried to soothe her. And to make the screaming stop. It tightened my muscles and hollowed out my breath. I clenched my teeth to dam my fear in the vast waters outside my awareness. I smiled and cooed; she ignored me. We'd ridden our first plane together the December before, the two of us bright and nervy with excitement, attached and attuned to each other's feelings. But that was before I left her, like her first mother.

My dad sat next to me looking out the window. He'd scored Clare's American visa to bring her home two days before, the miracle Jeff and I had prayed for daily over the past year.

Don and Karen worked for Missionary Flights International in Haiti, and we were flying on their converted cargo plane. Not pressurized, the DC-3 flew at only six thousand feet; we saw the whitecaps of the sea below us. It enthralled my father.

"Look, Lynn, the Bahamas." He pointed east.

"It's beautiful, Dad." I took his hand and leaned over to look at the deep blue of the ocean.

The echoey cabin held eight rows of four oversized, reclining seats with a deep open space for cargo behind the cockpit—a perfect place for our thirteen-month-old toddler to play on the floor. Once Karen had calmed Clare, she sat there on a blanket, teething on the triangle arm of her octopus. Her ever-present pacifier bobbed on its pink teddy bear clip on her shirt. Two more hours to West Palm Beach, Florida, en route to home in Waco, Texas.

~

Jeff and I had driven into Waco four years earlier to join a nonprofit and church, Jeff pulling a U-Haul behind his red Jeep Cherokee, and I in my silver shoebox Volvo 240. After three years of newlywed, graduate-student life in Los Angeles and then Austin, we had let roots sink into the Blackland Prairie of Central Texas. We believed in a Christian God with special concern for people on the margins of society, so we lived and worked in an area forsaken to poverty and all it bred. Generosity, community, laughter, and resilience alongside violence, substance abuse, and defeat. I'd hung my crisp, new Licensed Master Social Worker certificate on the wall as Social Services Director of the nonprofit, and Jeff his Master of Marital and Family Therapy diploma as Pastoral Care Director. We set up home, worked, and dreamed of having a baby.

Almost a year later (still no baby), we took our first work trip—our introduction to Haiti. The sultry Caribbean air rushed in as the plane door opened. Our line of twelve White, middle-class young adults streamed into a sea of dark faces in the airport. We gathered our bags inside the open-air building to a swirl of Haitian Creole, a hybrid of African dialects and French. Outside, our Haitian leader corralled us onto a flatbed truck rigged with splintery wooden benches and rebar railings, and we began a three-hour, dusty drive to the village of Ferrier.

I sat wide-eyed as we left the sparkling blue, open expanse of the sea and entered Cap-Haïtien, Haiti's second largest city. Cars honked, diesel engines revved, and people *tap-tapped* the sides of carnival-painted pickup truck taxis. Chickens huddled on laps squawked above the din. Bicycles and motorcycles skidded past us on the narrow roads shared with braying donkeys carrying sacks of charcoal into market. People called out *Blanc! Blanc!* to us, turning our white skin into a name. Each time the wind shifted, a pungent brew of animal droppings and rotting food replaced the scent of sea water and diesel fumes. As we emerged from town and entered the rolling countryside, brown with drought, I tucked my long skirt around my legs to keep the fierce sun from burning my pale skin. I laid my head back against the railing, pulled my hat down, and closed my eyes.

"You okay?" Jeff asked.

Opening my eyes, I took his hand. "Whirling in sights, sounds, and smells. I'm glad we're here."

"Me, too. I forgot how much I love to serve in a world so different from mine."

We reminisced about my high school work across the Haitian border in the Dominican Republic and his in Mexico City. We eased into silence as we bumped and jostled down the road in the hot wind, watching emaciated cows attempt to graze. I knew famine loomed. *What compelled these people in the poorest country in the Western Hemisphere to make it through to another day?*

I turned back to Jeff. "Living in Waco has already opened up the box I had God in. I think Haiti might explode it. If God answers prayers, rewards faithfulness and good works, why do so many people who love him suffer?"

"I don't know, babe. It's hard to see so much pain in the world and keep believing. I guess that's why it's called *faith*."

I nodded and closed my eyes again. I wasn't sure what was happening to my faith, but it was definitely changing. My mantra had been "God is sovereign." Now I wondered.

I leaned my head on Jeff's shoulder and said, "Our life is an adventure. I'm grateful we're in it together." I trusted Jeff to follow God anywhere, and he trusted that faith in me, too. That's what had brought us together. But how could I continue to believe in prayer and simple answers? I looked at Jeff through the swirling dust. He was already tan, even though it was only May. He seemed relaxed and happy. His legs stretched out into the center of the truck bed. We'd celebrate his thirtieth birthday a few days later. We had partnered with World Hunger Relief, Inc., to build a school and with Hope for the Hungry to repair their orphanage. As our talk melted again in the heat of the sun, I closed my eyes and slept a bit.

During our week in the village, we worked alongside Haitians digging trenches, laying cinder blocks, mending walls. Their strength put us to shame. We laughed and played soccer in dirt fields with the village kids until cactus thorns popped the balls we'd brought. The people's exuberance and hospitality enchanted us. We fell in love with Haiti. On our way back to Cap-Haïtien, I rode on top of twelve suitcases in the bed of a mini pickup as dirt gusted around me. It occurred to me that relationships drove the Haitians I'd met to keep going. Not wealth or possessions or even working for peace and justice. Staying alive for the sake of keeping the ones they loved alive. On that long dirt road, that seed lodged itself inside me and waited to grow.

The next summer, two years into trying to make a baby, we saw a fertility doctor. Over the fall, I took crazy-making drug therapy to increase progesterone, but no baby. Winter surgery revealed severe endometriosis, and a new medicine—also crazy-making—suppressed my estrogen to kill the endo, but no baby. Spring break took Jeff back to Haiti leading a team; I stayed home—the faint hope of pregnancy kept me from taking malaria medicine. One night I opened our front door and walked to our porch swing before bed. Darkness enfolded me. The metal on metal of the swing's chain scraped and creaked. A swell of feelings I usually trapped inside erupted.

I yelled at the sky, "Why won't you answer us? We've given our lives to you, and you won't even give us a baby!" My eyes burned as they filled. "Teenagers and drug addicts around me get pregnant all the time. What is wrong with you?" I wiped my nose on my sleeve and shoved the swing back with my foot. Hot streams ran down my face. "I hate you!" Three years of challenges and disappointments had pushed me over the edge: inner-city violence and systemic oppression, infertility, up-close abject poverty in Haiti and Calcutta. I felt the suffering in my bones. My concept of God wasn't big enough to hold those realities.

When I was spent, a gentle voice inside me said, "I'm sorry it hurts. I'm sad, too. Can we just be sad together?" The profound sense that I was not alone blanketed my fire. I didn't understand, but I unclenched my fists. *If God was sad and yet didn't swoop down to right things, had I misunderstood how he worked?* I let my shoulders fall and took a deep breath. I cried until I was empty.

Jeff brought me a painting from the Caribbean. A Haitian woman with full lips and deep-brown-into-black, serious eyes. Her elegant neck rose out of a bright pink shirt to her broad face, framed by a cobalt headwrap and gold hoop earrings. Her dark-brown arms reached up to steady a woven basket full of orange mangoes that rested like a living crown on her head. The background was the brilliant blue of the Caribbean sky. The painting held the reality of the Haiti we loved: strength and vibrant life.

Jeff also brought home an idea that he told me about over dinner. "Rebecca from Hope for the Hungry pointed out an American couple at the airport yesterday. They've lived in Haiti for twenty years and fostered children waiting for adoption. She thought we might want to talk to them."

I took a bite of beans and rice. "About adopting?"

His eyebrows raised. "Maybe?"

"I can't even imagine. I'm so tired." I pushed my food around.

"I thought you wanted to adopt."

"Not on the heels of three years of infertility. International adoptions are arduous. Maybe later."

"I just thought it might be a possibility." Jeff turned back to his dinner.

But one day soon after, driving my Volvo home from a workout at the YMCA, I recognized the front-porch voice inside me: *I want you to adopt from Haiti*. A settled clarity ran through my core; it felt familiar, my sense of being led. My insides quickened. At home, Jeff was in the kitchen making dinner.

I walked in and said, "I think we're supposed to adopt from Haiti."

He paused and focused his beautiful green eyes on me. When I held his gaze, he smiled and said, "Okay." Just like that. Jeff's signature openness and faith.

Over a few days, we grappled with questions: Could we take a child from her home and culture? Was it okay for a Black child to have White parents? What if I got pregnant? We wrestled with the injustice of our privilege and the poverty of Haiti caused by brutal slavery. Then we agreed theoretical arguments wouldn't help a particular child. We deferred to the still, small voice inside me. Maybe I knew it was our only way to create a family.

Rebecca connected us to Don and Karen, and we met them for lunch as they passed through Texas in June. They looked like well-worn grandparents. We listened to their stories about riding Harleys in Wisconsin in their younger days. When we said we felt called to adopt, they encouraged us, "Start a home study, and we'll see what happens when we get back to Haiti in a month." I felt pregnant: a bit nauseous, excited, and scared.

On July 8, 1999, my endometriosis again raging, I'd accomplished the herculean task of showering. My hair dripped rivers down my neck and shoulders as I talked with Stephanie, a Baylor University student who lived with us, and sat resting on the floor of her room. When the phone rang, Jeff bounded up the stairs two at a time with the cordless receiver in his hand, kicking aside the wallpaper we'd torn off the walls and left in the hallway. We looked up, surprised that his predictable calm had been disrupted.

"Rebecca's heard from Don and Karen in Haiti."

I thought I heard Jeff's heart pounding; I caught my breath. *But haven't they only been back a few days?* "Put her on speaker!"

"Lynn and I are both here, Rebecca," Jeff said.

"Don and Karen emailed, and they have a five-week-old, five-pound baby girl named Katiana living with them." I reached up to grab Jeff's hand as Rebecca continued, "She came to them last week."

Could she be *our* baby? Years of yearning and disappointment filled me. I'd thought I was pregnant so many times; I couldn't let myself believe.

Rebecca recounted the story. The day after Don and Karen had returned to Haiti, a Haitian man had carried an emaciated baby girl to an American medical clinic a half mile down the road from Don and Karen's home. He'd waited for hours in the heat on a wooden bench. I imagined his sagging shoulders and hollow eyes. Finally, he carried her into an exam room. I saw the open windows, cement floor, and metal table that stood in the middle like an island. A nurse named Rachel from Waco entered. She was doing a year's stint in Haiti at seventy years old after being widowed. Through a translator, the man said he needed someone to love and care for the baby. They'd lost her mother from a fever two weeks before. The baby had diarrhea and threw up everything she ate. Limp on the table, her rib cage and head overwhelmed her twiggy arms and legs. The father had no one to care for her while he worked to feed his four other children. The day before, Rachel had gotten a letter from a mutual friend of ours in Waco telling our story and mentioning Don and Karen. Rachel told the desperate man she just might know of someone.

Stephanie scooted beside me and held my hand. We all barely breathed, like three animals stunned by headlights.

Rebecca went on. "A few days later, five-week-old Baby Katiana moved from her thatched-roof hut to Don and Karen's. But she almost died over the weekend."

"No," I murmured, clutching Jeff's hand.

"Karen squeezed beads of water into her tiny mouth with an eye dropper all night and prayed. First thing in the morning, she sent to town for lactose-free formula, and the baby sucked it down." Rebecca slowed and took a breath. "She's gained two pounds in three days. Karen says she's like a little piggie." Stephanie and Jeff both chuckled, the spell broken.

"She's okay," I choked out with a smile.

"Karen says she seems healthy. She'll take her back to the clinic this week for a checkup. This must be a shock, but she's asking if you want to adopt her. She'd like to know as soon as possible. And if so, whether you have a name picked out."

Everything fell away besides Jeff and me and our desire to have a baby. And her need. He offered me his hand and lifted me up to stand. We nodded at each other, eyes swimming. Stephanie grabbed her camera and snapped a picture.

Rebecca asked, "You guys still there?"

I leaned into Jeff as he said, "We would love to."

We named her Clare Katiana. After St. Clare of Assisi because of my long infatuation with St. Francis and his companion St. Clare. And a good French name since Haiti was a French-speaking country.

With Clare came an ending. My endometriosis pain made sitting or standing for more than a couple of hours unbearable. My doctor scheduled a complete hysterectomy for the end of July. I made light of it: *This surgery is just my version of a cesarean section; I have Clare waiting in Haiti.* But as they wheeled me to surgery in a blue scrub bonnet, I choked out the last words of our infertility journey to Jeff.

"I'm so sorry about the babies." The ones we would never have. The ones that might look and act like him or me. Tears seeped from the corners of my eyes onto the bed.

Jeff's face screwed up, his own eyes moist. "Oh, Lynn, it's not your fault. We're in it together, forever." He kissed my hand as they rolled me away and spent the next few hours steeping in sadness in the OR waiting room with my parents. When I lay awake that night, he climbed into my hospital bed beside me. I pushed my morphine button, and we held hands. We watched reruns of Seinfeld through the night.

It took three months to recover from surgery and its complications. And the adoption process seemed stuck in a morass of cross-cultural communication. I had eased my way back into work over the fall, but I decided to go to Haiti at the beginning of November, desperate to meet Clare and push the adoption along. Karen invited me to stay as long as I wanted; I bought a one-way ticket. I stared out the window as the pilot announced the final descent, straining to see Karen on the taxiway with Clare. My reflection startled me: a round face after three years of eating frozen lasagna with work groups at the nonprofit, not much exercise, and the menopause into which the hysterectomy had catapulted me. I was creeping up on thirty, and my short brown hair failed to cover the few new lines around my eyes that proved it. The wheels hit the ground and snapped my attention back. I instinctively held my sewn-up abdomen as we bumped along to a stop. Then I saw Clare.

Karen had fancied her up in an aqua-blue dress with white lace trim and tulle underneath, so it puffed out like a 1950s prom dress. When the pilot opened the door, the salty sea air pressed in around me. I held the rail and descended step by step to Karen, standing in her white airport uniform with five-month-old Clare on her hip. I wrapped one arm around Karen and tried to inhale. My heartbreak, infertility, waiting, longing rose into my throat, pushing against my vocal cords and silencing them. I tried to swallow it all, but it flowed out my eyes as Karen handed Clare to me. She was real. And tiny underneath that puff of a dress. Her petite eleven-pound body curved around my side, and she grasped my earring in her tiny hand. Joy and wonder burst through me.

"Hi, there, little one." I felt the softness of her skin, inhaled her baby smell, and looked into her big, bottomless eyes. And that smile; the sun lived there. Someone snapped pictures, and we walked into the small terminal to get my bag. A swarm of employees said, "*Bonjou, Manman Clare!*" Clare's *mom*. Astonishing.

In the days that followed, Emmail, a friend of Don and Karen's, drove me around and translated for me. He had a bright smile and a tender heart, and he loved Clare. He came over after breakfast on my fourth day and drove Karen, Clare, and me to the clinic lawyer's office in downtown Cap-Haïtien to sign papers with Clare's Haitian father, Roubnert. We walked upstairs to the office where Roubnert sat waiting. The small, short-haired man looked stunned to see Clare. Four months before, he'd left a dying, emaciated baby at the clinic. I carried a thriving five-month-old girl with bright eyes, a deep chortle, and a toothless broad smile. His mouth fell open and spread into a wide grin.

Insecurity pricked me; I held *his* child. I mumbled to Karen, "Should I hand her to him?"

She shook her head. "It's not a good idea."

I deferred. *But why did I have the power? How could I keep his daughter from him?*

To my relief we hurried off to see the judge. Roubnert, Clare, and I sat in the back seat of Karen's car with her and Emmail in the front. I turned Clare toward Roubnert and singsonged a smile from her. He clapped and clucked at her, reached out, then waved instead. His yearning undid me, and I handed her over. She laughed and gibberished on his lap while he spoke Creole to her and mirrored her smile.

I pointed to Clare and said, "*Remen ou.*" *She likes you.* He smiled and nodded. My jaw unclenched, my shoulders released, and my chest expanded a bit.

Emmail parallel parked on a narrow street by a corner building with giant archways, wooden doors pushed open wide. We navigated the dusty sidewalk teeming with people.

"*Merci anpil,*" I said to Roubnert as we crossed the threshold into the tribunal with Clare on my hip again. *Thank you so much.* I longed to be able to talk to him. My stomach churned, and people milled around, all eyes on me, the *Blanc.* We followed Madame George, the Haitian lawyer, into an open area with a long, old wooden table at one end. A man plopped down a huge red book and opened it to a page filled with handwritten Creole. He handed Roubnert a pen; Roubnert signed and passed the pen to me. I shifted Clare to my other hip and turned to the lawyer, asking what I was signing. After getting a few scraps of English, I paused, chose to trust her, and signed my name. Karen smiled through deep wrinkles on her face tanned from years of the Caribbean sun and asked us to pose for pictures, Haitians watching from every corner. My head swam.

Back at her office, Madame George, Roubnert, and Emmail talked a hundred miles an hour in Creole while I sat in a daze under the ceiling fan, thankful the electricity was working. Madame George had realized Roubnert's name on his birth certificate didn't match his signature in the big red book. He'd have to see the magistrate in his village then make the ten-mile trek on his bicycle again to Madame George's office with another document.

Clare and I both slept hard back at Don and Karen's. When their generator came on at eight o'clock, I emailed the story of the day to Jeff. I ended with: *I wanted you to be with us today. To meet Roubnert and experience the Haitian court with the big red book. I hate being without you and for Clare and you to have to wait so long to be together. Is it time for you to come? I love you. P.S. The ants ate my estrogen I left on the nightstand. Ugh. Could you refill my prescription at Eckerd and send or bring it to me?*

Jeff weighed coming to Haiti with responsibilities at work while I lived with Clare at Don and Karen's, worked on the adoption, and transformed into Clare's mom. Don moved Clare's crib into my room. I fed her every bottle. We spent hours at the lawyer's office hoping to move things along—I sang, walked, and napped her there in my arms. But each document I got led to two new papers to find. On the way back to Don and Karen's, we'd pick up sugary, crispy elephant ear pastries from the French bakery in Cap-Haïtien or stop for chicken Creole in the warm, saltwater breeze on the open-air patio at the hotel in town owned by a French expat.

Every night at eight o'clock, I sat at the old desktop computer and emailed Jeff the day's news and my heart; Karen called them my epistles. I read his responses at nine each morning. We discovered a freedom writing our thoughts and feelings to each other: complaining, disagreeing, extending grace. Our intimacy deepened. Miraculously, our crises in starting a family had hollowed out a fertile place, and our marriage had grown. And just before Thanksgiving, Jeff came to

Haiti. His first night, he bathed Clare in a plastic refrigerator drawer on the card-table-turned-kitchen-island and laid her on her belly on our eggplant-purple, batik bedcover. We took pictures of her perfect naked bottom and bright gorgeous smile.

Jeff took on the trips to town, and I drank in the slowness, Clare, and Haiti. Afternoons we sat on the front porch watching lizards and red hibiscus blooms that swayed in the wind. And dodging a vibrant green hummingbird who nested in the eaves and torpedoed us to protect her babies. One Friday morning, Jeff and Emmail drove around the car-eating potholes into town for an appointment with Madame George. Jeff sat on the yellow concrete wall outside the office all day, but she never showed. He came home fuming.

"How can she not show up? I had an appointment." He paced and ran his fingers through his brown hair. I noticed his receding hairline but didn't mention it.

"Different culture, babe." I played with Clare on the bed. She smiled and gurgled at me.

"Well, it's wrong. And nothing happens over the weekend. It means another week here at least. If that lawyer says, 'two more weeks' again, I'm going to hurt her." She'd told Jeff when he arrived in Haiti two weeks before that we'd have the US visa two weeks later. Now we knew *two more weeks* meant *not yet*. But I didn't care how long it took as long as I was with Clare. At bedtime, Jeff and I swayed and sang Clare to sleep, snuggled her blue flannel blanket around her in her crib in the corner of our room, and read *The Lord of the Rings* trilogy to each other. We had a lovely afternoon tea with Clare's four siblings, father, and grandmother at nurse Rachel's cottage on the clinic grounds over the weekend.

On December fifth, Clare turned six months old and sat up on her own. I told Jeff I knew he had to return to work, and his pacing was driving me to distraction. His face lit up with relief then went slack. He hated to leave Clare; he felt guilty for missing work;

Haitian inefficiency drove him crazy. A few days later, he plopped Clare in the nest of clothes in his green Eagle Creek backpack, pretending to smuggle her back to Waco. But Clare and I stayed on with Don and Karen. We'd become a strange sort of family. I loved them very much.

By mid-December, Madame George assured me we had everything for Clare's US visa and our homegoing. Emmail, Clare, and I boarded a plane to the US consulate in Port-au-Prince after a tearful goodbye with Don and Karen. That was Clare and my first flight together, all excitement, joy, and connection. Mother and daughter.

The next morning, an electric jolt flashed through me when the consulate official said, "You lack almost all the papers necessary for an international adoption." I burned as he explained Madame George hadn't known US requirements. And signing the big red book had granted us guardianship directly from Roubnert against US policy. A third party had to be involved. I ransacked my ever-present, get-out-of-a-trap tool bag. *How to circumvent this barrier?* Nothing came to me. We took a taxi back to the hotel, and I kept searching: calling Jeff, US officials, Don and Karen, the attorney, a new attorney in Port. Nothing. After a few days, Emmail went home, and Jeff came back to Haiti. When he entered the hotel courtyard, I ran to him. We held each other with Clare between us, and I cried.

"I'm so sorry I couldn't get it done and you had to come back," I said. His face softened, and he looked down into my eyes. His warm fingers touched my cheek.

"Not your fault, love. We'll figure it out. We're in this together."

After a week of phone calls, emails, and long days of waiting, the truth came into clear, terrible focus. Our new Haitian lawyer said *six weeks in the US to sort out the American paperwork.* We couldn't take her home. I emailed friends and family and closed with: *Our understanding of God, the way we relate to Him and He to us has been stripped back to basics. We aren't sure anymore in* what *we are supposed*

to have faith or what the purpose of our prayer is, but we do keep asking
God to help us believe. That's about all we've got.

Clare and I boarded a plane to Cap-Haïtien as Jeff boarded
American Airlines to Texas. We were in a movie being rewound. Jeff
landed in Dallas alone. I deplaned with Clare on my hip and handed
her back to Karen. Then I flew north to the States without her. I
arrived home on Christmas Eve with bacterial dysentery and a shattered heart.

Don moved Clare's crib back into their bedroom in Haiti. Clare
started to crawl and powdered her knees on the cement floor as she
wandered the house looking for me. They said she sat on a blanket in
the living room as if under a shadow. In Waco, I rocked in a cham-
bray-covered glider by the big front window in the corner of Clare's
empty room. I cried or stared unfocused or sang "Amazing Grace" and
muttered the Lord's Prayer—I had no prayers of my own anymore. I
felt hollow and dead inside. *How I could miss someone so much who*
had never been there? My doctor diagnosed depression. Looking back,
I realized I'd had my first major episode at thirteen, missing the last six
weeks of eighth grade with mysterious headaches and stomach pain.
I'd suffered from depression all my life.

Jeff dominoed paycheck stubs, tax returns, and bank statements
on the wood floor of the study. We stacked them up with notarized
medical and psychological exams and educational records. We'd
wrangled papers not for six weeks but for five months. By the end of
May, an African, French-speaking graduate student had translated it
all into French, and we FedEx-ed it to Washington, DC, for certifica-
tion at the Haitian Embassy. Clare had long since stopped looking for
me in Haiti. She cruised the sofas and practiced standing. In June, she
started walking and celebrated her first birthday without us. I turned
thirty, resigned from the nonprofit at an impasse with my boss, and
the Haitian Embassy stapled a velvet red ribbon—proof of authentic-
ity—on top of each section of the dual-language encyclopedia of our

life. The packet arrived back in Waco a year after Rebecca's call about Clare.

I bought a one-way ticket to Port-au-Prince to fight for Clare's US visa. I had no illusions of control this time, mine or a sovereign god's; I believed the adoption might never happen. But I wasn't giving up. Jeff stayed home to work while I sussed things out. My dad ached to help me and offered to come along. On the Fourth of July, 2000, Dad and I took our seats on American Airlines.

At the consulate office, Fred—the stout, sandy-haired man who'd denied Jeff and me Clare's visa in December—sat again behind his metal desk and again shook his head. We had all the documents, but the guardianship paper from Roubnert, still in our file, was still illegal.

"Anything you can do to help us, Fred? Lynn and Jeff have worked for a year to make this happen. To give Clare a good home." Dad's sky-blue eyes held Fred's gaze.

Fred shifted in his seat. "I appreciate your situation, but there's nothing I can do." He looked at his desk and rustled papers. I sat still and remained quiet.

"You must have some power here," Dad said. "I know you're in an important position."

Fred looked up and sat a bit taller. "It is important work."

"Protecting American interests," Dad agreed. Fred nodded. I seemed to have disappeared. "It occurs to me that the document has already been approved." Fred and I both raised our eyebrows as Dad continued, "A Texas congressman walked the case through Immigration and Naturalization Services for us eight months ago."

Fred shifted again, looked at me and back to my dad. He shuffled through our file until he came to the INS paper stamped *Approved* with a date of 11.20.99.

"I realize you're in a bind, Fred. The two things conflict. It's a hard position for an official." Fred let his shoulders relax a bit.

My dad took the opening. "I wonder if you could defer to the original INS approval in this case. That signature seems to me to give you some leeway."

Fred leaned back in his chair. "I guess it's the INS guy's job at stake, not mine. You're right about that." He sat up and banged his red stamp on our two-inch-thick packet of papers.

Dad reached across the desk to shake Fred's hand. "Fred, you've given a baby girl a good home today."

A single sob and choking gasp escaped me when Fred passed us Clare's American visa. Two days later, Dad and I climbed the stairs onto the DC-3 in Cap-Haïtien with Clare and Karen, who was coming to help Clare transition to life in Waco.

Skating

I sat with Clare on her blue blanket on the floor of the plane making her octopus dance. She reached for its colorful arms like a kitten batting a ball. Her laughter gurgled up and out her wide-open mouth between four little white teeth top and bottom. She was as happy as she had been enraged an hour before at takeoff. My dad laughed and clapped with her, his blue eyes twinkling. The few passengers watched her—a performer on a stage. Clare seemed plugged into extra wattage. Bright and shiny. Magnetic. And I got to be her mom.

But then Karen stood up to go to the bathroom, and Clare froze. She reached for the seat and pulled herself up, raising her arms to Karen.

Picking her up, Karen said, "You stay with your momma while I go to the bathroom." I got to my feet, and Karen handed me Clare as the plane shimmied over a pocket of rough air. But Clare grasped Karen around the neck like a noose.

Shifting Clare to my hip, I leaned over and grabbed *The Very Hungry Caterpillar*. "Let's read a book, love." Clare twisted her little body to wriggle free.

Karen pried Clare's hands off her neck. "It will be just a minute. You'll be fine." She walked down the aisle while Clare struggled to get back to her.

I used my softest voice, sang, swayed back and forth with her. Nothing abated the wail that filled the cavernous body of the DC-3 or stilled the writhing. I walked the wide aisle to the bathroom with Clare, and Karen spoke reassurances through the door. Clare's eyes darted back and forth as she tried to find her escape, an animal in a trap. The toilet flushed, and Karen opened the door. Clare lunged out of my arms and into Karen's. She buried her head in Karen's shoulder and went silent. My heart took up the writhing.

After the DC-3 touched down in West Palm Beach, we walked through a set of glass doors into the USA. Karen carried Clare over the threshold while I looked over my shoulder, expecting to see someone chasing us: *You can't take her out of the building! It's not finished! Stop!* But no one came. The door closed behind us, and the Florida summer heat engulfed us. It was like walking in a dream.

When we landed in Dallas, friends and family met us at the gate with a WELCOME HOME, CLARE sign, the kind our high school football teams burst through after halftime under the Friday night lights. My sister, Kim, had painted the neon pink, yellow, and blue bubble letters. My mom held one end with my three-year-old niece, Annie, and my sister held the other beside her round and drooping belly full of my nephew Ben, who was to be born four days later. Our closest friends from the Waco nonprofit, Jason and Angel, held another sign. They had sent me off to Haiti in November and covered for us at work. They had gathered us up at their table on Christmas after we crawled home without Clare. They stood at the gate now with tears of joy and their one-year-old son, Isaac—Clare's soon-to-be first best friend. Jeff stood front and center.

Karen held Clare's hand as they stepped through the gate. My dad and I followed. Clare beamed her full-sun smile as she walked her own personal runway in denim overalls and a bright orange shirt with white trim around the neck for her grand entrance into our family. Until Jeff approached her. She dropped Karen's hand and her smile and leeched onto Karen's leg like most scared one-year-olds who need the security of Mom. Karen picked her up.

"You're okay, babe. This is your new family." But Clare maintained her death grip.

Jeff wrapped his arms around me and squeezed, "Thank you for bringing our baby home."

My tears splotched his shirt. "You're welcome." I smiled, looking up into his eyes.

I turned to see my mom offer a white stuffed dog with pink tulle ribbon around its neck to Clare. "Hi, Clare. I'm your Mimi. Would you like this?" Clare reached out and snuggled the puppy to her chest, burying her nose in it.

After a few moments she wriggled down from Karen to walk around. Annie's blond hair swung at her shoulders as she followed Clare, patting her tiny Afro. Clare had never been in a modern, international airport. She'd never seen an escalator. She'd never smelled McDonald's french fries or Auntie Anne's pretzels. She'd never ridden in a car seat. With Karen beside her, she inhaled all the new. It seemed like her pores opened up extra wide to let it all in at once. America.

We arrived in Waco after two hours southbound on I-35. Jeff, Karen, Clare, my mom and dad, and I climbed the steps onto the porch of the big, ramshackle house we'd bought three years before. Jeff unlocked the wooden front door, and we walked into the open expanse of our entryway. We'd painted the walls café au lait, and a mahogany staircase with a turn halfway up led to the second floor. Clare went straight for the stairs, scrambling up on all fours with us following behind.

"Here's your room, love," I told her and led her inside. A crib from our nonprofit's thrift store had been on one wall for ten months already, and the blue mourning glider still sat by the window. Annie's old changing table with red and blue drawers underneath sat between the front windows, and a daybed filled the wall opposite the crib. Clare knew what a crib was for. Karen changed her diaper, plopped her in, and she went right to sleep.

That night Jeff and I lay talking in bed, wonderstruck that Clare lay in the crib in the adjacent room.

"We did it," I said.

"You did it. You and your dad went and got her." He turned toward me and gazed, our eyes inches apart, his hand resting on my hip.

"*We* did it. He just sealed the deal." My fingers traced his cheekbone. "What do we do now?"

Jeff laughed. "I guess we get up in the morning and feed her breakfast."

I nestled into his chest and smiled. "Right. First breakfast."

After a couple of days settling in and visits from Jeff's parents and what felt like hundreds of friends, Karen left for two nights to visit a friend a few towns away, and my mom and dad went home. When Clare woke up from a nap to just Jeff and me, her face crumpled into the wrinkled folds of an old woman's. She toddled from her bedroom into the guest room and sniffed Karen's vanilla perfume but couldn't find her. The wail began. She dropped to her knees to race the hall that spanned the length of the house like a police dog looking for drugs. As I mumbled reassurances that Karen would be back, she started for the sweeping staircase, so I caught her hands, stood her up, and we went down together.

"It will just be a little while, baby. I'm here." I carried her into the backyard. Jeff joined us, and we took turns holding her. We showed her leaves and lizards. We sang and bounced. But nothing abated the desperation, the crying. My heart squeezed; my breathing shallowed like hers. *What the hell have we done?*

Time—an hour? more?—morphed the wails to cries to whimpers to silence. She took her pacifier and let me rock her until dinner, when she ate a few bites of banana and avocado. Back upstairs, she tottered to her crib, grabbed on, and lifted her leg to climb in. When Jeff picked her up, she dove over the side. She popped a pacifier in her mouth, clutched one in her hand, her blanket in the other, and went to sleep. In the morning, she woke up subdued.

A friend had offered to take family photos, so we put Clare's overalls back on and gave her Mudge—the stuffed white dog from Mimi. He made her smile. We walked out back to the paint-peeling detached garage. Clare leaned against it as if resting at a farmyard barn. She reached out her tiny, dark hand to touch the rough wood. When we asked her to show us Mudge, she grinned. After a few minutes, her full, shining smile broke through, showing the resilience we'd see over and over again throughout her life. We sat under a big pecan tree and sang "Itsy Bitsy Spider." As we all danced our hands, Clare lit up. Her few teeth framed her Ronald McDonald smile—all horseshoe open-mouthed with a straight upper lip. Her nose crinkled up, and her deep-brown, wide-set eyes shone like each one held a diamond at its center. Little elfin ears and short, tight curls atop her broad forehead rounded out her face. I felt equal parts ravenous and grateful for this "normal" family ritual and at the same time like one of those unrelated models in a PC multicultural photo in a frame at Target: a real family and not yet real all at once.

The next afternoon, Karen came back to finish out the week. Clare snubbed her at first, but by bedtime she climbed in her lap to read *Good Night Gorilla*. After Clare was asleep, Jeff and I told Karen about Clare's devastated search for her.

"Sounds like when you left Haiti, Lynn," Karen reminded me.

"I'd forgotten."

"That little one has had a lot of changes. But she's stubborn and strong. She'll be fine," she assured us. I wanted to believe her.

A few days later, I loaded Clare into her car seat in my Volvo and put Karen's luggage in the trunk. The three of us drove two hours south to the airport in Austin. We walked Karen up to her gate where Clare sat on Karen's lap and played pat-a-cake while we laughed and ate donut holes. Karen wiped Clare's chocolate milk mustache off with a napkin.

"I'll never be able to repay you for all you've done," I said. "Thank you."

"I'm happy you're together. She's a special one, this girl." Karen looked down at Clare who was twisting a long lock of Karen's brown hair in her hand.

"You've loved Clare so well. You welcomed me into your home. You came home with us." My voice cracked. The last year's elation, desperation, fear, and relief rolled inside me like waves.

"We love you all." Karen tilted her head and smiled. She seemed joyful at Clare being home; she'd done her work and could return to Haiti at peace. Maybe tears came on the plane.

When the loudspeaker called her flight to board, she handed Clare to me for the last time and stood up. We hugged with Clare on my hip. Clare held on to my neck, wide-eyed and silent, as Karen handed the attendant her boarding pass. I waved when she turned around to see Clare one last time. Clare raised her little hand and waved goodbye to her second mom. She watched Karen disappear through the gate. My chest hardly expanded as I sipped the air. Clare wriggled to get down. She grabbed my hand. She never looked back.

One morning the next week when Jeff left for work, I scooped Clare up from her usual flow of constant movement, babble conversation, and climbing my body like a jungle gym. I would teach lifespan development at the Baylor University Graduate School of Social Work in the fall but first spend July and August giving Clare my undivided attention.

"Here you go, love." I buckled her into her Safety 1st booster seat—bold, royal-blue plastic with one red and one green side—strapped onto a tall chair at the bar above our kitchen counter. I offered her half a peanut butter and jelly sandwich and strawberries and sat next to her, eating peanut butter toast. When she got distracted by a bird flying past the window, the neighbor's dog barking, the Raffi CD playing, anything, everything, I chanted, "Chew, swallow, take another bite. Chew, swallow, take another bite." *Would she just eat one day?* After a full hour, I wiped her face and hands with a wet cloth and took off her footy pajamas. Dry diaper and jumper on, we loaded up with Angel and Isaac to go to a splash pad.

Water jumped, bubbled, and sprayed at all different levels and trajectories from a dozen holes in the squishy mat covering the playground. Angel asked if I had a swim diaper and swimsuit for Clare. No, embarrassingly. Clare—in her pink, plaid jumper next to Isaac in his swim diaper and swim shorts—stood at the edge and surveyed the kids. Soaked children shrieked, and parents called, "Slow down!" Shades of green stretched up the hill and reflected in the Brazos River that ran along one side of the playground. I held Clare's hand and walked her toward the water fountains in my cutoff shorts and T-shirt. Water tumbled from the highest points, separating into individual droplets that drifted through the sunlight to splatter the ground. When Clare got splashed, she stopped.

I knelt down, put my arm around her, and looked in her eyes. "Do you want me to hold you?"

She reached around my neck and held on tight. I picked her up, and we went in together. The water hit her arms, bounced into her face. A stream that had sunk to bubbles at the ground shot back up just in front of us. We both gasped, and then I laughed. I reached my hand out to touch the cold water. Tentatively, she reached her hand out, too. A smile spread over her face, and a little laugh came. After circling the fountains for a while, I walked right through one. We both squealed, and I ran to the edge and set her down. She found Isaac playing there and walked over to join him. Before long they were both full in; they careened around, laughed, and played. Clare looked up as the streams broke into drops and let them splash her face without a flinch. Her pink-and-white jumper clung to her wet skin. Water droplets balanced on her tight curls.

After thirty exuberant minutes, Clare got tired. I didn't have a towel or change of clothes. Ugh. I needed an outing-with-a-child checklist. Angel toweled Isaac off, put on dry clothes, and strapped him in the car seat beside Clare. She gave him his water and both of them a handful of goldfish in brown paper bags.

Clare was screaming nonstop by the time we got home. Her hair dripped water onto her shoulders and ran in streams down her back. I wiped the cold wetness off her skin and pulled dry clothes on her. I tried to think over her screams. *Would food help?* I threw frozen strawberries and bananas in the blender with a splash of apple juice. She wedged herself in between the cabinet and my legs, begging me to hold her like she did every night while I cooked dinner. The shrill grinding of the blades and motor made her scream louder. Then she wouldn't drink. *Was it too cold? Did she not like it?* I begged her to have some. I sat on the kitchen floor with her; I tried to force it into her. Defeated, I rocked her for an hour until she fell asleep. Five more hours until Jeff came home.

I wanted us to slide into life as a family, step in mid flow as if we'd been together from the beginning. But so many things happened the first year—developmental milestones and deep attachments, parents and babies learning each other: expressions, cries, temperaments, rhythms, and needs. Our transition felt more like stepping onto an ice rink without knowing how to skate, arms shot out to keep balanced, wobbling from one side to the other with a few smooth glides in between. And guilt washed over me when I felt anything but grateful for being Clare's mom, the thing I'd wanted for so long.

Luckily, Clare woke up smiling every day. My depression had always made me feel like I moved through molasses, but with Clare I danced and sang and went on walks. She took hour-long baths in the kitchen sink, banged the water, and squealed with her pacifier fixed between her teeth. I laughed, enchanted; she brought me to life. She darted from place to place, pausing to rest her wings like the hummingbird on Karen's front porch in Haiti. She also dive-bombed me at random. I thought back to the video tapes Karen had sent while we waited for Clare to come home. When Clare's face squinched up and turned red, they cut out. They picked back up with Clare laughing and clapping. At home, I couldn't stop her screams and flailing once they started. I had to wait them out. Karen had called her strong-willed. I called her a blazing fire, giving life or consuming it.

I couldn't wait to introduce Clare to the Waco giraffes who had saved my life. Before Clare came home, I had slipped through a red brick archway into the fifty-two acres of the Cameron Park Zoo in the early mornings to exercise. Solitude, animals, and forest. It balanced my stress and deconstructing faith. My favorite spot sat at the end of the road that wound from the zoo entrance to the African savanna habitat. A small pond separated two white rhinos from greater kudus, dik-diks, crowned cranes, and giraffes roaming two acres. Elephants galumphed farther along in a separate yard. The lion enclosure ended the circuit.

I'd fallen in love with the giraffes while resting on a bench after my walks. Nothing hurried them. They lumbered around big limestone rocks and fallen logs through dirt and grass. Until they heard the lion's roar. Then I saw power and beauty in their rhythmic running. At the edge of the enclosure, they reached their long black tongues up into the trees and wound them around leaves, pulled them down, and ate. They chewed, ruminated, chewed. Watching them in the makeshift savanna was my meditation, though I didn't call it that yet. My confusion and heartbreak over the pain and injustice in the world and my own life receded; space opened up inside me for breath.

Clare, Jeff, and I began our visits on the wood plank lookout to Gibbon Island. The musky smells of animals and their dung wafted over the water. At one end, a waterfall sang as Clare swung her petite body on the rope fencing. The lion's roar carried across the water from our path's end.

"Listen," I said. "Hear the lion talking to us?" Her eyes grew wide, and we ventured on around the path.

When we got to Grammy Nell's playground, Clare ran through

the wooden mulch and up the dirt path to the treehouse. After a look through the telescope, she flew down the yellow slide fashioned like half of a hollowed-out tree. Jeff ran to catch her, but she crashed to the ground, not minding the impact at all. With a laugh, she jumped up to run through the hollow gray-and-black stone snake with bright yellow eyes and out its wide-open mouth.

As we completed the circle, I sat and talked to my beloved giraffes, and Clare ran back and forth around the curves of the path, Jeff following behind her. She raced up the ramp to the treetop lookout and screeched a call to the fuzzy-legged elephants flapping their ears and eating from the bamboo forest. She ran back down past my bench to stare at the wrinkly rhinos. She got out tons of energy—of which she had tons. After an hour, just before she crashed (I could set my watch by it), we scooped her into the stroller and handed her peanut butter crackers and a sippy cup of apple juice to avoid it. As she munched, I strolled her past prowling lions to the island of ring-tailed lemurs.

"Goodbye, lions. Goodbye, zoo," I called out. Cracker crumbs spilled from Clare's mouth as she burbled a one-year-old version of "Goodbye, lemurs" toward the trees where they sat, arms and legs outstretched, bellies to the sun.

As summer ended, our housemate, Stephanie, arrived home from an internship in time to watch Clare two days a week while I worked. I was grateful for an infusion of social work and adult conversations. Clare loved Steph, a huge relief since Clare was loath to leave my side. Somehow, I felt like it wasn't about me, though; I might have been a mama gorilla—fulfilling a basic animal need for protection and nurture. Stephanie had become a little sister to us and now became Aunt Steph to Clare. I could work at ease. As the semester unfolded, though, I struggled to transition between Clare and Baylor. Lesson plans and grading took me forever. At home, I swam in Clare's passions all day, and it wore me out.

One day, gratefully done with classes for the week, I sat drawing with Clare on our front sidewalk with fat pieces of white, pink, and blue chalk. A friend walked by under the cerulean-blue, fall Texas sky with her kids, a red metal wagon jangling behind her. She stopped to lift Clare in the air and singsong to her; Clare struggled to get back to me. My friend sat her in the wagon instead.

"Come for a ride with us, Clare! It'll be fun!"

Clare looked at me and started to cry. I froze. *Defer to my friend's confidence? Say no and rescue Clare?* I watched her pull away. Clare's cries escalated as they turned the corner. I held my breath, hoping I'd done the right thing. *But how could this teach Clare it was okay to leave me?* Clare's persistent wail crescendoed several minutes later as they rounded the corner again. I ran to her and scooped her up. A familiar pain shot from my lower back down my left leg as I held her close. I ignored it. She pressed her face, covered in tears and mucus, into my shoulder.

My friend said, "Good first try! Next time will be easier. We love you, Clare!" And they went on. I carried Clare inside and eased into the glider with her. She cried herself to sleep. I felt I couldn't do anything well—Clare or teaching.

When my back pain continued to sear, the doctor discovered a herniated disk near the base of my spine. My body screamed that I couldn't transition from no child to a twenty-pound toddler without gradual learning and strengthening. I declined a spring semester class to focus on parenting and scheduled back surgery after the holidays. It coincided with Stephanie's February move to Miami, so we enrolled Clare in a Parents' Day Out program two days a week during my physical therapy. Clare cried and cried and cried. For weeks. The kind women tried everything: comfort, distraction. Resorted to time-outs on a stool. Nothing worked. We bought the trying-for-Hallmark photo they took of Clare eyeing a black-and-white rabbit in an Easter basket, and they kicked her out by end of April. Surgery had relieved the nerve pain, and physical therapy gave me tools, so I settled in with

Clare and tried to find energy to do my exercises after Jeff got home each day.

My mind said love healed anything; God was faithful. But our fierce love for Clare didn't make life with her easy. It also didn't reconcile our differences with the founders of the nonprofit and church. They broadcast seeds of hope, justice, and healing, creating a cascade of programs; Jeff and I wanted to go deep. They overflowed service to marginalized people; living full throttle was unsustainable for us. We couldn't find balance there. But Jeff had become a bridge between the passionate, demanding founder and the staff and volunteers. Loyal above all else, he couldn't imagine leaving. And where would we go?

"We have to get out of here," I said one night. Jeff had described another confrontation at a staff meeting. We sat on our hunter-green couch and held hands. The *How long must we stay?* conversation was stuck on repeat—the decision-making paralyzed Jeff. We prayed together and went to bed believing we would somehow discover a next step we could agree on. A few days later, my dear college friend Christine suggested a sabbatical in the fall. A semester at Regent College, a graduate school of theology, in Vancouver, British Columbia, Canada. We'd been visiting her and her husband, Cliff, there over the last several years—a refuge from our Waco storms. The international student body explored Christian spirituality through art and literature, in the workplace and on retreat. Jeff could enroll and get a student visa, I could audit classes cheaply, and we could explore what work was ours to do next. We had a destination.

We celebrated Clare's second birthday in June with a pool party at a friend's house. I had swim diapers and towels. Our small group from church, my sister's family from Dallas, and our parents from West Texas all came. Jeff and I held Clare between us as she blew out two candles and, just beginning to speak, said a wobbly *Happy Birthday* to herself. Angel took a picture, and I realized we weren't a PC photo of a family. Somewhere along the way we had become an actual one.

Two months later, I dripped with sweat on our front porch in the humid August heat. Angel and I shooed mosquitos off Clare and Isaac as Jason and Jeff loaded the last chairs and clicked our U-Haul trailer shut. We'd sold our house to our neighbor's daughter and pocketed the cash to live on for a while. Jeff had a Canadian student visa in his backpack. After hugs and tears, Jeff strapped Clare in her car seat and started the engine. She wore purple kid headphones plugged into a small TV/VCR combo that balanced on the console. Lala the yellow Teletubby and Clare's pink-and-white, candy-striped bunny flanked her, Mudge in her lap. The blue handle of her pacifier dangled to her chin. The U-Haul weighed down my Volvo's back bumper to hover over the ground.

I reached over and ran my hand through Jeff's short brown hair as we pulled away, "You have tears in your eyes." He lifted the gold wire rims of his glasses and wiped the drops away as they fell. His green eyes shone.

"A huge weight just lifted. I had no idea how the battles of these years had flattened me. I don't know who I am anymore."

"I still know you. And love you," I said, and he pressed his lips to my hand.

"Why did it take me so long to leave?"

"We're leaving now," I said. "We'll make it."

Arms Out Wide

As Christine and I crested a hill two weeks later on a sunny September day, I gasped. The deep blue expanse of English Bay opened to Howe Sound, and the Georgia Strait reached out for the Pacific. Not like the Gulf of Mexico on Texas shores, vanishing over the edge of a very flat earth at the horizon. This had texture and dimension. Islands popped up here and there like the dark green hips of luscious, curvy women diving into the sea. And the sun wasn't the southern sun that bellowed. The gentle, kind Canadian sun offered its light. Probably apologizing for making me squint a bit.

"Do you ever get used to it? Not notice the extravagant beauty?" I asked Christine as we returned from an IKEA trip. "I hope I never do."

We rounded the bend to St. Andrews Hall on the University of British Columbia campus. It curved around a grassy courtyard in a horseshoe and housed mostly international students and their young families. Jeff, Clare, and I moved into Cliff and Christine's rented townhouse as they returned to Texas with their two young boys. Clare ran amuck with children from around the world there. The Canadians two doors down said she was the loudest child they'd ever heard.

During Regent College orientation, Jeff and I slid into two seats in the chapel a few rows from the back. Students and faculty filled the hundreds of chairs in the auditorium. They punctuated our silence with side-shuffle steps, the rustle of backpacks, "good to see yas," and quiet chatter. The rows descended to a pit at the front that buzzed with folks tapping microphones and tuning instruments. High above them, five bright banners depicted a Hebrew creation story and the Jesus story in blues, greens, purples, pinks, and yellows. The late summer sunshine streamed in from a massive skylight behind them. I pulled my feet up into my chair and wrapped my arms around my legs.

I whispered my stream-of-consciousness thoughts to Jeff: "There are so many people. Think Clare is okay in childcare? I can't believe we're here."

"I can't remember the last time I wasn't in charge of a gathering. It's weird to just sit here. Kind of makes me feel guilty," Jeff said. A chime sounded; the room quieted.

A tall, White woman with short brown hair and a flowing green skirt took the microphone. "I'm Donna. We are so grateful you're here. Welcome to the first chapel of the year. To this place of beauty and rigorous thought. To community. For many, a refuge from years of ministry. Some arrive disoriented, looking for a new path. Others arrive in certainty and find themselves deconstructed while they are here." After more welcomes from administrators and a few songs, Donna invited us into silence. Nothing but breath and awareness. The whole auditorium paused and paid attention to Spirit. Jeff's fingers entwined with mine, and warm, gentle tears rolled down my cheeks. My muscles released—like the first time sitting after a long day of hard work outside. Weary bones. And relief.

Jeff took just enough courses to keep his student visa. I audited classes, and we shared parenting fifty-fifty. We became partners in a new way. I joined a book club and laughed until it hurt with Regent women who taught me about canned peas from England and global writers. I walked to the beach at Spanish Banks, spending time alone with the waves, sea lions, and sand while Jeff cared for Clare. Towering evergreens, ferns, and blackberry bushes flourished all around us, nourished by the annual six-month drizzle from November to April. Jeff, the West Texas boy of wide skies and blazing sunsets, felt a bit claustrophobic. I unfurled and drank deeply.

One October Sunday morning, Jeff took Clare's small hand, and we walked up the main mall to the UBC Botanical Garden Apple Festival. We swung her high in the air between us every few steps. Clare shone in a bright orange tunic spotted with fuchsia flowers as she and I skipped and sang Raffi songs at the top of our lungs:

"Baby Beluga in the deep blue sea/ Swim so wild and you swim so free/ Heaven above and the sea below/ And a little white whale on the go/ BABY BELUGA. . . ."

I picked up a giant maple leaf and made it Clare's hat. We paused at a red wooden apple with a white arrow that pointed the way. In Texas: the state fair, football, and sweating in line for fried twinkies. Here: a tent full of fresh apples, piles of caramel and candied apples, and singers strumming. My smile filled my whole face. *This was my home?* Volunteers welcomed us. Clare grabbed my pant leg, and I peg-legged over to a young woman holding a paint brush.

She crouched down to Clare's eye level as the breeze blew her long blond hair across the unicorn painted on her cheek. "Want me to paint your face? Maybe a rainbow?"

"I like rainbows." Clare's chin-to-eyebrow smile broke out.

The woman looked at me, and I smiled. "Please."

Clare scrambled into the chair. A few minutes later a bright rainbow arched from jaw to jaw, and Clare jumped down and ran on. Jeff and I held hands, walking along behind. Drawn to the ring of children's laughter, Clare led us to a puppet show. Jeff lifted her to his lap as we found a spot on a bench and joined in. Afterward, Clare wandered over to a pumpkin twice her size, climbed on, and hammed for a picture. Our beautiful girl. We followed a fresh, sweet scent to the tasting tent of small local growers where long tables covered in red cloths dripped with the juice of sliced apples. After about ten minutes of tasting—honeyed, tangy, mild, robust, crunchy, soft—Clare lay on the ground between the tables. Bored, tired, her rainbow smudged.

"Time to go." Jeff hoisted her onto his shoulders for the walk across campus to our apartment for a nap. As we walked, I stretched my arms out wide and twirled under the clear autumn sun.

One thing Clare had always done well was sleep. But in Vancouver she woke up in the middle of every night. She lost her pacifiers. She had bad dreams. Jeff and my double bed got crowded with six arms and legs and three bodies—especially the little one who preferred a head in one set of grown-up ribs and feet in the other. Our solution: ditch the pacifiers. Two-year-olds were supposed to be ready. Losing them kept her, and us, up. My sister was pregnant again with baby number three, so we made a letting-go ritual out of sending Clare's pacifiers to her.

We talked with Clare about it for a week. She was ambivalent and, at almost two-and-a-half, quite articulate with her strong opinions. We prepared. Clare colored a special box, and I wrote baby Kate's name on it. Then Clare climbed under a vinyl rain cover into her stroller. As I pushed her to the post office at UBC, her breath steamed up the inside. Raindrops pattered the outside and slid to the ground. Inside the post office, she emerged from her dry cocoon and popped the box of pacifiers into the mail slot. Clare skipped home in the misty shower, proud for baby Kate to have her pacifiers. Until bedtime.

"I need my pacis! I need my pacis!" she screamed and sobbed.

Jeff cooed, "Let me hold you, sweetie." She hit his arms and face with her little fists. I reached for her, and she dove into my arms. I carried her up the stairs to her bunk bed. When she saw her bedroom door, her arms flew to the door jams to stop us going through.

"*Noooooooooo!*" her scream pierced the air. I wrestled her through the door and onto her bed. Her feet battered the wall and top bunk.

"Calm down, babe. I'm right here. It's okay. You're a big girl now." I didn't convince her.

"I want my pacis back! Get them now!"

I heard the door open downstairs and the neighbor's voice.

Alarmed by the screams, she'd come over to check on us. Exhaustion turned down the boil to a simmering, whimpering *paci,* and our late-night regret for this awful idea and *whose was it anyway*? I tossed and turned with her in her twin bed all night long.

Naptime the next day was worse. Our rule was no coming out of her room; we came to her when it was time. She slept or looked at books and snuggled her blankie. Except now she couldn't settle without the pacifier. She ripped off her onesie and diaper and peed all over her bed. I was stunned. She flung the door open and stormed down the stairs begging, "Spank me! Please spank me!" Anything to get us close to her.

After a week we were soooo tired. We tried everything: sleep with her, let her sleep with us, hold her and rock her to sleep like when she was a baby. Nothing worked. Her wail reminded me of something: the airplane. The animal pain and desperation that had exploded from her when Karen went to the bathroom on the plane on the way home from Haiti. It was the same cry. But we had agreed *no more pacis* and wouldn't reverse it. That would teach her that if she wailed enough, she'd get what she wanted. Because that was how positive and negative consequences worked, damn it. Consistency.

After a couple weeks of everything we thought we knew about parenting not working, my sister suggested Benadryl. One little pink pill thirty minutes before bedtime for a week. It worked. She fell asleep without her pacifier. And woke up every night and climbed into our bed to press against our ribs. Until she was eleven years old. Part of me had just given up the struggle. But another part of me was desperate to regain some semblance of control. As much as I loved being her mom, her mercurial and fiery spirit had exploded and was wearing me down.

I needed help. Between the constant, gray drizzle, Clare, and depression, I was sinking. I called Judith, a psychiatrist/therapist/spiritual director—miraculously all three in one—who Christine recommended. We talked about infertility, our work in Waco, spirituality, marriage, parenting. She prescribed a new medication for depression and got it right. When I'd been diagnosed in Waco, I'd tried antidepressants. At first it was amazing. I felt like I'd entered a commercial I'd seen in Los Angeles. Camera focused on a beautiful, muted scene of a mountain. After a dramatic pause, a hand appeared as if wiping the inside of the TV screen. With each swipe the picture behind became crisper, colors came alive, and you realized you'd been looking at the world through the smog. I'd noticed the beauty around me. I didn't have to drag myself out of bed and work so hard to brush my teeth twice a day. *This is how other people lived?* But within weeks the effects had worn off. I'd tried different meds. On one, I bought my first pair of cowboy boots—bright red—on a whim and returned to my office, grabbed anyone who happened to be nearby, said, "Dance with me!" and twirled them around the office. Then I went home and crashed. I filled our porcelain claw-foot tub, stepped into the hot water, and considered sinking under and never coming up. Then I'd quit meds. But I trusted Judith.

The medicine she prescribed wiped away the smog but left me feeling like me. Just without my Eeyore side so pronounced. I still struggled with Clare's emotions and behaviors but also saw all that sparkled in her: her impromptu performances, clowning around, snuggling for stories, dancing with her whole body. The way she lit up the world with her smile. I laughed with her when Jeff snatched her up as he came in the door and flipped her upside-down, cheered when she reached her feet up and walked on the ceiling. Life was not just hard or just full of joy. It was both—full force either way.

One day Judith asked me, "What does it feel like when you need space from Clare?" I looked out the window at the giant evergreens.

"Like she will consume me, devour me if she can. But it wouldn't be enough. She's insatiable. She climbs on my lap while I use the toilet." We sat in silence. I curled my feet up under myself on the sofa as a few red leaves fell from the trees. "Like she'd crawl up inside me and stay there. Until she gets mad and wants to claw her way out." The silence stretched until I met Judith's gaze.

"Those aren't emotions, Lynn," Judith said. "I'm talking about sad, mad, glad, scared, and all their variations. It sounds like terror. And maybe exhaustion."

I nodded and let my head hang. My main survival skill was not feeling my truest feelings; I knew *they* would consume me.

Judith continued, "We need to explore the root of that sense of being consumed or devoured, a powerful image." Relieved our time was up, I agreed to take it up another day. I drove home through the rain.

When I arrived, Jeff was cooking dinner, and Clare stood on a chair at our kitchen sink full of suds, washing dishes shirtless—one of her favorite pastimes.

"Mommy," she squealed as she rubbed her chest and pouchy belly with white suds. A warmth filled me; after a few hours away, I was so happy to see her.

"Hold on there, babe," Jeff turned from the pasta sauce on the stove and wrapped his arm around her so she wouldn't slide off the chair. I walked over and squeezed her at arm's length to keep myself dry. She grabbed the water sprayer and whooshed the soap down her legs onto the floor. And all over me. Jeff and I laughed. At least the floor got cleaned in the process. I dried us off and laid a long piece of gauzy fabric the deep blue of the sea on the living room floor. Clare and I danced in it like a river with tambourines as Jeff finished dinner to our Putumayo Caribbean music. Clare swayed her hips, twirled, and flung her light around the room.

When we got to Texas for Christmas, I hung my head out the window on the way home from the airport to drink in the sun. But we weren't finished with Vancouver yet; we had just begun to find our way. Back in B.C. that winter, Jeff skied at Whistler with friends. He snowshoed to a cabin and chopped wood for their cooking fire. And we discovered Galiano Island. Regent professors Loren and Mary Ruth Wilkinson lived there. They oversaw Regent community groups and hosted them for work, conversation, and meals around their table. Our group of twelve gathered at Tsawwassen Ferry Terminal and traveled an hour and a half to the Southern Gulf Island.

After helping clean up our first breakfast, I stepped onto the wooden back deck overlooking the cove. The salty sea and fecundity of the forest permeated the air.

Jeff grabbed some of the last of the season's apples and pressed them into cider with the hand press. "I'll take a turn," I said and squirted sticky drops of juice on myself. Clare flitted from person to person, flashing her smile. When our friend Dan picked her up and flung her over his shoulders with a tickle, her squeal rang across the water.

"Are you good with Clare hanging out here with you for a bit?" I asked him.

"My pleasure," he said.

I slid the glass door open and walked with Jeff through the living room with its floor to ceiling books. No one hanging on my leg for a few moments. We paused for a deep breath and a hug.

"If we could live on Galiano, I'd stay in B.C. forever," Jeff said.

"Deal." I smiled and kissed him.

I wandered into the kitchen and poured a cup of Earl Grey tea from the always hot pot under its cozy. The smell of bergamot filled the air.

"How can we help?" we asked the crew in the kitchen.

I whisked bright yellow eggs into flour and cranked dough through a pasta maker. Mary Ruth hung the long strips of fettucine on a clothes rack to dry. I walked with Jeff down the stairs to the basement, pulled frozen blocks of basil from their summer garden, and whirred them up with oil as he gathered braided garlic from the rafters. Loren showed us how to press a flat rock onto a clove of garlic to open the skin so I could peel and chop it to add to the basil for pesto.

By four o'clock, the weak, winter sun had slipped under the water. Our friends brought Clare inside and washed her hands. Before dinner, I lit the candles in the chandelier over the table. I settled into my place next to Jeff and blew a kiss to Clare sitting on Dan's lap. I laced my fingers with Jeff's as we sang a blessing.

We watched the Wilkinsons and others in Vancouver live in harmony with the planet. They sought justice for it as well as for disenfranchised people. Our theology of creation, community, and beauty expanded like the Georgia Strait into a vast sea. On Tuesday evenings, I talked through it all with a friend. Wai Mei and I sipped tea in her townhouse just down the horseshoe from ours as her husband Wan and Jeff put the kids to bed. We discussed evolving ideas of God. Also, how to get dishes done with toddlers and carve out silence for ourselves. She had a brand-new baby girl. I loved to hold her and smell her baby smell. And a hole opened in me as I watched Wai Mei nurse her.

One night I let the pain spill out. "Sometimes, even though I'm so happy for you and Wan that you have Alisha, and I wouldn't want it any different, and I'm so grateful to have your friendship. . ." I stammered and pushed my new, sea-green glasses up my nose. I started again, "Sometimes, it hurts to watch you nurse her when I want so much to have been pregnant and nursed a baby. Sometimes I have to walk away."

She leaned toward me on the couch. Her black hair framed her face that mirrored my pain.

I confessed, "Loving Clare doesn't take away the sting of not doing what almost all women do. Make, grow, deliver, and nurse a baby. One that 'has your eyes' or 'his nose' or 'looks just like her aunt Kim.'" I put my glasses on the table and wiped away a tear.

"I'm sure that's true, Lynn. It's okay to feel whatever you feel."

I nodded. "Jeff still mourns not having biological kids. It's like a cloud over him when he gets still and quiet. We want more children. It doesn't feel like we're done yet. It's so hard with Clare sometimes, though. And we're not sure how an adoption would work in Canada as US citizens." Though Clare often overwhelmed us, it never occurred to us to remain a family of three.

Wai Mei encircled me with her arms. She let me feel. I laid my head on her shoulder as soft rain pattered the windows. She cried with me; she loved me.

One April day, the sun returned. People scrambled outside like ants fleeing their hill; Vancouver burst into life. Clare traded her red-and-black ladybug umbrella, raincoat, and boots for a blue Schwinn with training wheels and a Barney helmet. She raced around the courtyard with Brian, Wai Mei's son. People opened their windows, and the smell of spices from Korea, Singapore, India, and Malaysia swirled around the courtyard. As the days warmed and grew to their longest, we spent Sunday evenings on Spanish Banks.

We washed the dinner dishes, and Jeff grabbed the purple backpack we carried Clare in on hikes. He propped it open on the living room floor as Clare jumped up and down; then he picked her up and slipped her little legs inside. She had turned three on the beach a month before but was still petite.

"Ready, Freddy?" he asked.

"Yes!" she roared loud enough for the neighbors to hear.

"I can't believe we get to spend summer in Vancouver," I chimed in. "Let's go to the beach!" As we walked along the courtyard, I realized how much I'd miss St. Andrews Hall. We planned to move to the east side of Vancouver a few weeks later; we'd found people living a balance of contemplation and social action there at Grandview Calvary Baptist Church. But today, we still had Spanish Banks.

Jeff fed Clare blackberries as we walked down the hill. *Squishy* and *yummy* she proclaimed every time he plucked one from the huge bushes lining the sidewalk. My hands oozed purple from the gobs I gathered.

"Don't get them in my hair," Jeff said, laughing.

"I'm washing it for you," Clare said as she licked her fingers and ran them through his hair.

We rounded a bend and emerged onto Spanish Banks. On the grass yard above the beach, a guy with long, blond dreadlocks started to tap a djembe drum. Soon a woman in a bikini top and shorts joined in. The rise and fall of the singing of the drums laid down the beat for dancers. Jeff slung off the pack and sat it on the ground. Clare climbed out, already thumping to the rhythm. I spread our quilt out and sat down. My body moved, too. The drums woke up my shoulders and torso and pulled them into the dance.

"Can I go, Mom?"

"Sure, love." I watched her glide toward the music. The drum circle absorbed people as the slap of the djembes carried the low resonance and high-pitched tones across the water.

Clare inched her way closer and closer. Her first and most brilliant language was vibration—motion and rhythm. Her body hummed with it until she couldn't keep from dancing. Jeff lay down on the quilt. His khaki shorts and golf shirt seemed out of place, but he was at home anywhere. Still and always a bridge between worlds.

"I'm going to miss this," I said. "But I also miss daily life with disenfranchised people." I watched Clare dance—she glowed—as Jeff and I talked about the church service on the Eastside at Grandview that morning. I said being there felt like home. He agreed. We were glad we'd live down the street soon. He pointed to Clare and said how amazing she was—twirling like a dervish. I stood up and walked over to Clare, took her hand and danced with her.

"It's almost time to go, love." Pinks, oranges, and reds streaked the sky behind Bowen Island in Howe Sound.

"No. No. No!" she chanted.

"You can have another ride in your backpack." I knew the snack I'd brought and the sway of Jeff's amble would put her to sleep by the time we made it up the hill. If I could get her in the pack.

Jeff appeared, scooped her up and twirled her around like an airplane. She giggled her way right into her backpack. We climbed toward St. Andrews, me feeding Clare bites of a granola bar along the way until her eyes drooped, her head rested, and she slept.

At a Slant

In July, we drove our things to the third floor of a baby-blue, Victorian house on the east side of Vancouver. Yellow daisies, lavender echinacea, and fat pink dahlias in the front garden welcomed us. Clare left her fourth home in her three years circling the sun.

She missed St. Andrew's courtyard full of kids; she wanted constant companions and entertainment. It exhausted her introverted parents. We discovered a community center preschool around the corner on Commercial Drive. Eighteen months had passed since the Parents' Day Out debacle in Waco. Maybe she was ready? She loved it when Jeff and I visited with her in September. Big windows brightened the space filled with centers—dress up, painting, puzzles, and books. We signed her up. I tried to coax her to stay without me over the first few days, but when I crept toward the door, she tailed me and latched on. No way. Kelly, the young director, suggested a quick departure.

The next morning, I stood in our doorway in my pjs and kissed Jeff goodbye as he left for the Skytrain to Regent. After Clare and I finished our oatmeal with the last of the blackberries and walnuts, I wiped white and purple smears from her brown cheeks and dressed us. Blue jeans and a bright purple shirt for Clare. Blue jeans and a favorite old olive-green V-neck for me. We held hands as we walked down the hill to Commercial Drive. A few red and orange leaves drifted down to the sidewalk. Clare kicked at them, sang, and traded smiles with everyone who passed. I'd had her hair braided for the first time at a Jamaican shop, and her braids danced as she walked. She was enchanting. Black women had stopped me in the grocery store the whole first year she was home, advising me how to keep her hair healthy and styled. I had no time or energy for them then, ignorant of how Black hair had been used both to oppress and empower. I was learning.

Clare slowed as we approached the glass doors to the school. I saw our reflection there. She stood just past my knees. The contrast between us surprised me: her amber skin against my ocher; her vibrant clothes beside my subtle shades; newly super-short-clipped, straight hair on my head and the russet braids on hers. In my mind, we were like any other mother and daughter. And yet, so not.

"I'll come in with you, love," I said. The director emerged from her office with a big smile.

She knelt. "I'm so glad you're here, Clare. I put out some red and blue paint for you."

I hugged Clare and pried her from my leg, "Be back soon, honey. I love you."

Kelly reached out and held her. My teeth clenched as Clare began to wail. Kelly's arms encircled her. Clare's arms and legs writhed like tentacles stretching toward me. I looked over my shoulder as I walked toward the door. All the children stared at Clare. But it seemed she didn't see or hear anything. She looked like an animal fighting to survive. Her fire consumed all the oxygen around me, and I felt a crush like the moment before surfacing after a long swim underwater. As I walked through the door, I lectured myself: *Three-year-olds are ready for time with friends apart from Mom. Child development 101 says so.* Shaking, I crossed Commercial Drive to a coffee shop.

Notes for my creative nonfiction class strewn across the table, I cupped a steaming Americano. I took a sip. It burned my tongue, and I jerked the mug back, staining my papers with brown splotches. I ran my hands over my hair and stared out the window. An imaginary cord glimmered there, connecting Clare and me across the two blocks between us. It burned at both ends. I pretended to ignore it and turned back to my work.

For a month, I left her like that three days a week. I ruminated: *It shouldn't be so dramatic to start preschool . . . She's not ready . . . I'm traumatizing her.* I needed to make it work, though; I needed to make *her* work. Kelly said Clare's intense feelings alarmed her. But in time, Clare settled and engaged. Thirty minutes of wails became fifteen. Kelly encouraged me to not give up. After two months, the writhing and screaming abated. Clare perfected her survival skill of adaptation that she'd carry into adulthood. She made friends and donned a red plastic firefighter helmet for the requisite preschool visit to the neighborhood fire station.

Clare also joined a theater class on Granville Island that fall when my mom mailed us some "fun money." Clare told stories with gusto at home, directed Groovy Girl dolls and her bunny in plays. She seemed made for the stage. Mom sent twice as much as the fee, so I invited my new friend Thetena to bring her daughter Lina along, too. We'd met at Kinbrace House—Grandview's nonprofit housing for refugees across the street from us.

I dropped Thetena and the girls at theater one day and wound my way through narrow streets to find an elusive parking space. By the time I'd walked back, class had begun.

I chatted with Thetena in the lobby. "You know you're my hero, right?"

She'd been telling me about her escape from the war between Eritrea and Ethiopia. How she'd sought asylum with Lina in Canada.

"Stop. You're an amazing mom, Lynn. And Clare's not easy. Fantastic but not easy."

I changed the subject. "I'm happy the girls have each other in class." I wondered how Clare was doing right then. *Better that I wasn't here when she went back,* I thought. Thetena told me about the sleepover Clare had the night before. They'd danced and sung. She told me Clare cried a little at bedtime, but Thetena lay with her, gave her a blankie. Clare slept through the night. I couldn't believe it. The teacher appeared and invited us back for the end of class.

"Kids, we're going to show the adults our story." Cheers filled the room.

"Places, please," the instructor clapped.

Clare shone front and center wearing a red cape and white boa. The teacher began to narrate an abridged *Orphan Annie*. *Ugh, always the abandoned kids stories.* Clare dropped to the floor at *scrub*, looked wistfully out the window at *parents*. She jumped into another child's arms when the kind man adopted Annie at the end.

"Woohoo!" we all cheered, and the kids took a happy bow.

Thetena and I walked over to Clare and Lina, the two Brown girls in a room of Canadian Whiteness. We both sank to our knees and hugged them tight, then helped gather props into a basket.

"Thanks for today," I called to the teacher as we headed toward the door.

"Always a delight to have Clare. She's got some charisma, that one."

"She lights up a room." I agreed. I thought how so few people saw the other side of Clare. Thetena had. After one happy playdate, Thetena watched Clare hiss, screech, and spit in Jeff's face—transformed into an enraged cat when he asked her to come home. On Commercial Drive, we'd bop into a store, and then she'd melt down when I said no to new Groovy Girl clothes she *needed*. I dreaded shopping. Finally, we made a rule to never buy anything on the spot; we'd talk and maybe go back another day. The same rule every single time seemed to bring her self-control online—at least sometimes.

As we headed out of the studio, Clare got belligerent. She didn't want to leave. A few steps later, she wanted the candy store. When I said no to feeding pigeons, she sat down.

"We have to get home for lunch, babe." I felt my insides twisting up.

"Come on, Clare. It's time," Thetena said.

"I want candy!" Clare screamed. She was hungry and tired, and transitions were always hard.

We'd crossed over to crazy. There was no escape, only walking through to the other side. I took a deep breath, steeled myself, and picked her up. She thrashed. I gave Thetena the keys and asked her to go on. No audience, please. I couldn't contain Clare's flailing arms and legs. In one swift motion, I swung her onto my shoulders. I clamped a hand on her thigh and one on her back. She pounded my chest with her heels.

"Help me!" she roar-chanted on our long walk to our car where I wrestled her into her seat. Canadians, docile I presumed, scowled at me. For being a terrible mother, I was sure. I got in the car and rested my head on the steering wheel. Thetena held my hand. I turned on the ignition and headed home as Clare's howls reverberated off the windows.

When Canadian Thanksgiving arrived, we celebrated with thirty-odd Regent students at a community house. Leaves crunched under our boots, and lodgepole pines towered over us in the drizzle as we walked to the door. Inside, I helped Clare out of her newest ladybug raincoat. We hung our coats on wall hooks and slipped off our wet boots. Clare ran into her friend's arms, eyes shining. She picked him up with signature exuberance. I laughed as they ran off to play. Jeff and I followed the aroma of Thanksgiving to the yellows, reds, and oranges of the buffet—turkey, sweet potatoes, cranberry chutney, roasted roots, pecan and pumpkin pies. I added my purple Thai rice pilaf, a little embarrassed I couldn't be normal for once. People chatted around the edges of long tables set in a U with autumn leaves and stalks of red berries down the centers. After a while, we gathered the children and sat down to share our gratitude.

When my turn came I said, "I'm grateful for the sea and the islands, healing and community." I looked around and smiled with a deep sense of belonging I'd never known before.

Next, Clare said, "Beluga whales and rainboots." Everyone laughed, and she flashed her smile.

Jeff said, "I'm grateful for this season of study, hikes, Lynn, and Clare." I looked in his green eyes and felt the spark I had ten years before, the day we met on his balcony in Austin. He slid his hand into mine under the table and squeezed. The kids ran off to play after a few bites, but the adults popcorned up around the table to toast our abundant blessings.

The next week, I left Clare and Jeff at home and drove through downtown into Stanley Park, emerging from a tunnel of cedar, fir, and hemlocks to cross over the Burrard Inlet on Lion's Gate Bridge. In North Vancouver, I parked at my therapist's office. On her red couch, my body recognized safety; my muscles softened, breath deepened. I exhaled. I updated her on Jeff and my ongoing conversation about another adoption. As I recounted Clare's alarming sexual explorations with friends, fear, shame, anger, and confusion rose in me. Clare had no physical boundaries. She lived in and through her body, in tune with all its sensations. So much of her behavior was like typical development but exaggerated and at a slant. I felt like we lived in a Salvador Dalí painting—things recognizable but as you'd see them in a dream.

Judith asked me to close my eyes, "Let your mind wander back to other times you've felt similar emotions." Her clock ticked in the silence.

I sank off the couch onto the floor and curled into a ball. I saw myself crouched behind a chair, shaking. I remembered for the first time: my friend's older brother, a teenager to my preschooler, coaxed me to "play" with him. He reached into my pants and touched my vagina. It felt good at first, but I got scared. I told him to stop; we both got angry. I screamed, kicked, and punched; he puffed up and yelled, pulled down his pants. His long, hard penis thrust at my vulva like a weapon. He fought to get inside me. I felt searing pain. Suddenly, he was done. Human again and laughing.

"Don't tell anyone or I'll do it again." He walked away.

I was alone—no one coming to help me. I bled. I told no one.

Judith's voice brought me back. She asked me to feel my body touching the floor, to notice sounds in the room; she grounded me in my senses. Finally, exhausted, I pulled myself onto the couch and she handed me a box of tissues. I blew my nose again and again as we talked. I settled, though the shock remained. We agreed on friends I would call right away for support and to meet again the next week. I'd call her if I needed her in the meantime.

I drove back over Lion's Gate toward home, rolling down the windows to let the cold rush in. Its sting kept me in my body in the present and screamed that I was alive. I stopped halfway and bought a pack of Marlboro Lights, though I'd given up smoking nine years before, and dropped a quarter in a pay phone to call Jeff.

"My session sucked," I said. "Tell you about it later. I'm staying out for a while to recover."

"Are you okay?!" Worry rang in Jeff's voice.

"I need some time." I swallowed hard.

"Take all the time you need." Silence hung between us. "Are you safe?"

"I'm safe. Don't worry. Kiss Clare good night for me."

Next, I called Jodi and Michelle, two close Regent friends. They met me moments later outside a coffee shop. We trudged the streets in the cold. I smoked, talked, yelled, cried, and went silent. Then started again. They held my hands and held me upright when I thought I would crumple to the sidewalk. When I was spent, they walked me to my car and drove me home where Jeff sat on the top step of the porch. He stood as I climbed the stairs.

"Can I hug you?" He reached for me as I hit the top step.

"No," I pushed past him. Jodi stayed with him.

Michelle walked me up to my bedroom. I sank into bed, clothes still on, and turned my back. Her auburn curls brushed my shoulder as she pulled the covers up. My mind escaped my body, habitual after almost thirty years of practice dissociating. I slept.

Jeff came with me to see Judith the next week. We dropped onto the red couch hand in hand. Judith talked about how to walk together through my new memories of abuse, explaining that Clare's experiences and behaviors triggered my trauma. I described myself curled in a tight ball rocking on Jeff and my bed, heart pounding the day before. I'd squeezed a pillow over my head to block out Clare's howls from the adjacent bedroom where Jeff was trying to calm her, my own trauma too triggered for me to help.

Judith spoke a possibility, "This experience can be an invitation to healing. To become more whole and free."

Afterward, Jeff and I walked the seawall in silence. A slate-gray sky hovered over us. A sea lion popped its head above the choppy water. The air worked like smelling salts and woke me up from the fog that had descended in session. Drizzle began to fall, and I snapped the front of my raincoat.

"I'm scared, Jeff. I don't know who I'm becoming."

"What do you mean?"

"I don't know who God is at all anymore. I don't know who I am. Clare brings out so much shame and anger in me." I remembered yelling at her the day before.

I looked at Jeff and thought how much I wanted him to rescue me. To lead instead of follow—in parenting, spiritually, and health for our minds and bodies. But would I ever follow if he did? I said I'd been waiting for him to create some ideal version of our life, ourselves. But not anymore. I was responsible for my own healing, growth, and life.

I fell silent, looked at the Sound, and waited. Giving him enough space and oxygen to speak meant keeping silent way beyond my comfort level. Across the water, I saw Spanish Banks. My sacred place.

"I don't know where *my* healing is. Or how to find it. But I want to." Jeff had been despondent since Waco, still mad at God for our infertility. And our old boss's favorite criticism played in his head: Jeff lacked initiative and passion. He'd been flattened. When he took my hand, I turned and looked up at him. The rain dripped down my face.

"I'm so tired. And afraid," I said. "What if as we become our truest selves, we don't fit together? What if we grow farther and farther apart?" Silence hovered between us.

"We will accept and love each other no matter who we become," Jeff looked at the sea stretching south to the Gulf Islands. "God knew who we'd become when He brought us together. He will see us through."

I had married him for that simple faith and confidence. It tethered me to the firm, good earth my passions threatened to rip from under me. I wasn't sure I believed him, but I did believe we were in it together with Clare no matter what.

Spring finally returned, and a Regent friend called with a question. Would we want to meet her pregnant friend Monica? She was considering placing her child for adoption. A serendipitous baby excited us. Maybe it was time? We took the first step and invited Monica to dinner at our house. Clare was ecstatic; her three-year-old brain didn't register "we're just talking about it." The baby under Clare's small hand in Monica's belly was hers. After baby boy Riley was born, we visited. Monica was still undecided. One day, she moved back East with Riley. Our heartbreak made plain how ready we felt for another child. Clare cried; was her heart broken, too?

The next day she reared back and slapped me hard across the face. We both froze for the seconds it took the sting to fade. Heat and redness rose on my cheek. When my breath and thought returned, I grasped her hands hard.

"I can't let you hit me," I plopped her on her bed and walked out. Jerking her door closed, I slid to the floor outside it.

Clare screamed, "Let me out!"

"You stay in your room until you're sorry and in control."

Her shrieks drowned me out, "I want you!"

My fear turned to resolve. "I love you. I'll never go away, Clare. But you have to calm down." Time crawled through her endless screams. I stared at the pile of dishes in the sink. The remnants of a burned quesadilla stuck to a plate. The charred smell hung in the air.

Then an eerie silence invaded the space. A moment later, the door lurched, and glass exploded on the other side. My body shook with the vibration and fear. I flung open the door. Her lamp and CD player lay hurled to the floor. *How could my tiny, four-year-old child do that?* I held her and rocked us both until our hearts slowed their racing.

I ached to understand. And control Clare. But nothing controlled Clare. We'd tried spanking in Waco but seeking peace through violence felt dissonant. And it had no effect. We'd employed my social work and Jeff's marriage and family therapy skills to no avail. We turned to our Canadian family doctor who sent us to play therapy. Clare loved the dolls, but her behavior continued to escalate. One morning on a camping trip with our St. Andrew's friends Wai Mei and Wan, she slapped me several times. Jeff stepped in and gave a time-out, I talked, we dished out positive and negative consequences. The last time she slapped me, I picked up her thrashing body and took her into our tent.

My voice came out soft and low. "I'm not mad at you, but I'm going to slap you. So you know what it feels like when you hurt me. You have to stop." She went still and silent, staring at me.

"I love you, Clare. I don't know how to make you understand it's not okay." My voice and hands began to shake. "I'm going to count to three and then slap you."

And I did. Hard. She didn't flinch or cry. Or ever slap me again.

Somehow the chaos and violence in our home didn't dampen our longing for another child. My research led me to Adoption Link, a Chicago adoption agency that collaborated with Canadian authorities.

As summer school began, and Jeff took his last classes for a master's of Christian studies degree, we took virtual classes on interracial adoption. Margaret at Adoption Link called us a few weeks in. Keanna, an African American woman in Chicago, wanted to talk with us. Her baby boy was due in late August. She couldn't parent him. Our White privilege and the injustice of the situation weighed on us again. She was a poor, single, Black woman, and we were a White, married couple from wealthy families with access to everything. But we set up a conference call.

We talked about the summer heat in Chicago and Texas. Keanna's shy, Midwestern voice sounded hunched over and tired, "I'm calling him Antonio," she said.

"Our daughter's name is Clare," Jeff said. Clare wasn't on the call; we'd learned our lesson.

"What's she like?"

Jeff continued, "She just turned four. She loves acting, dancing, and music. She's passionate and funny." We chatted a few minutes more. That was it. We agreed to pay her doctor bills over the summer and have regular phone calls. In August, we would adopt her son. We called him Patrick Anthony, after St. Patrick. Pax for short. Our hope was that he would bring peace into the world. Clare would have a brother; we would have a son. We'd fly to pick him up as soon as he was born. Gel as a family over the fall while Jeff finished his thesis. Then move our happy family of four to Dallas in December—back to family, a strong Black community, and Jeff's deep Texas roots. Clare needed stability; maybe planting roots would ground her. Seamless.

In late August, Margaret called. Keanna thought she was in labor. We should buy plane tickets when it was definite. Jeff compartmentalized and studied. I bounced from task to task like a pinball. We waited. And waited. In two days, we called back. They hadn't heard from Keanna again but would check in on her. We waited. And waited.

And waited. They couldn't find Keanna. Maybe she would call. The butterflies in my stomach turned to wasps.

On September 6, Margaret called. "The hardest thing is we will probably never know." Keanna disappeared. They were so sorry. *Sometimes it happens. Let's put you back on the list.*

That day in my beloved Vancouver, lightning crashed into the earth. Thunder roared. Her gentle rain turned into a sky-splitting storm. Our dear friends Cliff and Christine were visiting on Bowen Island, so we took the ferry over, flattened by despair. Cliff raced Clare and their boys around the yard in a wheelbarrow. Jeff held their new baby girl to his chest and silently wept. I fell into Christine's arms on the couch and sobbed.

Six weeks later, we were gone.

Hope

In early October, Jeff, Clare, and I rolled into Oak Cliff across the Trinity River from downtown Dallas. We turned on Bishop Avenue. Eyes peeled for the likeness of the online picture: an old, wooden, two-story house with black lampposts in front of white brick columns. Baby blue, like on 16th street in Waco and Venables in East Vancouver. We'd rented it sight unseen, a hurried escape after losing Patrick. Brad—the stocky, dark-haired owner of the boxy fourplex—met us at the door and led us upstairs.

As he unlocked our door, he said, "Welcome to Dallas."

I looked down at Clare. "This is our new house, babe. Welcome home."

She looked up, eyes wide; her hand gripped mine.

Jeff walked through into our new living room, "Home again, home again, jiggety jog." He'd said that in seven other doorways in the ten years we'd been married.

I felt a familiar sinking disillusionment when I landed in a place I'd only imagined. Clare reached her arms up. I lifted her onto my hip, glad to hold something between me and this new space. Her legs dangled down to my knees. A faint musty smell lingered under a biting bleach odor, and the carpet was old and worn. But light poured into each room through big, wood-framed windows.

We followed Brad through the front bedroom onto the balcony. The still hot, fall Texas sun slid down the western sky and waltzed with the branches of the big pecan tree in the front yard. I exhaled deeply.

Back inside, we walked to the back of the apartment across smoky blue linoleum that tiled the kitchen floor.

"The downstairs neighbors have three kids. You'll like them, Clare," Brad said. Clare perked up and leaned toward Jeff. I passed her to him.

"You'll have to use your ballerina feet," I said. We'd worked on that for a year on Venables. Clare's normal walk sounded like a sumo wrestler—so loud in such a little body. *Walk softly* meant nothing but she knew how to dance. We crossed into the second bedroom, an enclosed back balcony. I raised my eyebrows and nodded to Brad's marketing job. A washer and dryer hugged one wall. Under a back wall of windows was just enough space for our low IKEA bookshelves. We started setting up home.

Jeff's prospective job at an urban nonprofit that had seemed certain a month before evaporated within a week. He looked for ways to pay our bills. God love him. (Unable to multitask while parenting Clare, I'd officially joined the long-term unemployed.) He always did whatever it took: sandblasted furniture between counseling appointments in Austin, continuously cleaned bathrooms, handrails, and doorknobs at Regent during the 2002 SARS virus scare, re-tiled our bathroom on the east side in exchange for rent. A friend called and said her son-in-law had a clothing warehouse that needed organization. We said, "Yes, please." Jeff tucked his graduate degrees in his back pocket and went to work at Consolidated Clothiers.

Clare and I kissed Jeff goodbye one morning as he headed out in blue jeans and a T-shirt. We pulled on shorts and T-shirts and went for a long, slow walk. At the top of a hill, nestled between pecans, elms, and oaks a mile north of us, we found the Kessler School on the second floor of a Methodist Church, wandered inside, and introduced ourselves. The director smiled and led Clare, clutching my hand, to the open doors of the four-year-old class. Clare pulled me in behind. Her wide eyes scanned the room. Huge windows let morning sun filter through the trees onto colorful carpet squares. Red and blue beanbags marked a reading corner. Clare let go and began to explore and smile, looking over her shoulder at me every few moments. The kids seemed friendly—mostly White but a few Brown, thank goodness. The teacher was kind and respectful to Clare and me both.

A little dark-haired girl tilted her head and looked back and forth at Clare and me. She walked up to me and spoke.

"Are you her mom?"

"Yep."

"Why is she brown and you're not?" A hundred eyes had asked us over the years. Once at the beach in Vancouver a woman asked *Where'd you get her?* as if Clare were a pair of shoes. All eyes scanned a playground when Clare called out the chorus *Mom, Mom, Mom,* looking for a color match anywhere. When I answered, the gawking began; sometimes Clare got peppered with questions on the monkey bars.

"She grew in another lady's tummy who was brown, too, and we adopted her. Her long-ago family came from Africa and mine came from Europe." I was ready for this, preparing since she came home from Haiti. Melanin and how different skin tones evolved based on exposure to sun. I could bring books—*Extraordinary Black Americans, The Colors of Us, African Dreams*—for story time. But she was four and satisfied. She ran off to play.

Miraculously, Clare nodded and turned back to the dress-up clothes when I said I was going down the hall for a minute. I knocked on the director's door and asked to enroll Clare. She went happily Monday, Wednesday, Friday from nine to noon. I had a break from direct-service parenting, and Clare had new friends and learned to read. Hallelujah!

A home, a paycheck, and a preschool. Check. My eyes opened wide for an adoption agency. We were like couples doing round after round of in vitro fertilization—whatever it takes. Or maybe aggressive, unashamed animals mating on the Discovery Channel. Trying to propagate the species. Not that we could procreate, but the instinctive drive must have overtaken us. Parenting Clare sure wasn't bliss, though we loved her fiercely.

After a few dead ends, I found Hope Cottage. The receptionist connected me to a young, upbeat social worker named Jeriva. She said they could accept our paperwork and training from Adoption Link in Chicago. *It sounds like you've been through a lot.* Her compassion and kindness made me cry. We scheduled an update for our home study and by January our name landed on the waiting families list. I let the longing slide back in.

One month later, Clare stood on a chair beside me at our kitchen sink. She washed plastic containers and crooned "Brown-Eyed Girl"—like Jeff did to her each night: *Sha-la-la-la-la, my brown-eyed girl, and you, my brown-eyed girl.* Metal measuring cups became cymbals. I swished my hips and washed plates and knives. We stacked dishes on a slatted, wooden drying rack next to the sink. When the phone rang, I grabbed a dish towel and turned around to our long pine table. Our kitchen counter, island, and dining room, it held a pile of cookbooks, a glass jar of pens, a notepad, and a cordless phone plugged into the jack on the wall. I dried my hands and picked up the phone.

Jeriva's voice said, "Hi, Lynn. How are you?" My breath caught. Clare felt my energy shift and turned.

Jeriva chuckled into the silence. "We have a baby girl who was born five days ago. Her young birth mom is not able to parent. She chose your profile."

A baby girl. I sank to the floor; Clare's face registered alarm. She climbed down and sat in my lap. A tear slid down my cheek as I hugged her.

"She is a quarter Black but looks White. I've checked her fingernails and behind her ears. She's probably not getting any darker." Jeriva knew we thought Clare needed a Black sibling—not White like us. It was the one thing we specified. We could handle drug exposure or a history of mental illness; we'd love so much and so well it would all work out. My mind went numb. The silence stretched.

"Jeriva, what do I do now?"

She laughed, "Call Jeff and then call me back."

"Right. I'll get right back to you."

I set Clare on the floor. "Everything is okay, baby. I'm okay." As I put the phone on its cradle, I said, "Want to watch some Teletubbies?" The creases on her forehead smoothed, and she ran to the living room. The Vancouver fiascos had schooled us: leave her out of specific baby conversations. Luckily, TV mesmerized her. I handed her some fruit leather, popped the VHS tape into our little TV, stole to my room, and called Jeff.

"Hey, babe . . . Jeriva called."

"Really?" his voice climbed an octave above his usual baritone.

"There's a baby girl."

"For us?"

"Maybe. Her birth mom chose us."

"Already? Wow!" He was starting to stammer.

"She's White. Well, biracial but looks White."

Jeff asked what I thought. I recounted our conversations about race. Hard enough for Clare to have White parents without a White sibling, too. Wouldn't she feel left out, like she didn't belong? He agreed but wondered if the birth mom's choice was providential. I looked out the back windows at the clear winter sky. A scarlet cardinal sat on a branch.

"Could it be right to reject a child because she looks White any more than because she's Black?" I asked.

"Maybe we stop thinking and just allow." Jeff was good at that: float along, trust.

I opened my clenched hands in my lap. My thin gold wedding band glimmered in the sunlight. Jeff had surprised me, too. I hadn't been looking for a fraternity boy in a red Jeep Cherokee. But I'd followed my heart to him.

"A baby girl, Jeff," I choked out.

"How soon can we pick her up?" he asked.

I laughed.

When Jeriva answered the phone, I said, "Yesandcanwepick heruprightnow?!"

She chuckled, "Maybe by tomorrow. Come at ten thirty to sign paperwork. And, Lynn, her birth mom didn't name her. No pressure, but do you have a name picked out?"

I named her that second: Anna Josephine Alsup. Anna who worshiped in the temple, waiting for the Christ and my sister and aunt's middle name. Josephine, my grandmother and mom's middle name. The legacy of strong women; the matriarchal line.

I called Jeff. "I sort of named her. Is that okay?" Kind, generous Jeff agreed.

We dropped Clare off at the Kessler School the next morning and drank coffee from colorful Italian pottery at a coffee shop near Hope Cottage. We sat hand in hand, waiting for ten thirty. We stared at each other. We pretended to read *The New York Times*. Then we drove a few blocks and entered Hope Cottage. We sat with Jeriva at a long conference table, signed a million papers, and wrote a check to cover social workers and lawyers. We planned to meet Jeriva at six at Anna's Hope Cottage foster home fifteen minutes south of our apartment; she'd be home with us by bedtime. We walked to our car in a daze. This was real.

Afterward, I dropped Jeff at work, picked Clare up, settled her down for a rest, and called my sister, Kim. "We pick her up tonight, and I have nothing. We haven't told Clare yet. I can't think." I'd donated every baby thing to the refugee house in Vancouver.

"You need a car seat and diapers. I've got you covered," Kim said through her own tears. She lived forty-five minutes north; she'd stop at Baby's R Us on the way down.

We must have told Clare when Jeff got home, but Anna's arrival eclipsed that conversation in my memory. Kim brought a bassinette from her attic and half of Baby's R Us. The changing pad lay on the dryer in our bedroom, diapers and wipes on the shelf over the washing machine, and the bassinette full of clothes at the foot of our bed. Jeff, Clare, Kim, and I went to pick up our baby.

The low winter sun reflected in pools of rainwater on the street as I wrapped my red scarf around my neck. Clare held Kim's hand and they followed Jeff and me onto the porch. Light shone through a small square window in the top of the door. I knocked and looked right and left through the glass on tiptoes. Jeriva's eyes sparkled when she opened the door. She seemed so settled and comfortable; I took a deep breath, and my shoulders relaxed.

"Come in," she said, smiling. We walked over the threshold. In a brown La-Z Boy recliner, a man with graying temples, bushy eyebrows, and a kind smile rocked a tiny, pink baby. Jeriva said, "This is Bill." His slight wife introduced herself as Jean and picked Anna up from his lap. She handed her to me.

Anna's six pounds filled my hands, and I rested her head in the crook of my arm. I felt the heat from her little body. *How could this tiny, perfect baby be mine?* She looked up at me. Nine months before in Vancouver, I hadn't known she'd been created. I hadn't felt her movements, seen elbows and heels press out through my belly. I hadn't ever talked to her. In utero, she'd heard her birth mom's unique heartbeat and breath. Familiar voices at home and school. Knew her birth mom's favorite foods, rhythms of sleep and wakefulness; felt her emotions. Those all disappeared when she emerged at noon six days before. Bright lights and machine beeps in the hospital nursery accosted her for days. Now I had her in my arms.

I whispered, "Hi, Anna. I'm so happy to meet you. I'm your mom." My whole body quickened.

Jeff gazed at her over my shoulder; I handed her to him. His green eyes stared deep into her blue and vice versa. They seemed to lock into each other in that moment. Jeff and I sat down on the couch with Clare between us. She added her hands to Jeff's on Anna's back and bottom. Kim sniffed, wiping tears from the corners of her eyes. We passed the bitty baby across the gray sectional to her. She laid Anna along her thighs and rested her small head at her knees. Anna's tiny feet pressed Kim's hips.

She held Anna's head in her hands, "Welcome to our family, baby Anna. We love you."

Clare needed to use the bathroom, so Jeriva pointed us down a hallway hung with generations of family pictures. We went into the bathroom together, and when she finished peeing, I propped her on my leg at the sink to wash her hands. She lathered the rose soap into bubbles between her small, chestnut hands.

As she reached into the stream from the faucet, she said, "I thought she was supposed to be brown, Mama."

I took a deep breath, "I thought so, too, love." I turned off the faucet and set her down on the ground. She dried her hands on a ruby-red, terry cloth towel.

"This baby has long ago grandparents from Africa like you. But she doesn't look like it, does she?"

"No." She studied the towel.

I knelt, eye-to-eye, "This is the baby God gave us, honey. Daddy and I believe we're meant to be a family."

Her face went inscrutable, and she held my gaze. Then she turned and darted out the door back to Jeff, Kim, and Anna. I stood up and wondered how I'd done. I wanted a rule book to navigate parenting, race, and adoption, but I was making it up as I went along.

After a bit, we hugged and thanked Bill and Jean. Kim took a picture of Jeriva and me with Anna in my arms under the streetlight. Jeriva's dark-brown chin and long locks squeezed to my temple.

"How can I thank you enough?" I asked her.

"It's the best of my job. Thanks for letting me share it."

I clicked Anna into her car seat and climbed in beside her with Clare on the other side. We each held one small hand as Jeff drove us home. My mom, nieces, and nephew waited there—Anna's welcome party.

After a few days of my mom's help, determined for Clare's life to remain as normal as possible, I slung Anna around me in a Malaysian cloth Wai Mei had given me in Vancouver and walked to the Kessler School to pick Clare up and picnic on our way home. Friends brought dinner and made homemade Valentine cards with Clare—a tradition I couldn't swing myself. I met Kim at the Dallas Zoo, strapped on a navy BabyBjörn carrier, and slipped my two-week-old baby inside.

My sister's kids Annie and Ben ran wild through the children's zoo with Clare. Two-year-old Kate sat in my lap holding Anna in hers. Kate loved Anna; Clare didn't. Instead of a playmate, she'd gotten a baby that slept, pooped, and ate. And competed for attention. Clare preferred being an Altizer with Annie and Ben. And at Kim's, the Altizer house, an unlimited supply of cookies and Rice Krispy treats flowed from the pantry; *Rug Rats* and *SpongeBob* always entertained: a sugar-TV-cousin heaven. A distinct contrast to our house. Kim called me The Sergeant. I defaulted to control, and Clare's volatility strengthened my grip. Out-of-control still triggered me. Jeff acquiesced to Clare's demands, but I became a despot. (Maybe Jeff wanted to be an Altizer, too.)

Nighttime became my favorite time. On my night to put Clare to bed, I turned on her bedside lamp and slid under the covers of her twin bed. Crisp cotton sheets lay smooth against our skin, a warm comforter pressed down around our bodies. She draped an arm and leg across me—as close as possible. We read a few books and turned out the light. I stroked up and back, up and back, up and back from wrist to elbow on the softest underbelly skin of her arm until she fell asleep. I lifted her limbs off my body and crawled out. Kneeling next to her bed, I watched the rise and fall of her chest, her smooth face, body relaxed, braids fanned out across the pillow. Warmth ran through me.

I tiptoed to the living room and gave Jeff a kiss. On a good day, I brushed my teeth. The unique exhaustion of newborn baby days pushed me into bed. Jeff, the night owl, gave Anna her bedtime bottle and snuggled her into her bassinette. Around three in the morning, I woke to soft murmurs and gentle cries, slid to the end of the bed and lifted her up.

"Hi, little love. You're hungry?"

She immediately calmed. We rounded the corner to the kitchen in the early morning quiet. I dumped premeasured formula into a bottle Jeff had filled with water, and we settled back into bed. No one else wanted anything from me during night feeds. The world stood still. The refrigerator hum soothed us, and the moon lit the room, turning everything silky, dark blue. I held Anna belly to belly, the bottle's nipple right next to mine. Our breathing synced, and her satisfied sucking promised all was right and good. I gazed at her perfect, pink face. My tiny, happy baby. She smelled like me, knew me, snuggled down onto my chest when she was ready to sleep again. I fell headlong in love. I was almost sad when Anna started sleeping through the night. Almost.

When Mother's Day came, we drove to meet my parents at my sister's. My mom, sister, and I settled into the shade by their new pool—hiding my light skin and freckles from the sun—with Anna on my lap, a white sun hat strapped under her chin. Jeff, tan already, stood immersed at the edge of the deep end, a pale imprint where his T-shirt usually blocked the sun. Clare gleamed wet and deep brown alongside lounge chairs on a tall, wide wall in her blue-and-white tankini.

"Come on in, babe. You can do it." Jeff jumped on one leg to get water out of his ear.

Clare looked nervous. White beads swung at the end of her braids. "Promise you'll catch me?"

"Already promised ten times. Yes!"

"Go, Clare!" we all chanted. She closed her eyes and flung herself into the water. Flying through the air, muscles etched in arms and legs, no baby fat left on her almost five-year-old body, she looked like an athlete. Jeff stretched out his arms and caught her as she smacked the water. She came up laughing.

I cheered and turned back to Mom and Kim. I said Anna had rolled from back to belly and back again; she'd sit up soon. Early at three months, but she was in a hurry to keep up with Clare. Anna watched everyone as we talked, the pink of her cheeks deepening with the heat. Clare jumped off the wall again and again into Jeff's steady arms.

"I gotta take a break, babe," he said.

"One more time!"

"Okay, but then I'm out."

"You need some food, too," I called. I fed her before, during, and after swimming to avoid meltdowns. Her body seemed to burn twice as much fuel as others.

"I'm sure Kim has some cookies."

I knew she needed protein and fat, but I could slip those in with some sugar. A spoonful and all that. The offer triggered Clare's sugar addiction, and she leaped, then climbed out of the water. Anna beamed her toothless smile for Jeff, her favorite, while Clare and I went inside and she settled in front of the television with food and Annie, Ben, and Kate.

It was after dark when we started the forty-five-minute drive home down Central Expressway. Risky. Clare needed much more sleep than most five-year-olds; by eight o'clock, she was overtired and hyper; she hated leaving the Altizers; sugar and TV both put her over the edge. Changes in rules, food, sleep, transitions all fractured Clare. But we had chanced it to enjoy a family celebration.

And so it began. No words, just wails. I tried music. Her feet pounded the back of the driver seat. She screeched, face flushed like fire. Her eyes squeezed tight as adrenaline strengthened her. Arms flailed. Distracting or demanding she stop was futile: she was too far gone. I fended off her arm nearest Anna as Jeff pulled off the highway. I knew I'd have bruises. Anna stared, frozen, as I jumped out, ran around and unclicked Clare's seatbelt. I held Clare in the cool night air and said we couldn't go until she calmed. I rocked. I squeezed. Each time she slumped, I moved toward the car. And it began again.

After ten minutes, Jeff traded out with me and held her beside the highway for ten more while I sang to Anna and stroked her face. Finally spent, Clare let Jeff strap her in next to me in the backseat where I sat between the girls to keep Anna safe. Clare held my hand, and both girls nodded off as I sat numbed, the adrenaline draining from my body. At home, Jeff carried Clare's limp body to bed. But a few hours later, her shrieking startled us awake. We ran to Clare's bedroom and worked to wake her. Her night terrors had begun when I'd taken Anna to Vancouver—desperate to introduce her to my people—a month before. It felt like Clare was breaking; we sought out a new play therapist.

At our first meeting, Jeff and I talked about night terrors and Clare devolving into what seemed like primal states. We described Clare's shifting identities: *I'm Rachel,* she'd say. Changing every week or so, she'd insist we call her by her new name. On Clare's visits, she played with a dollhouse as the therapist took notes. The therapist said we needed to keep Clare from fragmenting. It terrified us; we had both studied multiple personality disorder.

A bit of comfort arrived with our friend Michelle from Vancouver. She'd walked the streets with me reeling from my memories of abuse; she'd sat at our table in East Vancouver. Now we lived twenty minutes from her parents. The day Michelle visited, she joined our house hunt in Oak Cliff. I loved having part of our chosen family with us. I missed belonging. I missed beauty. I missed Vancouver—the place I'd found home.

Jeff drove us from house to house with Michelle in the back seat with the girls. "I used to hang out in Oak Cliff with my high school boyfriend," she said. Her chortle filled the car as she told stories. When she spotted Aunt Stelle's snow cone shop, she said, "No way! You have to stop. Pink Lady is the best; it tastes like cake."

Jeff pulled over, and we joined the line. Michelle wound her long, amber hair into a bun. A few stray curls bounced out. Sweat ran down our backs as we passed Anna back and forth, her cheeks turning from pink to red. Bees buzzed around a trash can full of paper cones stained red, blue, and yellow while Clare spun around people on the curb eating snow cones. She paused, lifted her face to the sun and drank in the heat.

When we bit into the cold, shaved ice, I agreed with Michelle, "Crazy worth the wait."

After we added our cones to the trash, Michelle climbed in the backseat with the girls for one last stop where Jeff and I jumped out to look at a house. After dinner back home, Michelle gave Clare a bath, read books, and put her to bed. We sat in the kitchen with peppermint tea and rich, dark chocolate while the girls slept. Michelle unloosed her bun. She looked worried. She described how Clare had leaned over her to Anna while Jeff and I were at the last house.

"You know they'll leave you and never come back," Clare had said to her little sister sucking her pacifier. "That's why they're looking for a new house." Jeff's face wrinkled in pain. My forehead dropped to the table, and I exhaled slow, long, and loud.

The next week I dropped Clare at a friend's, put Anna down for a nap, and sipped coffee at the kitchen table while I waited for a call from Clare's therapist. Grabbing the phone on the first ring, I told her about the day with Michelle.

She said, "First, I want to compliment you on a lovely child who has disturbances but is not disturbed. Sometimes when a little girl has had a lot of moves, she gets sad about a past move even though this move is happy. We can call the sad feelings 'early move feelings.'" She said to talk to Clare like she was talking to me. I scribbled notes. We moved on to Clare's nightmares and changing personalities.

"Maybe her nightmares come from memories. We can call them 'baby feelings' and rock them away. Let Clare know she can hold her sadness and go on. She doesn't have to become different people."

I shifted in my seat as I hunched over my paper. The usual soreness in my back flared, still there even after two years of Canadian physiotherapy. *Could a five-year-old understand these things?*

It sounded so sensible, simple as I read Jeff my notes that night in bed.

New Terrain

Clare began kindergarten and, as fall unfolded, I revived my practice of silent retreats. I had taken my first one in Vancouver with my friend Jodi—two nights in a condo near the Washington border. I walked the forest, read, wrote, napped. At dinnertime, we'd cooked veggies, beans, and rice, and she'd introduced me to hard apple cider from the Skagit valley. We went away every couple months after. Dorm rooms in an old church on UBC campus, Rivendell retreat center perched atop Kate's Hill on Bowen Island. Each time, I found my center; I discovered a home inside myself and came back refreshed, more patient and kind. In Dallas, I ferreted out a monastery and retreat center run by Discalced Carmelite friars twenty minutes from our new house. On a Friday afternoon, I put a sweater, pajamas, and toothbrush in a bag; filled another with greens, beans, oats, and soymilk; and waited for Jeff to get home.

As he walked in, I walked out with a kiss. "Dinner's on the stove. You're the best. Please not too much sugar or TV."

He nodded. "We'll be fine. Enjoy."

On the way, National Public Radio played *All Things Considered*, and red brake lights pulsed as cars inched closer to a traffic signal. Rain shimmered in bright white headlamps. Red and yellow leaves shone slick on the ground. With no kid music playing, no screams, no demands, I noticed it all. I turned off the paved thoroughfare onto a dirt road where a wrought-iron gate opened onto forty-five acres across a hilltop. My body recognized what was happening. My breath deepened; I exhaled completely.

The administrator met me at the massive front door. "Welcome, Lynn. I'll show you around and up to your room."

"Thank you. I'm so grateful to be here," I said.

She took my forty-dollar donation and pointed out the kitchen past a white statue of Mother Mary looking down at me from her pedestal. I followed her down a red-carpeted hallway hung with icons of St. Teresa of Jesus and St. John of the Cross— penetrating brown eyes, gazing heavenward. Concrete stairs led to a small room with a single bed, a desk, and a bathroom.

"This is perfect. Thank you," I said and closed the door. The silence. I turned to the bed and fell in for a short nap but woke the next morning, fourteen hours later. A whole day ahead to hike, eat, read, and pray.

When I got home, Clare said, "Mommy, you're so much nicer now." Yes. Yes, I was.

My friend Angelle, a yoga therapist, suggested I attend to my body as well as my spirit. I'd met her through Hope Cottage the year before. Angelle had called me two weeks after Anna came home—they'd been matched with a newborn, too, named Isabelle. Their baby looked like a fairy, maybe an elf: petite, small brown eyes set wide apart taking in every movement, tiny ears and feet, light-brown skin, a broad forehead. She was coiled tight. Angelle's life and mine had knit together with simple living, art, mindful parenting, and cloth diapers over eight months of Friday morning coffee with our babies. One Tuesday morning, I dropped Anna with Angelle and, at thirty-four years old, took my first yoga class—Explore the Body.

I entered the storefront studio into silence. The kind that permeates a space and embraces you. I slipped off my Simple clogs, placed them in a cubby, and walked through opaque, pastel curtains flowing between the entryway and classroom to find an open space on the floor.

"Anyone new to yoga?" A woman a bit older than me with messy, short blond hair surveyed the room. Five other women looked toward me at the back as I raised my hand.

"We'll take good care of you," the smiling instructor said.

By the middle of class, I lay on my back with the instructor digging a channel around my right hip and down my inner thigh with her fingers, stretching the muscle that strangled my hip. My tears and terror spiked, stored there for decades.

"Breathe through it," she said. I breathed.

"Let's get partners and come to hands and knees."

My partner sat facing me as I curled my toes under and straightened my legs into downward facing dog; then she grounded her hands in front of mine and placed her heels near my shoulders. She lifted her bum off the ground and walked her heels up my back, massaging it. My head hung loose under her legs. Such vulnerable poses.

"Your back feels like a steel plate, Lynn."

My imaginary armor. My body alert for danger since my childhood sexual assault. And Clare's explosiveness jabbed my wounds. She ran away from me in stores, at parks, at home; she screamed that I wasn't her *real* mom, cried, and hit.

"Imagine exhaling into the place of tension. Imagine expanding," the instructor said.

It was terrifying, but Angelle was convincing. After a few sessions, I was hooked.

As I explored this new terrain, Jeff followed a path deeper into the for-profit world. Winter creeped into North Texas, and he left Consolidated Clothiers to work with his closest friends on the top floor of an old building five minutes from the house we'd bought. They thought it was cool—in a run-down, vintage sort of way—drinking pour-over coffee and dreaming up projects in front of space heaters. Jeff did finances for his friends' entrepreneurial dreams in real estate and marketing. I hated the world that called humans "revenue producers" and lured people into consumption, but Jeff wanted to bring compassion and integrity to the marketplace. *Were my fears about us drifting apart materializing?* Anna and Clare took all my energy and kept the lurking question at bay.

As Jeff and his friend Wayne worked together, our families' friendship deepened. We'd met Wayne Strong on a reconnaissance visit to Dallas before moving from Vancouver. As we sat outside Einstein Bagels, his long legs jutting out from under the table, he told us about a rental house in Oak Cliff. He talked about his experience of race and justice in Dallas as a White man with an interracial family at a Black, urban church. He laughed easily and gave generously of his time and knowledge; his eyes sparkled. He and his wife, Avis, had a daughter and two sons, one Clare's age. When Clare and I spent time with Avis, people assumed Clare was Avis's daughter because their skin tones matched. Clare loved that. (She flinched when people said to me with Anna, "Look at the baby! What gorgeous blue eyes. She looks just like you.") And she idolized Jordyn, their daughter three years older, who was friendly, creative, funny, and beautiful. The Brothers—as they called the boys—were wild and fun. Before long, Clare wanted to be a Strong as much as she wanted to be an Altizer.

Another found family was our church. Jeff had visited Oak Cliff Presbyterian just after Anna came home the year before. Traditional church didn't interest me, but he'd called it friendly, multiracial, and multigenerational. That piqued my interest. And the pastor focused on Jesus stories. I didn't want theological proclamations, but I did want Jesus. We'd found home there.

Anna toddled across the parking lot one Sunday in white tights and a blue dress, watching her breath condense in the morning air. Her left hand grasped Jeff's finger and her right mine. Clare skipped, colorful skirt swishing as she went. Our friend opened the church door, and Clare flung herself around her legs. The stately Black woman—a retired principal—stood tall and thin in a stylish black suit.

"Good morning, sweetheart," she beamed. "And how's the birthday girl?"

Anna smiled from behind Jeff's leg. "Anna's great," Jeff said.

"We brought cake for everyone after service." I opened the box I carried, and she laughed. Clare's perfect kindergarten creation: cake glued together with strawberry icing where it had fallen apart; pastel pink, yellow, purple, and blue sprinkles crowded the top with candles to match. She'd plunked down a big, white, number one candle just off center.

After we left the cake in the kitchen, we walked on to the nursery.

"Happy Birthday, Anna Nanna!" Ms. Gardner called, her West Texas twang mixed with a North Carolina drawl. Our chosen granny. Her deep-brown arm rested on the closed half of a Dutch door, a grandson Clare's age by her side.

"Good morning, Granny," Jeff said, kissing her cheek. "Can you believe she's one?"

"Nah. Seems like yesterday I met y'all. When you wouldn't leave Nanna," she exhaled her sly chuckle. No way had I left my brand-new baby in the nursery. I had relished snuggling her in the pew without Clare climbing on me for months.

Clare ran through the door when Granny opened it. Anna lifted her arms, and Granny picked her up. Anna scrunched up her nose and laughed with one hand on each of Granny's cheeks, squeezing. Clare grabbed a fistful of animal crackers and sat next to her friend with a puzzle.

"Please come have some cake after service," I said as Jeff and I turned to go.

"I made it with my Mimi," Clare mumbled, spewing crackers. "It's white with strawberry icing, sprinkles, and a big number one." She bobbed her head, sassy and proud. She strutted around church—surrounded by aunties, uncles, and stand-in grandparents—like she owned it. Jeff wrapped his hand around mine as we walked toward the sanctuary and an hour of respite. After church, Anna sat in an old metal highchair and dug into the cake with both hands. Curious and delighted—her primary stances in the world. She could paw her hooves, yell, and sit immovable like a bull when someone tried to control her, but she laughed with her whole body: rocking, shoulders shaking, full of joy.

Anna, meds, yoga, and retreats confined depression to my borderlands, but it still took all of me to contain Clare even some of the time. The therapist's sensible suggestions had changed nothing. Clare ripped up calendars and artwork, chucked things at walls, at us. We restrained her. Our love for her still ran deep, but Jeff was bewildered, and I was exhausted.

By spring's end, Clare and I had played with the therapist's doll house for nine months. One morning, I sat at my grandmother's oak dressing table and listened to her latest theories over the phone. Out my bedroom window, cilantro was going to seed in our circular garden bed. Our rescued mastiff, Bowen, sniffed the gate and raised his leg to pee. The therapist said because Clare lost control leaving playdates, to always have the next playtime already set up. I doodled around the edges of my paper.

"When Clare's blowing up, she needs a redirection of her passions. Think of her temperament as expressive versus explosive."

She's expressive when she dances. A Roman candle when she rages, I thought.

"She doesn't have to hurt herself or others. Get controls in place. Teach her no with understanding and nurturance."

I've tried no for years. My *understanding and nurturance don't match* her *passion.*

"She fears annihilation. If she can hurt you, it scares her; she could make you go away. That makes her too powerful. She can't be allowed to overpower you."

Weeds poked out among the spinach. I'd need to get to that. *I don't want her to overpower me. But I am so tired. And she is so powerful. At only almost six years old. What's ahead?*

"You must get control of her for her own sake."

Nothing controls Clare. Not even Clare.

I thanked her and said we wanted to take a break for the summer. *Maybe forever.*

Anna, Clare, and I walked the stream that wound through our neighborhood that summer. It curved past a mulberry tree, and we stained our fingers popping its purple fruit into our mouths. We passed a blackberry bush where the train tracks crossed the stream. Its white blossoms opened to the bees, dropped as green bumps grew, and ripened into blackberries plump and juicy, worth all the thorn scratches it took to pick them. Clare wore out and climbed in the stroller, still small enough to fit at six and only forty pounds. Anna, stout and strong, toddled home with purple smears across pink cheeks.

Eighteen months with Anna made me want another child. I loved babies' smell, their weight growing heavy on my chest as they fell asleep, the world full of magic through their eyes. And it seemed wrong for Clare to be the only Black person in our family, even though Avis sat on Anna's bedroom floor one day and told me Clare didn't need a Brown sibling to be okay. She said Clare and Anna ran me ragged and maybe that was enough. I couldn't hear her; I wasn't done. We called Hope Cottage and began again.

I stitched yellow thread up the spine of a pressed-leaf paper book to make our profile: what matters most to us—people and the planet, diversity, beauty, hospitality, church, and family. I pasted pictures onto card stock pages. Family, friends, Clare and Anna on backyard, fallen limbs in autumn leaves and perched in the window of their wooden playhouse. Clare pointed off in the distance with a smile; a new permanent tooth peeked out where her right front baby one had been. The orange-and-red scarf that held back her twists—my newly perfected hair style—matched the leaves on the ground. Anna looked up from under blond bangs, basking in Clare's elusive attention. Jeff wrote a letter I tucked into a pocket in the front cover. We finished the paperwork two years after Anna's.

Our social worker, Jeriva, called six weeks later, on January 6, 2006, about another baby girl. Biracial, three months old, in Hope Cottage foster care since birth, light brown skin. This time the birth mom, Diane, wanted to meet us. Jeff and I pulled up to Hope Cottage the next day, took a deep breath and went inside. A tall, White woman with long dark hair sat next to an older, blond version of herself. We chatted with Diane and her mom about faith, interracial families, and our desire for another baby. At the end of an hour, we agreed to an adoption ceremony. An acknowledgment of the intertwined beauty and pain of adoption.

We took Clare and Anna to Norma's Diner for breakfast and the announcement a few days later. After birthday celebrations, family gatherings, and daddy/daughter dates, the waitress knew us. "Hey, Clare and Anna!" She led us to a shiny red vinyl booth and a metal table on a pedestal.

"We'll take eggs, pancakes, and hot chocolate, please," Jeff said. Clare looked suspicious. Hot cocoa for breakfast?

The girls gave themselves whipped cream mustaches while I said, "Mimi and Pop will pick you up from school today." A typically wide-eyed Anna looked from me to Jeff to Clare as I continued, "And a new baby sister will be there when you get home."

Clare squealed and squeezed tight a silent, grinning Anna.

After dropping Clare in her first-grade classroom and Anna at Parents' Day Out, we met Jeriva at Hope Cottage. She led us to the playroom where Diane sat on a low stool holding a baby whose big, brown eyes filled her face. Diane stood as we came in. She smiled and handed the baby to me, and I was on the tarmac in Haiti marveling at a bundle of life and beauty being given to me all over again.

"Oh, Diane. She's beautiful," I got out a whisper. "Hello, Faith. I'm so happy to meet you." Jeff gazed at her over my shoulder. I handed her to him, and he lifted her above his head, tilting his face to match hers. She smiled, and a dimple creased her cheek.

I pulled a baby blue pouch from my purse and handed it to Diane. "We want you to have this."

She took out a silver ring of Celtic knots, intertwined and unbroken. Jeff had given it to me in Vancouver, and I sometimes wore it as a wedding ring. I told her it felt like adoption to me. A sort of marriage between parents. The first who gave life and the second who nurtured the child into the person she'd become.

"Thank you," she said as she reached out, and we embraced. She unclasped the necklace she wore, slid the chain through the ring, and I helped her clasp it back.

Jeff handed Faith to Diane, and Jeriva ushered us into a living room. Faith and Diane joined her mom, sister, and older daughter in one corner; Jeff walked to our family and friends clumped in another; Faith's foster family talked with Hope Cottage staff in a third. I floated between them as if hosting a party as a grandfather clock ticked on.

Jeriva began. "Jeff and Lynn, come to my right and Diane with your family to my left."

I wondered how Diane felt. My body tingled with anticipation and nerves. I looked out at Angelle and Matt, Avis and Wayne, my parents, sister and brother-in-law and Jeff's parents. Their presence upheld me and filled my eyes with tears.

Jeriva continued, "We welcome Faith Faye in love and hope. We welcome Diane, who witnessed the miracle of Faith Faye's entry into the world. We welcome Jeff and Lynn who participate in the miracle of loving choice." Diane shifted Faith to her chest, glancing at her mom and sister.

"Diane, we offer this rose, a symbol of life unfolding and offer you comfort during this difficult time of your noble decision for adoption for your child. May joy come from your sorrow, hope from your pain, and strength from your adversity." Jeriva handed Diane a yellow rose and motioned for her to hand Faith to me.

I sipped breath, afraid a wave might crash out of me—relief, gratitude, sadness, guilt—into the silence. Diane passed Faith to me. It felt as if we stretched to reach each other, might drop her in the chasm between us. Faith looked from Diane to me—one woman she knew in her bones and one she didn't know at all. I held her to my chest and breathed in her baby scent. Jeff's hand touched the small of my back. My eyes overflowed.

Jeriva turned her attention to us. "No flower grows alone, apart from sunshine and rain, apart from the soil in which it lives. So, too, no child grows alone. Jeff and Lynn, accept this rose in honor of your dedication to your children. Upon you rests the sacred joy of nurturing this young life between birth and maturity."

I looked up at Jeff and we nodded.

"To the best of your ability do you promise to nurture and instruct this child in the way of good living for her and humankind?"

"We do." The whole room shifted and sniffed.

"We give thanks for the blessings bestowed upon this family in giving them a child. We wish them calm strength and patient wisdom as they seek to bring this child to love all that is true and noble, just and pure, loveable and gracious, excellent and admirable."

Jeriva picked up several roses, handed them to me, and used the name we'd chosen for the first time, "Lucia Faith, these roses symbolize a beautiful life unfolding. I dedicate you to the service of truth, justice, and love. May the Spirit of Life be with you always. Jeff and Lynn, we acknowledge you as parents of Lucia Faith Alsup and celebrate your newly formed family. May I introduce the new family." Jeff and I turned to face everyone, radiant.

As I lay in bed that night, I'd grieve how Diane must have felt. But in that moment, I cuddled Lucy on the Hope Cottage couch for her first bottle from my hand. The foster family gave Jeff photos of Lucy's first three months and a blanket and cried as they said goodbye.

Anna and Clare sat on our front porch wicker bench with my

mom and dad as we pulled in. My smile grew even wider as I brought Lucy in her carrier seat onto the front porch.

"Want to hold her, Clare?"

Clare, who had bounded down, scrambled back up next to Anna. I lifted Lucy onto Clare's lap, and she cradled her like a doll. Anna rested her hand over Lucy's tiny one and kissed her chubby, tan cheeks.

Jeff knelt down in front of them. "Meet Lucy, you two."

And we were five.

Schooling

The story I imagined people conjured about the girls and me: I married Clare's Black father, brought my Anna with me, and then we had Lucy. I watched them work it out in their minds. In grocery stores, parks, airplanes, classrooms. When Jeff joined us, the story scrambled. No one recognized us as family out in the world.

A year plus into our family of five, Clare snapped her bike helmet strap under her chin and jumped on her blue Schwinn. Jeff helped three-year-old Anna onto her purple one; her round, pink cheeks glowed with familiar joy. Lucy scrambled into her stroller, curls akimbo on top of her head, and I buckled her. I pushed her down the hill toward the creek a block over from our home, pausing to check out new spring-green leaves on the fig tree I'd forage from come late summer.

"Clare, watch for cars," I yelled as she careened across the street without a look to even one side. She hopped onto the greenbelt headed toward Kiest Park. Jeff helped Anna lift her bike over the curb and climb back on. We curved past a playground and waited together at a corner where a city bus rumbled past, coughing black smoke.

"Eww!" Lucy squinched up her nose, and we all laughed.

A few blocks later, we merged onto the park path with people of different races, sizes, abilities, and ages. That made it one of my favorite Dallas spots. Winding around soccer fields still winter yellow, we ducked under pecan branches, budding oaks, and mulberries. A breeze cooled us enough to need our jackets but the sun warmed our faces. I paused beside Jeff to drink it in. Clare raced ahead; Anna's training wheels *clickity-clacked* as she tried to catch her. When Clare paused at a fork in the path, Anna came from behind, her tire bumping into Clare's as she passed. Anna steamed ahead, thrilled to be in the lead.

Clare jumped back onto her seat, put her head down, and aimed for Anna. I saw ten seconds into the future, let the stroller go, and tore off to intercept Clare. Her wheel rammed Anna's hard a second before I got there. Anna's handlebars twisted out of her hands; her bike tipped. As she lurched to the ground, I remembered eighteen-month-old Lucy strapped in the stroller. I spun around as Jeff missed the handle of the stroller I had thrust forward. It hit a rock and fell over; Lucy's lip split on the metal hinge. A breathless pause hung in the air as Jeff reached her, then her shriek. *Clare hurt* both *of them*, I thought.

I knelt down to Anna. And screamed at Clare standing astride her bike, glaring at Anna. "You *hurt* her," I yelled. "She didn't *mean* to bump you. She can't control her bike!" My chest tingled and tightened; my heart hardened. "She's *three*. You are almost *eight years old*!"

Silent, Clare's eyes blazed. I turned my back, disgusted. Anna looked up and sniffed, tear-stain stripes on her flushed cheeks.

I noticed her scraped knee. "Are you okay, honey?" As she hid her face in my pant leg, I hugged her close. "I'm so sorry that happened."

Jeff had righted Lucy and dabbed blood from her lip. With her in one arm, he pushed the stroller to our stormy circle. *Could he see my body vibrate with rage?* Clare loomed over Anna and me: arms crossed, face impassive.

When I stood, Lucy lunged into my arms. I covered her face with kisses and picked grass from her hair. "I'm so sorry I let you go, sweetheart. Are you okay?"

Lucy didn't use words yet, but she nodded as her big, brown eyes filled. Her lip was already swollen but had stopped bleeding. I wiped the tears from her cheeks and squeezed her to my chest with my hand on her curls.

Jeff—the peacemaker—said, "Clare, come with me while Mom helps Anna."

"No way," I growled. "Clare stays with me. You guys go ahead." I buckled Lucy in her stroller, helped Anna stand and brushed the grass from her shorts.

"Come on guys," Jeff said. "Let's see if that grumpy old troll is under the bridge."

As I turned to Clare, all kindness drained from my face. She glowered at the ground. I lectured her about unacceptable behavior, shouted, "*Look me in the eye!*"

I snarled through clenched teeth, "In our family we practice kindness and peace." She could practice obeying me and walk by my side all the way around the park.

I snatched up her bike in one hand, balanced it beside me and rolled it away with me. Clare walked ten steps behind; I yelled, "*Catch up!*" When she didn't, I waited, then grabbed her arm and pulled her. She twisted free, dragged her feet, complained: she was hot and couldn't carry her jacket she'd taken off. I yanked it from her hand, threw it to the ground, and left it there. I bulldogged my way through a mile and a half. My own meltdown.

Clare and I crossed the wood plank bridge—sweating and red faced—and emerged from the trees. Anna and Lucy sat on a bench swinging their legs next to Jeff. Other families laughed on the playground, but Anna and Lucy had slid and swung for forty-five minutes already. They were tired. And maybe worried. A question flashed through my mind: *How* did *the volatility of our life shape them*? We went home in silence. It took hours for my adrenaline to dissipate and shame to surface. I felt guilty, out of control. Not who I wanted to be.

That night, Jeff tried to make love with me, to connect and release the stress of the day. Exhausted and ashamed, I didn't want to. But didn't say. Easier to let the rest of me float away from my body—my superpower. I didn't catch my breath at his touch, open to him, or press closer. No tingle, shudder, or quiet moan. After a while, he gave up.

"How can you just lie there? Not move or say anything?" His tone reminded me of my own with Clare hours before. How could I explain? I didn't understand it myself. He'd tell me later he felt powerless to affect me; it infuriated, frightened, and confused him. I turned over and pretended to go to sleep. If only he knew his potency: he ignited my trauma with a touch.

In the morning, Jeff took Clare to school, and I entered the life I loved at home with Anna and Lucy. I recognized my innate rhythm in their toddler/preschool life: rest, eat, play, work, rest, eat, play, work. The girls trained me to stop, breathe, notice—each thing worthy of pause and attention. A black bug on the living room floor. The snail climbing a single blade of grass after a rain. Tiny yellow blossoms on weeds in the park. If I moved too fast, it ended in frustration, so I surrendered to curiosity—and *I-put-my-shoes-on-by-myself*. At that pace, we felt the cool, hard metal of the apple corer and the pressure it took to push the blades through. The juice on our fingers. The sun's warmth in the garden dirt.

The unshakable pull on my leg as I washed dishes, constant interruptions during phone calls taught me to face interruption squarely and listen. Or the volume turned up, up, up until I did. If I'd pause and sigh my way to the floor for ten minutes of play—cars, books, tickles—relief came for us all. Attention and response held the power.

But then we had to pick up Clare.

She slumped and scowled in the car transitioning from school to home; arrived exhausted and hungry not knowing what to eat. "How about some nuts?" *No.* "Popcorn?" *No.* "Apples and peanut butter?" *No.* I tried creative solutions for everything. A paper with three columns hung on the fridge—carbs, protein, fruits/veggies. I told her to pick one from each; she wanted sugar. She struggled with math; I taped a penny, nickel, dime, and quarter on envelopes. She sorted change into them for months to uncover the mystery of which was which. She complained that her friends left her out; I talked to another mom about it. Her daughter said it was hard to be Clare's friend. She didn't understand Clare. I didn't either.

In the fall, Clare wanted to play piano and do gymnastics but was too tired after school. Her bit of third-grade homework stretched to bedtime, many nights with us both in tears. On the weekends, she read voraciously, wrote vivid stories, and directed her sisters in plays that cracked us up. I wondered if homeschooling could bring Clare into rhythm throughout the week. Desperate, I gathered curricula and historical novels and painted our hallway with black chalkboard paint. In January, Clare left the Kessler School, and Anna continued morning three-year-old preschool there. I began a full-time job I'd never wanted: homeschooler. Our dining room table became Clare's desk while Lucy, at two, sat in a highchair nearby with Cheerios and matchbox cars and shouted her new words at us. Angelle, still my closest friend, said Lucy was the loudest child she'd ever met. Lucy burst with emotion—laughter as well as sobs and screams.

Anna asked Jeff to come to Pre-K–3 for show and tell. She loved school, and she loved Jeff. She wanted boots like the ones he wore when he mowed the lawn, except pink; she wanted a hat like he wore to string fences at his family's farm, except pink; she wanted guitar lessons when he started as Clare and I began piano. Jeff bought her a ukulele. He brought his guitar and her ukulele to the Kessler School for show and tell. He joined her on the alphabet rug and let the four-year-olds strum as Anna instructed them all.

Clare and my favorite part of homeschool was our three-person writers' group. She bounced around in front of our bay windows on Tuesdays waiting for Corrie, then perched on the arm of our hand-me-down, blue houndstooth chair and played with the new cowrie shell in her dreadlocks.

"She's here! She's here!" Clare swung the front door open and ran onto the porch.

"Hi, Clare," Corrie said.

I waved to Corrie's mom as she pulled away and called to her open window. "Thanks for dropping her off."

"How's it going, Corrie?" I asked.

She tucked a strand of brown hair behind her ear, and a bit of pink spread across her freckled cheek. "Good."

I loved having Corrie over; she was settled, mature, and curious. And she loved Clare—she drank in her passion and charisma. She was a couple years older than Clare and quiet; that helped. And Clare kept up with Corrie in writing. She excelled there.

I said the lesson for the day was observation and description with popcorn and oranges. They smiled and each raised an eyebrow. I led them to our old-fashioned popcorn popper on the stove. Clare screeched to a stop in front of it, and Corrie ambled in behind.

"Listen. Tell me what you hear." I grinned.

"Let's start!" Clare's exuberance about simple things was one of her gifts to the world. With one friend, structure, and me alongside for support, Clare could be a delight.

Corrie poured a tablespoon of oil into the pot. "I hear oil dribbling." She added a half cup of bright yellow corn kernels. "And kernels pinging the pot."

"I hear the blade spin them around," Clare said as she turned the crank. "And the *whoosh* of gas," when I ignited the burner.

"*Pop. Pop. Pop.*" Clare twinkled. We laughed; Clare's contagious enthusiasm with no storm clouds hanging over her was the best.

At the table with the bowl of popcorn, they opened their notebooks. I set a timer for ten minutes. They should free write about what they saw without stopping. Their pens flew as I turned back to grab an orange, cutting board, and knife to repeat the exercise.

"That's amazing, Lynn," Corrie said when the timer went off.

"What's that, love?"

"All you see if you pay attention."

"Can I read mine, Mom?"

"Of course, babe." Connecting in our joy felt good. One thing we could do together, Clare and I: words.

Clare stood up to read like a docent at the Dallas Museum of Art describing a masterpiece. "The popcorn is white but also brown and shiny in the center where the kernel still shows. It has bumps all around. The salt sits on top with a tiny shadow under it. I want to eat it up!"

Other parts of homeschooling weren't going so well. Clare recited all her math facts one day but said she didn't know them the next. I took away her beloved gymnastics class when she didn't try hard enough, and "just think" became my new favorite mantra. But no consequences affected her behavior except to make her shut down or melt down. When she stormed and screamed after Anna got home, I sat her on the back porch or at the bottom of the attic room stairs with the door closed to mute her. So, she gouged the door with a pen like a tiger scores a tree to sharpen its claws. We'd witness that fight in her—to survive and be heard—again and again throughout our journey. I wondered if Anna and Lucy believed me when I said Clare was okay. That I could take care of Clare and them. I wondered if *I* believed me.

Jeff and I took turns holding Clare while she cried at bedtime, thrashed or wailed that she missed her mom, *definitely* not meaning me. I scooted over in bed *every* night to make room for her (and often Anna and Lucy, too) when she woke up afraid. I dragged myself out of bed in the morning with barely a hello to Jeff to do it all again.

By Christmas, she begged to go back to school; my experiment had failed us both. In January, one year after we began, I walked Clare into the gym of our neighborhood elementary school, Rosemont. Her dreadlocks brushed the shoulders of her navy-blue polo; her khaki pants hung loose. (Thank God for the new button-up elastic inside waistbands that held them up.) A line of fourth graders sat and whisper-talked, waiting for a teacher to lead them to class. Clare's stoic face held steady, but she asked me to stay with her in line that first day. I crouched down where she sat, held her hand, and told her I believed in her.

Maybe public school was the answer.

Two weeks into the semester was President Obama's inauguration. Clare, Anna, Lucy, and I joined the 1.8 million people there in person via PBS in our finished attic where our television lived. We spread out on the floor as Aretha Franklin sang "My Country 'Tis of Thee." She stood tall in her gray suit and hat with a big bow studded with rhinestones right on top like the gift she was. I swayed as she belted out "let it reign" over and over again, clapped and whooped along with the crowd. Anna gave me her sideways glance, embarrassed by my exuberance even in the attic. Clare looked right through Anna and laughed and clapped with Lucy—her usual tactic to leave Anna out.

"See the woman in yellow? The crocheted coat? That's Barak Obama's wife," I said.

Clare propped herself onto her elbows. "She looks kinda like me."

"Yes, she does, love. Yes, she does," I pushed a lock from her forehead.

Itzhak Perlman pulled his bow across violin strings. Yo-Yo Ma joined on the cello. Anthony McGill blew his clarinet, and Gabriela Montero's hands danced across piano keys as the song reached its crescendo. Lucy climbed in my lap, made up her own lyrics, and we shimmied together. I jumped up to applaud with the crowd, and Lucy plopped to the floor, cheering with me. Then Barak and Michelle stood. While I sobbed as he repeated the oath, the girls inched closer to me.

"Okay, Mommy?" Lucy questioned for them all, always needing me to be okay.

"It's an incredible day for equality, justice, and love," I said, pulling them all close. "I never imagined I would see a Black president." I broke again. Anna and Lucy squabbled over who got my lap, and I shushed them. "Listen."

"The challenges we face are real," Obama declared. "They are serious, and they are many. They will not be met easily or in a short span of time. But know this, America, they will be met."

Clare stared at the television and reached for my hand. The littles got restless, so I offered them paper and crayons. When Elizabeth Alexander recited her poem "Praise Song for the Day," waves rose up from my belly, filled my eyes, receded, and swept up again.

"She looks like Lucy, Mom," Clare said. Lucy popped up and walked to the TV that sat at her three-year-old height. She touched Alexander's face on the screen.

"We walk into that which we cannot yet see," Alexander said. "What if the mightiest word we have is love?"

I walked Anna to her first day of kindergarten at Rosemont in the fall. Her khaki skirt and navy top matched Clare's who began fifth grade there the same day. Anna's ponytail, turning from little-girl blond to light brown, swished behind her. We found her name on a red laminated paper on a table for four in her new classroom. Across the table sat a girl with a shy smile and bouncy brown curls. They mumbled hello and I asked her name.

"I'm Annabella, and I love horses."

"I'm Anna. Me, too."

She turned to me. "You can go now, Mom."

She'd already turned back to Annabella to talk horses when I smiled and said, "Have a great day, love. I'll see you at three." Walking to the front doors, I held back tears.

Outside, I called my mom. "Hi, Mom." My voiced cracked.

"Is everything okay?"

"It's hard to leave your baby at school."

She chuckled. "Yes. But it will get easier."

I sniffed.

"How did she do?"

"Great. Didn't miss a beat. Miss Independence."

"I hope Lucy's first day of preschool goes great, too."

"I'm not so sure about that."

Lucy clung to me at the door to her classroom each day but always went in. She loved the stories, kids, music, and dancing. She lived completely in her body—so much like Clare. Drop-off got easier for Lucy when Jeff took it over in October as his friend's firm gradually closed during the Great Recession. I celebrated. I didn't care that we were unemployed again; I sighed with relief to be done with the slick and hip world of advertisers. Maybe Jeff and I could rebuild our marriage. Parenting had consumed me; chasing success had consumed Jeff.

∽

Five months before, we had sat down together with our bank account, planning a home-improvement project.

"Lynn, I have something to tell you." *Oh, no.* A close friend had just suffered a cheating-lying-husband situation. I was scared.

"It's not like Tom. But I haven't been honest." The ceiling fan squeaked into the silence. Jeff looked like he'd run over a puppy.

"Tell me." I turned to stone. I hated dishonesty above all else. And sometimes Jeff, avoiding conflict, changed stories or omitted details.

"I lent some money to the firm." He studied his blue jeans as he spoke.

"What?" My eyebrows shot up.

"We couldn't make payroll again. But a big deal was closing two days later. I'd pay us back and you wouldn't have to know."

"I wouldn't have to know?" My forehead furrowed, and the scent of the rice I'd burned at dinner hung in the room.

"It was wrong. I feel horrible. And the deal fell through."

"How much?"

"A lot."

"How much?"

"Thirty thousand dollars." Jeff whispered.

I gasped. "That's all our savings. Including the money for the house project. Bruce is counting on it." Jeff's guitar teacher, Bruce, was a carpenter who needed work. We'd decided to use money we'd saved over years to hire him. "You let us both believe."

"I know. I'm so sorry." The flush in his face seeped into his eyes, and tears dropped onto the carpet.

When I could speak again, I said, "I'm leaving for a while. I'll be back later." I picked up my purse and walked out the door.

I came home late that night, but I didn't talk to Jeff for days. When I finally met him at a park, I yelled, "*What the fuck were you thinking?*"

"Please stop yelling, Lynn." He looked flattened, two dimensional. "I was so afraid to fail I was willing to lie to you." Kids swung and screeched across a field, and yellow pollen swirled around us.

"You need help," I accused as the sun beat down.

He nodded, "Please forgive me."

"I'm not ready yet," was all I could say.

We agreed to begin counseling. The firm had folded before repaying us.

~

We drove together to the young elementary carpool line at Rosemont a week after Jeff lost his job; red and yellow leaves let go of their branches and drifted along beside us. Anna smooched Lucy and hopped into her kindergarten teacher's big hug. Lucy chattered as Jeff turned up the hill to drop Clare at upper elementary. Alongside the building, kids slammed car doors, shouldered backpacks, and ran inside. Clare sank down in her seat next to Lucy's booster. Like into quicksand. Or maybe cement. So far, a typical morning; she was tired and had refused to eat much. I thought low blood sugar scrambled her brain.

"It's time to go, Clare," I said.

No response.

Jeff said, "Clare. Grab your lunch box and go."

"You'll be late, Clare," I added.

No response. Lucy had turned silent, too.

"Clare, it's time," Jeff repeated.

Jeff and I exchanged glances. *Why couldn't she just go?* I said I'd help her if she wouldn't do it herself. Her eyes widened, but she didn't speak. I walked around the car, opened her door, and counted to five. The fresh air did not clear my head.

"You're getting out. Dad and I are going for coffee." Five months into counseling, I mistrusted Jeff still but was working to reconnect, to remember why I married him. We needed the coffee date. "You're not ruining it." I grabbed Clare's arm and started to pull, determined to win.

"Mom, stop," she whisper-shouted even though the other kids had long gone inside. She slid out of the car and stood on the sidewalk. I picked up her lunch bag, saw Lucy's scared face, and cringed at myself. *Poor Lucy.* When Clare refused her lunch, I put it on the sidewalk, slammed her door, walked back to the passenger side and got in.

"Please go inside, Clare," Jeff pleaded through the open window. She stood motionless, tears streaming down her cheeks.

"We have to drive away, Jeff." My gut clenched. I was appalled with myself. But I'd tried keeping her home; that didn't work either. Maybe this would teach her. I texted Clare's teacher as we pulled away and admitted what I'd done. She praised me for holding firm boundaries, not giving in to Clare's drama. She'd send someone to watch out, keep Clare safe.

I met Lucy's teacher later that week for a parent conference. I walked up the familiar Kessler School staircase and watched the leaves fall from the tree outside the two-story window, pausing when I saw my reflection. My cheekbones stood out again; I'd lost ten years of weight gained through infertility, hysterectomy, and creating family. My always short hair had bits of gray I hadn't noticed before. Right on time for my fortieth birthday coming up. I looked ragged—saggy jeans with a hole at the knee and an old T-shirt. Makeup was long gone. Maybe I'd get myself together soon.

Lucy's teacher sat at a preschool-sized table with red and yellow construction paper projects spread in front of her. "Hey, Lynn. Good to see you. I can't believe Anna's moved on to kindergarten, and we're meeting about Lucy." Her rosy cheeks lifted in a smile.

"Seven years we've been at the Kessler School. Amazing," I said as I joined her in a little, red plastic chair.

"How's Anna?"

"Great. Loves Rosemont. And she's started riding horses."

"Awesome. Lucy's doing well, too. Friends with everyone. Loves to make them laugh." Her brown eyes twinkled as she chuckled.

"She is hilarious, that's for sure."

"She creates whole worlds with the red, cardboard blocks," she pointed to the blocks on a blue rug behind her. "I'm sure you know how she rules the room," she laughed.

I tilted my head. "I'm not sure what you mean."

"She's kind of a police officer, making sure everyone follows classroom rules or whatever game she invents." She smiled like I'd recognize her description.

"That's surprising. At our house, she follows whatever Anna or Clare dream up."

"Hmm. Here she's in charge. Kids look to her for permission, even when *I* ask them to do something." She laughed again. I had no idea Lucy could assert herself like that.

She looked down at her notes and continued, "She struggles with letters and numbers unless we're singing, but it will come. Writing, too. She works hard, but her hand can't seem to write what she wants. It frustrates her, and she shuts down."

I nodded. I recognized that description. Lucy's face went blank when things were hard, or she didn't understand. She seemed to live in a very confusing world. I shared that I'd tried teaching Lucy to buckle her seat belt for months; she couldn't translate my words into motions her hands could do. Desperate one day, I took her hand in mine and buckled it with her. She'd buckled it herself ever since.

"I'll try that with handwriting. Maybe fat, rubber grips would help her hold her pencils. Her fine motor skills are a bit behind."

I sighed. More problems to solve. I told her a friend had encouraged me to get a speech therapy evaluation. Lucy's deficits hadn't qualified for services, but something was up.

"Don't worry too much. All kids develop differently. She'll get it. She is a delightful, helpful, happy child. We love having her in the classroom."

As she walked me out, she motioned to OUTLAW WANTED signs—kids' pictures pasted onto descriptions they had dictated to parents—covering a wall.

"There's Lucy."

Rats: I hadn't done her hair on the day of the picture. The French braid was fuzzed out, and she looked a bit dazed. Her light-brown skin complemented her bright purple shirt, though. And her eyes sparkled. I remembered filling out the form below the picture with her:

Name: Lucia Alsup
Nickname: Lucy in the Sky with Diamonds
Color Eyes: Brown
Color Hair: Brown
Crime: Blaring The Beatles from her bedroom
Identifiable characteristics: No answer when called
Last place seen: On bedroom floor playing
What to do if seen: Calmly turn down music and wait for it to crank back up
Special Warnings: Might be dancing wildly

"That's Lucy," I said with a smile.

Preparations

In January, Jeff became executive director of the Well Community. It provided safe, purposeful days for people with severe mental illness. He said it felt like coming home. Healing from what he called affluenza: the slickness and consumption of Dallas; trying to outdo everyone; more, more, more. Our seven years in Dallas—two babies, parenting Clare, and Jeff's dive into the for-profit world that I judged—had pummeled us. The simple joy and acceptance from people tossed aside by dominant culture mended him. His face shone at weeknight church services he led for the community as he exchanged bear hugs, laughed, and joked in the big fellowship hall of the church that housed the Well. He stood tall as he preached and served. I began to recognize him again. He had gray around his temples and lines around his eyes, but the man I married had resurfaced. Our relationship's threads began to knit back together, preparation to face Clare's impending unraveling.

Clare had joined adolescence, and her life was mostly volatile and unhappy. And, as always, she got sick a lot: asthma and allergies, perpetual sore throat and stomach, fatigue. We turned to a special-needs nutritionist named Faye Elahi who formulated supplements for the many vitamin and mineral deficiencies she uncovered. Jeff sat at the end of our pine table and pushed the powder into lines like cocaine every Sunday night, filling capsules for Clare. I cajoled and yelled at her to take them each morning. She gagged and complained, sometimes made herself throw up. She could do that on demand. She often stashed them in her closet or under the seat in the car but ingested enough to level her out a bit.

And we turned to Haiti. I wondered to Jeff if a trip back could fill a hole and stabilize Clare. He trusted my instincts—often yielded decisions to me. I made lists and planned ad nauseum; he didn't over-think, went with the flow. It seemed to me I created the flow with all my kicking and pushing and both resented and appreciated his easygoing nature. As he did my intensity. I suggested we talk to Clare about the three of us going to Haiti for a week over the summer.

"I bet we could stay at Don and Karen's. Eat beans and rice at the hotel in town. Visit the clinic where Rachel worked," I said, repeating thoughts floating around my head for days. "Maybe we could find your biological family." As I put my arm around Clare's shoulder, she leaned into me on the couch. I brushed her dreadlocks from my cheek. Jeff and I exhaled in the post-little-sisters'-bedtime quiet.

"I'd be excited to see Don and Karen," Clare said. They'd stopped in on a trip to the States the summer before and watched Clare on stage at Camp Broadway. "And I'm scared. I hope I could see my family. But what would that be like?" She stared off.

"We don't have to go if you're not ready." Jeff took her silky brown hand in his tan one, three shades lighter. His green eyes looked worried.

I drifted my fingers through her locks. "It might be intense. It's very different there." Jeff and I had talked about how the extreme poverty might affect Clare. "And I'm not sure we'd find them. But we'd be in it together." I rubbed her back while she thought.

"I do want to." Clare's face rode the roller coaster of her emotions, lit up and open, then clouded over and furrowed. The ceiling fan whined above us as we sat. After a few moments, she nodded her head. "Okay. Let's go." She scooched down, laid her head in my lap, and smiled up at me.

"If you're sure," Jeff said.

Come July, Jeff's parents picked up Anna and Lucy and took them to the family farm while Jeff, Clare, and I traveled to Haiti. We spent a night in Miami at the home of our Waco friends, Jason and Angel, and then flew to Haiti where Don and Karen welcomed us back. It felt like a circle completing itself.

When we walked out of the airport in Cap-Haïtien, people bombarded Clare with the music of Haitian Creole. They recognized her as one of their own. She slid between Jeff and me, surrounded herself with us.

"I think there is going to be a lot of hand-holding this trip," she whispered. When we merged into the sea of people, she blended in perfectly for the first time since we'd left that airport ten years before.

I woke up the next morning unsure where I was. As my eyes focused on the gray, cement block walls of the house, the fecund smell of the tropics reminded me. I rolled over. Clare, still asleep between Jeff and me, looked small and fragile, twisted in the white sheets from a night of her usual constant movement. Heat rose from my stomach to my throat: *My mom's fear was right. I was crazy to think Clare needed to reconnect. At only eleven years old. To find belonging and patch her identity together by inhabiting this place, even just for a while.* Then my therapist's words echoed in my mind: my best gift to Clare was to believe in her strength, not spare her from pain; stay close as her companion on her journey. I swallowed my fear.

We joined Don and Karen for Kellogg's Corn Flakes and Haitian coffee and waited for Emmail. Emmail who had translated Creole to English and back again ten years before at Met George's office with Clare's Haitian father; in Port-au-Prince, when I believed I'd be bringing Clare home, when I realized I couldn't. Miraculously, his visit from his new home in Chicago overlapped with ours for one night. At seven in the morning, he arrived, smiling bright and big, believing in · something much larger than himself. He remembered where Clare's family had lived. The four of us drove off to ferret them out before he flew home that afternoon.

Clare held Jeff's hand in the back seat as we bounced and stuttered over potholes. Men hoed the fields against a backdrop of mountains robed with green; women squatted next to metal pots of steaming food—ready to sell breakfast to passersby. We chatted as children laughed, racing beside thin bicycle tires they pushed along with sticks. We turned left off the paved road onto cobblestone. I remembered it. My breath quickened; I worked to deepen it again. We came to a Y in the road where we'd turned in 1999 to find a judge. I knew it marked L'Acul du Nord—where Clare was born, where her family might still live. Emmail stopped the car, closed his eyes, prayed. Then he got out.

Clare asked, "Where's he going?!"

"To ask people in the village. To find your family. These people know them." I clambered into the backseat to wait with Jeff and Clare.

An old woman sat beside a cooking pot ten feet from my window. Black liquid poured from a mesh bag she held. Another woman walked up with her own tin pitcher, and the old woman filled it. A tiny, white-and-orange kitten lay on the curb next to her.

"Never seen a cat in Haiti before," I said to fill the silence and distract us. Maybe level out the waves of energy coursing through the car.

"What is Emmail *doing*?" Clare's leg bounced up and down as she looked over her shoulder.

And then Emmail returned, pointing to a crowd who'd gathered. "They know Katiana's family. They will lead us to her home."

Katiana, Clare's Haitian name. Clare receded; Katiana emerged. We stared at each other. Seven forty-five in the morning on Day One, and we'd found them. As we stepped out of the car, Clare gripped my hand. Her face went inscrutable. A woman in a cherry-red shirt and cornrows stood nearby. Sweat dripped from her temples off her chin as she stared at Clare.

"Katiana," she said. "Katiana."

Emmail called Clare over to say *Bon jou*. Good morning. The woman touched Clare's face. Clare stood motionless.

She grasped Jeff's hand in her free one as we followed the

woman—and the crowd followed us—onto a footpath winding through dirt yards of two-room, reed houses. We crossed a trickle of a stream covered in garbage a herd of pigs was nosing through for breakfast. The smell we'd warned Clare about assaulted us: open-dumpster-in-the-alley smell. Her nose crinkled, and she worked hard to keep her face straight.

The path narrowed, and we loosed hands to go single file. Clare's adrenaline washed over me from behind; I took a deep breath. Living fences lined the path: bright green, pencil-thin shoots reached up from plants as tall as me. Our guide ducked inside an opening in the hedge to our left. Clare froze as a girl a few years older approached. She reached out, held our shoulders, kissed our cheeks and ran past us calling, "Filosane," Clare's oldest sister's name. I recognized the girl from our shared day at Rachel's cottage ten years before—Clare's youngest sister, Patricia. Clare's face was expressionless as we crossed the threshold into a dirt courtyard.

Katiana, Katiana, Katiana: a chant whispered by the crowd. She had come home. A boy who looked about seventeen plunged into the yard. Hands on shoulders, cheek kisses. I recognized him, too: Alex, Clare's oldest brother.

Emmail smiled, pointed to Clare and said *"Kiyes sa?"* Who is this?

"Katiana." Alex's face shone with sweat and a shy smile; tears almost came. Instead, he gave a quiet laugh, his mouth gaped, and he dashed inside the house. A gray-haired woman with deep folds in her face peeked out the curtain covering the front entrance. Clare's grandmother didn't emerge. Instead, Alex carried out two woven reed chairs and a stool. Jeff, Clare, and I sat. Clare relaxed a bit beside Alex. He shared her high cheekbones and iridescence. The red-shirted woman lifted up her hand and eyes to heaven, waved her arm, and praised God in Creole.

Emmail translated, "They were talking about Baby Katiana last night. And today she came. Amazing, they say."

A younger boy rushed in and Emmail smiled. "*Kiyes sa?*"

"Katiana." The boy shrank back. Clare smiled at Edras, her youngest brother.

We sat in the chairs in the dirt in the sun in wonder.

Patricia returned with Filosane, the oldest. I recognized her drooping eyes. I had seen those eyes on Clare's face. *What was behind them?* I interpreted it as disrespect, indifference, or sullenness when Clare looked at me that way. In that moment, I wondered how much of Clare I might have misunderstood.

Emmail said Alex would help us find Clare's father who'd left on an errand just before we arrived. We were to return the next day for a visit. Clare stood with a smile, hugged, kissed cheeks, and we followed Alex down the path.

Clare sat between Alex and me in the back seat with her hands in her lap. She leaned over and whispered, "It's strange to be called Katiana."

"In Spanish-speaking countries, people called me Lina," I said, "because they couldn't pronounce Lynn." But I was reaching. Clare Katiana meant something deeper. I had no words for that.

She turned back to Alex. Pantomimed, laughed. Clare and her brother—their features mirror images.

"*Li la,*" Alex pointed to a man pedaling his bicycle along the side of the road. Emmail translated, "There he is."

Clare reached for my hand but kept smiling and laughing with Alex. The air in the car felt electric. Emmail pulled ahead of Clare's father, turned onto a side street, and jumped out. I watched him recognize Emmail from the adoption days through the back windshield. When Emmail motioned to us, we emerged from the car.

"*Acha!*" Clare's dad laughed and covered his mouth like he'd discovered he was on *Candid Camera.* Clare gleamed. Her face said *they love me, they want me*—words she would repeat for a year back at home. He hugged and kissed us all, shook his head, and smiled. Alex sat down on the bike rack, morphing into a bored-looking teenager, the Haitian nothing-moves-me expression. Haiti: equal parts impassive and expressive. Like Clare. Again, the thought flashed, *How much had I gotten wrong about her?* I sidled up to Jeff and took his arm.

After supper back at Don and Karen's, I washed dishes with Vero and Betsy—two women who as girls had come and gone from Don and Karen's during the adoption.

Betsy said, "I told Vero today, Lynn, you kept your promise. You came back." Her eyes were soft and deep.

I squeezed her to me. "I'm doing my best."

Over the next few days, Clare opened up and drank in Haiti. We spent an evening with her family, swam at a hotel in town, visited Rachel's clinic and an orphanage on the compound of a Franciscan brotherhood who believed children deserved beauty and created a lush garden complete with peacocks to prove it.

Two things eclipsed everything else for Clare when we said goodbye to Don and Karen and returned to Dallas: the *Katiana* chant alongside the exuberant village welcome and the foreignness of Haiti. They loved her; she was wanted after all. And Clare wanted America—comfort and consumption—not Haiti. She stopped calling for her Haitian mom when she wailed. She stopped talking about her "real" family and that we weren't it. She settled a bit. Jeff and I did, too. Both the Well and Haiti awakened our initial connection: the call to restoration, wholeness, and love.

As things shifted, I imagined my life opening up. In a year, Lucy would start kindergarten full time. *Where to put my energy after a decade dominated by babies, toddlers, and preschoolers?* I wanted a spiritual director to accompany me through the transition. I'd first experienced spiritual direction in Waco, waiting for baby Clare to come home from Haiti. My spiritual director had listened for the Sacred in my stories and helped deepen my attention there for an hour once a month at St. Paul's Episcopal Church. I needed that again. Soon after I started my search for one, I'd heard the name Nancy Dunkerly so many times I felt I had to meet her. We made a date for the Cosmic Café where I'd sip my favorite chai and check her out.

Nancy walked in wearing white slacks and a crisp, blue, button-down shirt. She had short gray hair combed back beauty parlor style—just the description she gave me on the phone. She smiled, seeming to recognize me, too. I'd said brown hair, blue eyes, and a green T-shirt. I swayed to Sanskrit chants thrumming from the speakers. Nancy looked up at a gold-and-white lotus flower mandala on the ceiling and at the Buddha and elephant-headed Ganesh images scattered about as she walked to the table. My nerves hummed as I realized this might seem an unusual spot to discuss spiritual direction in the Christian tradition. But she didn't miss a beat.

"Interesting place." Her eyes sparkled. "I've never been here before." She ordered a pot of mint tea.

I breathed in the nag champa incense; my friend Angelle burned it every day, so it smelled like home to me. "It's one of my favorite spots. Thanks for coming."

"I love to explore new places." As the waiter set a metal tea pot on the table, Nancy asked, "Why did you want to have tea, Lynn?"

I told her about anticipating a transition into a new season of life. She asked about my experience with spiritual direction and my spiritual journey. I described my search for balance between rest and work, prayer and action. How life in Waco had exploded the box that held my God. She sipped her tea, leaned toward me, and listened. I said Regent College had taught me that beauty, art, and care for the earth mattered like care for people. That as a storyteller at our church in Dallas, I offered wonder rather than answers. She nodded and commented a bit. We connected easily, seemed to speak the same language. I felt at home talking about spiritual things with her.

After about an hour, she said, "Lynn, I wonder if you're supposed to be the spiritual director you're looking for." I leaned back and took a sip of my chai, gone cold, as she continued, "I work with HeartPaths. We offer spiritual formation and spiritual director training from a Christian tradition, but we are open to people of all faiths."

"That's not what I expected." I tilted my head, surprised. Flattering but crazy. I wanted to *see* a spiritual director, not *be* one.

"Isn't that often true on a spiritual path?" She smiled. "Year one small groups practice different contemplative prayers each week. We have seminars one Saturday per month. And you'd have the spiritual director you're looking for—a HeartPaths director." She handed me a flyer. Something stirred in me as she went on to describe the books, journaling, and community.

"We discern together each May about your continuing on for the full three-year program."

I said I'd consider it and thanked her for meeting me. She answered that it was her pleasure and picked up our bill.

As we walked out, she said, "Look forward to hearing from you, Lynn. And thanks for introducing me to the Cosmic Café." She almost winked at me.

"Thanks so much, Nancy. I'll be in touch."

I couldn't shake thoughts of HeartPaths. I frequented the website home page where an orange-and-yellow nautilus shell spiraled to a luminous center. The invitation to contemplative prayer and community wooed me; the interfaith openness scared me. It touched an old fear I'd picked up in college, taught to guard and speak truth. But words rang in my mind from a retreat I'd attended the summer before. Jeff had found it and arranged for our moms to split kid duties with him for a week. The best gift ever. Phillip Newell, a Celtic Christian, had led it in the high desert of New Mexico with Rabbi Nahum Ward-Lev and a Sufi Muslim teacher named Ramah Lutz. Phillip had said, "Jesus is the treasure Christians bring to the table where we sit together with people of other faiths and discover their treasures."

Jeff walked with me through my questions. He trusted me and

my faith even when I feared I would tumble over the edge. He trusted God to take care of me. I said yes to HeartPaths as Anna started first grade at Rosemont, Clare middle school at North Hills Preparatory Academy, and Lucy her last year of preschool at the Kessler School.

Each morning of September, I ferried the girls to school, then dropped into my grandmother's gold chair by my bed, sat up straight, and put my feet flat on the ground to practice Breath Prayer. I breathed in five counts and exhaled ten. I focused on my breath for five minutes. After a week, I worked up to ten minutes. The next week I lasted fifteen. But I felt crazy. *Do I believe I can be in, connect to the Presence of the Mystery we call God? Really?* It seemed ludicrous as I sat in my chair by my bed at nine in the morning. *What is God anyway?* I wondered. Still, I practiced.

The next month, I learned centering prayer. On my golden chair, I breathed and let a word rise in me. Jesus; Mother; open; love. I used it to bring me back to inner silence and awareness of Presence when my thoughts strayed. One day, I stayed quiet for twenty minutes, then journaled about my gratefulness. For stillness, quiet, and the blue fall sky. For breathing in and out, the aliveness of the tingling, cool in-breath and the warmth of compassion I exhaled back out into the world. My word stayed with me throughout the day, taking me back to stillness. But when I sat down to practice a few days later, it felt like the first time I'd even attempted contemplative prayer. I forgot to surrender to silence a thousand times, remembered, then followed a flitting thought or memory across the field of my mind and twirled back again. *What am I doing? Opening and emptying? Sitting still and straight; just being. How is that not a waste of time? What is happening in me? To me?* I wasn't at all sure. Still, I practiced.

Once a month, I met with my spiritual director. I drove thirty minutes north to Community Christian Church in Richardson and sat across from her as she lit a candle to remind us of the Sacred with us. I talked about my worries. Lucy was five and still only recognized letters or numbers some of the time; she seemed to have missing connections. I wondered what would help her brain work better. My toes clutched my brown Birkenstock sandal shaking on my foot as my director glided in her rocking chair. Anna at six had started to lie and steal. In the classroom; from friends. I didn't know how to stop her. I looked at my lap. My chest barely rose and fell with my shallow breathing.

My spiritual director's dark-brown eyes looked like a curious puppy's. "Where do you find God, Life, in it all?"

I looked back in my mind. Clare was having a relatively peaceful year at North Hills. She hadn't been violent since our return from Haiti. Is *that* where I found life?

"On the window ledge over my kitchen sink, I think." I said, surprising myself. I uncrossed my legs and recrossed them at the ankle. She looked surprised, too.

"It's become my altar. Right now, it holds a clear stone, a bleached white shell, and a delicate dried rose from Clare's bush that we planted when she decided to get baptized." I took a deep breath. "They remind me of timelessness and offer me hope when I pause there and breathe."

She led me deeper. "And what do you feel in your body at those moments?"

I closed my eyes to remember. "A warmth in my belly. My chest expands, and my shoulders drop."

"Maybe God is inviting you to notice that and release."

A new language for me: invitation and surrender.

"When you talk about your girls, it reminds me of a fist clenched tight." She tightened her hand. "You might practice gripping and releasing your hands when you notice you're contracted." She let her hand fall open, relaxed. I mirrored her movements and felt a release in my whole body. I agreed to try.

On my next retreat at Mt. Carmel, I noticed my mind's relentless chatter. It critiqued what I read or worried about the girls or what Jeff was feeding them, letting them get away with. Wondered what I would eat next. One morning, I lay under a cottonwood tree on the grounds as it danced with the wind. I looked through the branches into the expansive blue fall sky. And my mind *would not shut up*. Cortisol rushed through me. I felt helpless but looked for the compassionate observer inside that we'd talked about at HeartPaths. Just notice, no judgment. I was getting to know her.

The quiet, the Presence, permeated me even when my meditation was distracted and frustrating. It nurtured love in me—an answer to a prayer I'd written: *There is so little I know. Love. That is the whole thing, I think. Love God. Love neighbors. May I love more and better. May my children one day say, "She was crazy and made lots of mistakes, but she loved God, she loved us, and she loved people."*

As my final project for Year One, I co-led a retreat in May. Always willing to dip into my world, Jeff came. He practiced lectio divina, centering prayer, visual prayer, guided meditation, and a mindful eating meditation. He opened himself with his innate generosity and kindness. And then went back to his more traditional prayers when he got home. But I wanted more; I signed up for HeartPaths Year Two and the June session of something Nancy Dunkerly called Whole-Brain Prayer.

Exercises of the Imagination

Nancy stood at the front of the Episcopal Church of the Transfiguration classroom with a familiar twinkle in her blue eyes. She looked out over two sections of four tables each set at a slant, like the lead bird of a flock of white-headed swans flying north for the summer, my brown head the youngest among them.

"Most people use the left side, logical brain to pray. Recount worries and make requests. What if we engage our right side, intuitive brains? A practice I call Whole-Brain Prayer." She led us into silence to allow an intention, prayer or question to rise.

In my mind, a vision: *Jeff in bed that Saturday morning, his iPad propped on his belly; the girls' scowls when I said no TV; me flipping pancakes, hosting a tea party and trampoline romp instead—to avoid three angry screen-zombies after a morning of television.*

First, my jaw clenched, and anger heated my chest. Jeff said yes to screens because kids-should-get-to-watch-cartoons-on-Saturday-mornings no matter how many fiascos ensued. And to avoid conflict and be left alone. Same with donuts. I said no sugar to dodge the monsters Clare and Anna became. Second, I reached for compassion. *Maybe Jeff tried to balance me out?* I took a deep breath and wrote in my art journal: *How to release my irritation and judgment toward Jeff?*

Nancy invited us to collect glossy magazine pictures from long tables against the wall to make an intuitive collage. "Let go of the words you wrote. Don't think too much. Receive what calls to you."

My hands behind my back, I walked the length of the tables. An image stopped me. A man knelt between rows of vibrant green leaves with a trowel in hand. Wide hat, hunched back, beating sun. A bit farther on, a second picture called—a woman's full, bare brown breasts cradled a beaded seed necklace. A baby lay in her cupped hand, a bump of pink tongue at its open mouth about to latch on and drink.

When we sat down with our images, Nancy said, "Let the images and papers arrange themselves; don't worry about making beautiful art. Let go." She sat down to her own collage work at the front table.

The room rasped with tearing paper. Caps popped off glue sticks, and people patted down bits of images. The rhythms of an acoustic guitar streamed from Nancy's speaker, holding us all. I tore the hunched figure and the woman and child into rough circles and pasted them in the center of the page—the field worker hovered over the nursing pair. I glued crescents torn from a yellow fallow field, green leaves, sunlight and shadows around the edges. Black ink waved from corner to corner of my collage. After thirty minutes, Nancy passed around questions: What did you feel as you worked? Where in your body did you feel it? What questions arose? Where are you drawn in the collage? If it were to sing, what would that be like? If it could speak, what would it say? How would you reply?

I saw Jeff and me. Our work as parents differed, but we poured out the same life. He nourished our family through his work, tired and strong; I brought it from my body and soul. The collage said: *I am safe, I am nourishing, I am full, I am emptying, I am filling, I am bent, I am tired, I am alone but together. We are one whole.* The acceptance I'd prayed for washed over me. Back at home, I found Clare perched on the yellow arm of our vintage Salvation Army couch, Anna pouring tea for Lucy, and Granny Gardner from church reading *The Velveteen Rabbit* to them all. She was their Dallas grandmother, and she loved them fiercely. She offered to stay each Tuesday in June so I could go back.

The next week, Nancy began with a quote from Wendy Wright:

"Our relentless search for new ways of being and relating, our dreams of beauty, our longings for mercy and justice—these are exercises of the imagination." A prayer for nonjudgmental seeing arose in me. *How do I observe what really is?* We scribbled lines with our nondominant hand, eyes closed, and then used color to reveal what we saw in the shapes. The week after, Nancy quoted Carl Jung: "The energy of the center point is manifested in almost irresistible compulsion and urge to become what one is." We colored mandalas and noticed resistances, resonances, and dissonances.

The final class of June, we created our own mandalas by tracing a paper plate and using pastels to fill the circle. My question: *How can fire and water live together and one not consume the other? In their proper places?* Thick slashes of oranges, reds, blues, and grays overflowed the borders of my mandala with a coal-black infinity symbol laid on top. I'd discovered more dishonesty from Jeff the week before. We'd healed our relationship over the last year, so I felt sucker-punched. And any duplicity triggered my fear. He sat on the edge of our bed, devastated, as I threatened to take the girls and leave if it happened again. He promised it wouldn't. He asked for forgiveness; I withdrew. During the mandala prayer, I realized I didn't want to shut him out. It was too hard; I loved him; I needed him. Whole-Brain Prayer was a pressure valve, releasing tension. And a magic mirror, revealing my inner life. Jeff kept his promise.

I signed up for monthly Whole-Brain Prayer beginning that fall as Anna and Lucy joined Clare at North Hills Prep. They could all stay at NHP through high school. It solved the yearly find-good-public-school-programs-in-a-big-city dilemma. Anna left her friends behind at Rosemont and labored to catch up to her second-grade NHP peers. She didn't complain even when we added Lindamood-Bell tutoring across town three days a week for her reading and comprehension. Lucy's long journey to connect the alphabet song she sang to the shapes she saw on paper continued, but her teacher promised she would read by the end of kindergarten. And Kathryn, Clare's seventh-grade counselor, answered my call for help.

Clare missed assignments and argued with teachers. Her math teacher said Clare turned her work in to the wrong basket, incomplete or not at all. Clare's stories slipped and slid: she went to school early for tutoring, but her teachers never saw her; she said they weren't there; her math teacher was unfair, changed the rules, and didn't help her understand new concepts. They infuriated each other. Kathryn became their mediator. We needed one at home, too, where confusion and chaos deepened daily. My Year Two HeartPaths spiritual director, Eunice, companioned me through it all.

Eunice was a couple decades older than me and radiated strength, wisdom, and joy. I met with her every other week as a guide for my HeartPaths journey through the Spiritual Exercises of St. Ignatius—a five-hundred-year-old series of meditations on the life of Jesus and our life in the world—and all they brought up in me. We talked about fears that fed my perfectionism and domineering. My inability to control Clare. The shadows that threatened to swallow me if I gave them my attention in my practice of the Examen—a twenty-minute, prayerful review of each day. Depression always lurked nearby.

"I don't think you need the full Examen each day, Lynn," Eunice said. "You easily notice what drains life from you." She smiled and chuckled; she knew my Eeyore side. "Focus on life-giving moments. And maybe settle for peanut butter and jelly instead of organic, well-rounded meals now and then."

Through the focused attention of the Examen, simple things became profound: the coral, rust, and purple sky at twilight as Anna and I stood at the kitchen window washing dishes; a child laughing in the park; Clare and Lucy dancing; fat, furry tree branches budding in spring; Jeff holding my hand. I journaled: *We bump up against the Divine Love all the time. There is so much beauty and grace around*

*us, whether we call it God or something else. The continual creation is
enough to bring hope.*

Hope I needed as Clare continued to unravel. She roamed the
halls during class, racked up zeros on assignments, tried to flush her
phone battery down the toilet so we couldn't uncover her secrets.
She told Kathryn she thought her brain didn't work right. Kathryn
suggested we get a diagnosis to allow classroom accommodations, so
I took Clare to a psychiatrist. Clare met criteria for ADHD, anxiety
disorder, and major depressive disorder. A committee of her teachers
described Clare's challenges: forgetful, zoned out, lack of executive
function skills, and difficulty processing information and regulating
her emotions. And strengths: friendly, gets along well with others,
takes on strong leadership roles, makes and keeps friends at school,
creative, cooperative, and adaptable—things we would learn to count
on over the years to come. We put accommodations in place, and Clare
started anxiety meds. And running away. My daily centering prayer
held me together, but it also pulled me into my own murky depths. I
carried it all back to Eunice twice a month, creeping through morning
traffic on LBJ Freeway in my blue Civic from NHP to Community
Christian Church.

Eunice opened the door. She led me to a rocking chair where I
stared into the flame of a candle as it danced. Sunlight peeked through
closed blinds, and I asked if I could open them. Light flooded the
room when I reached over and twisted the white, plastic wand.

Eunice's smile raised her pink cheeks to the crinkles around her
eyes where blond bangs wisped across. "Let's take some silence to
begin, Lynn. Sound okay?"

"I need a reset. Traffic was crazy," I nodded and closed my eyes. My
shoulders relaxed as my breath deepened. Silence wrapped me up like
the arms of a close friend. After a while, I spoke. "Contemplation and
mystery have replaced the words I used to wield: sovereign, infallible,

faithful." *What did those things even mean?* I crossed my arms over my chest. My jaw clenched. Eunice stretched the silence.

"Notice your posture? You look barricaded sitting there. Like maybe the unknown threatens you. I wonder why these feelings are so strong?"

I had crossed my legs like tangled wires, hunched over. I listened inside myself. Ran my fingers through my hair. "If I have no words for God, who's been my center for twenty years," I took a deep breath and almost whispered, "I might disintegrate." Sobs erupted. The warmth of Eunice's hand covered mine. We sat that way for a long time. It felt like dissolving into goo inside a chrysalis. My eyes stung. The light fell across my foot on the blue carpet. I looked up.

Eunice's blue eyes flowed with compassion. "Sometimes we use theology as scaffolding. Especially when the world feels dangerous. Like it did for you as a child. Like it might now at home. It offers the illusion of security and control." In her words, I heard my lifetime strategy: figure things out, understand, and you'll be okay. Eunice offered the name of a therapist she trusted, and I returned to therapy—anything to lessen the pain.

At one session, I told my therapist how my fear had taken over that week. Lucy had stood in pajamas covered with cats in tiaras, stuffing her blankie in her Dora backpack along with Red Dog—a gift from her birth mom, Diane, the Christmas before our adoption.

"Whatcha doing, love?" I'd asked.

Her thin brown braids had whipped over her shoulder as she turned. "Leaving."

"Going where?" *Was this about Clare's nightly storms?*

"To find my brother."

Ah, adoption. "Where will you look?" I was well practiced at these conversations.

"Down the hill. I'll knock on doors and ask who's seen him." She zipped her pack and slipped her little arms in the straps. Dora hung down past her bottom.

"What's his name?"

Her forehead creased. "I don't know." At six, Lucy still had the magical thinking of a younger child.

"You're missing him, though. I imagine that hurts. I will miss *you* if you go."

Her bottom lip puffed out. "I'll bring him back here. We can put mattresses on the floor and all sleep together in one big room," she said with a gap-toothed smile.

"You'd like that. All of us together."

She walked past me to the living room and turned. "I'll miss you, too, but I have to go."

"It's dark outside; it isn't safe." I pointed out the window, and she turned to look as she put her hand on the doorknob.

"I'm strong and brave. I have to."

My face flushed; I shifted to mom-in-charge. "No, Lucy. You can't go."

Unfazed, she opened the door, letting the cool night air inside. "I told you. I have to."

My stomach lurched, and my voice got stronger. "Do not disobey me, Lucy." At the change in my voice, Anna rounded the corner. Lucy stepped onto the front porch, determined to reconcile her families. Dora smiled at me from her back.

"Lucy, there are bad guys out there, and they will get you." I knew I'd pay with bedtime fear for a long time to come, but Lucy needed specifics not generalities. And I couldn't let her walk out into the night. She paused on the top step and turned to me, eyes wide. Anna reached for my hand as Lucy moved toward me.

"When I'm bigger and stronger, I will find him."

Anna let go of my hand and took Lucy's. She led her back inside. "Come back in, Lu. You don't want to get hurt." As Anna had walked her back to her bedroom, I'd sunk onto the couch and dropped my head into my hands. I told my therapist how afraid I'd felt. My shame that I reverted to scaring Lucy to control her, keep her safe. We explored my childhood sexual abuse, one of the things that fed my desperate need for control and certainty. She guided me through visual meditations to heal further and suggested mindfulness training. Desperate, I did whatever she said.

My parents gave Jeff and me a reprieve for a nineteenth wedding anniversary gift—a long weekend away at a bed and breakfast. We left the girls with them and drove down I-35 lined with wildflowers—blue bonnets, red prairie fire, Texas yellow stars, and pink buttercups—toward Austin. We listened to *Wait, Wait, Don't Tell Me* on NPR and laughed at Paula Poundstone, our favorite comedian. At Rainbow Hearth in the Texas Hill Country, we slept in, made love, and ate a late breakfast of muffins and omelets with fresh sprouts grown in the B&B's basement. We took dark roast coffee back to our balcony, gazed at Lake Buchanan, and read. After our host, a massage therapist, worked the knots out of our glutes and shoulders with a padded disc fitted to her power sander, we took a long walk down to the lake. The land offered shells twisted and bleached white, memories of the sea once covering it. Space opened, strength gathered in us. All in time for the tsunami's crash into our life.

It crested after school one day at the end of April. Clare pressed her forehead to the car window the whole thirty-minute drive home. Braided hair extensions I'd let her get when schoolwork consumed even grooming the dreadlocks she'd worn for years hung like a veil over her face. The moment the car's gear hit park in our driveway, she bolted. To escape her trap: our house. I clenched my teeth then forced myself to relax and exhale.

"Don't worry, loves," I said as Anna and Lucy unbuckled. "I'm sure she's gone to Jamie's next door." Our twenty-five-year-old neighbor, Clare's favorite harbor. I settled the younger girls with paper and crayons at their round wooden table by the bay window and went to fetch Clare. I noticed the pecan tree between our houses had leafed out. A few blackened, empty husks remained on the branches like open, four-fingered claws.

Jamie answered the door with the sad, stunned expression of one who had seen Clare's meltdowns up close. I followed her to her bedroom. Clare lay curled up on the bed like a turtle in its shell, braids the same dark brown as her skin tangled around her. I pushed aside mounds of wadded up tissues and sat down beside her. Jamie stood by the bedroom door.

"You're always welcome here, sweetie, but not to run away. You are lucky to have parents who love you so much."

Clare looked up at her through red puffy eyes. After a moment, she nodded.

"I do love you, baby. And I need you to come home." Anger and exhaustion trembled under the surface, but I knew letting it out would only escalate things. Clare pushed up and dropped her feet over the bedside. After a long pause, she slid off the bed and walked out. We crossed the front lawn together, and I followed her inside to her room. The preternatural calm dissipated. She couldn't slam the door because we'd removed it a month before when she had shaken the walls and crashed framed pictures to the ground, but she thwacked the floor with her backpack and thudded a book against the wall. Papers hissed as she ripped. The beginning of a rage.

I stepped into the hallway and called Jeff. "I need help right now." No hello, no explanation. None needed.

"I'll be right there," he said, sighing.

I dialed a friend and asked her to enfold Anna into her snack-and-bike-ride-after-school routine. Dialed another friend and asked if I could bring Lucy over. My well-practiced drill: keep everyone safe; shield Anna and Lucy from Clare's terrors. I trudged to the living room, pausing in the doorway. Anna and Lucy wore hunter-green, navy, and white plaid school jumpers. Dried white yogurt from lunch swiped across Lucy's brown cheek. Anna leaned around Lucy's end-of-the-day, fluffy dog ears to write her name for her at the top of a coloring page. Anna's tongue peeked out of the corner of her mouth as she concentrated.

"You write it L. U. C. Y." Stray light brown strands had escaped Anna's ponytail, and she pushed them behind her ear. They both looked up as I sat down sideways in a tiny chair.

"Is Clare okay?" Anna asked. Lucy hunched her shoulders and sank back, eyes big.

"She will be. Dad's coming. How about playdates for you two?" They both lit up a bit.

"You'll stay with me?" Worry spread over Lucy's face.

"I'll go in with you." I held her hand and turned up the music to drown out their questions and the growls and crashes coming from Clare's bedroom. Anna saw her friend's car round the corner onto our street and raced outside. Her friend flew out of the car, grabbed Anna around the waist and lifted her off the ground. As I waved goodbye, Jeff pulled up. He looked haggard in wrinkled khaki pants, locking eyes with me. His green collared shirt brought out their color, but they looked weary.

"I'm sorry. You're busy. Thank you for coming," I said.

He touched my shoulder and nodded, "Of course." The wind ruffled his short brown hair and showed his ever-broadening forehead. He shuffled to the front porch and bent to his knee to hug Lucy who'd come out to wave goodbye to Anna.

"Hey, love. How was your day?" he said.

"Okay. But Clare is mad."

"I'm going to help with that." He tickled her belly, and giggles transformed her.

"To your playdate!" I whisked her off as Jeff walked into the storm.

Lucy and I kicked away piles of yellow catkins fallen from the oak trees as we walked up to her friend's door and knocked. When the door opened, my *Hi there* sounded preschool-teacher cheerful. I walked in and knelt, eye-to-eye with Lucy.

I smiled—as if I could fool her. "Clare's having big feelings and needs me." Lucy nodded.

"You have fun. I'll be back soon."

Lucy clutched me for a long moment and then ran off to the dress-up clothes. I stood and let my face crumple into folds of confusion and fear as my friend hugged me. I felt my wall crack. The one that held back my dread every day in the school parking lot as Anna, Lucy, and I waited for Clare. The one that shut people out while protecting me from whatever came next. Blinking away tears, I whispered, *Thank you.* My keys dug into my palm as I ran to the car.

Back at our house, Jeff—face creased with strain—paced the hall outside the locked bathroom door. I heard Clare's wails and snorts; she hadn't climbed out the window yet. I pictured snot running down her face, red with the heat of rage. She sounded fully into her animal self.

"Let's tag out," I said so Jeff could take a break. I knew he would sit on our bed and pray. I leaned my cheek onto the cool wood frame of the bathroom door, into Clare. Maybe a gentle voice would bring her down.

"Clare, how can I help you?"

I felt it first. Before I heard it. The whole door vibrated. Then the crash, like thunder after lightning, reverberated as glass shattered and smashed to the tile floor. The mirror clamped onto the bathroom side of the door? Jeff ran to me.

"Clare!" I yelled. But then shock calmed my voice—no feelings to muddle things, just heartbeat, breath, adrenaline. I murmured, "I need to know if you're okay. Please talk to me."

I heard a small voice, snatched back to human. "I'm okay. But glass is everywhere and I'm scared."

"*Please* let me help you, babe."

The deadbolt shifted. I turned the knob, afraid of what I'd see. Glass scraped across the floor as I pushed open the door. I gasped. Red splatters covered the subway floor tiles, the bathtub, up the white beadboard. *Oh, my God.* Then my nose took in a sharp, acrid smell. Fingernail polish. My eyes swept over the floor. They found the black plastic handle of the bottle. *Had Clare thrown it against the mirror so hard everything shattered?* Shards filled the sink and covered the floor, huge butcher-knife-sharp points and tiny shavings.

Clare huddled in the corner, all fury and life drained from her. "I'm sorry. I'm sorry. I'm sorry."

"It's okay, love. Just stay there, and I'll make a path. Jeff, I need the broom."

Jeff hurried away. When he handed me the broom, I swept then reached out for Clare's hand. Jeff followed us to the bedroom, and we three sat on the edge of our bed. I put my arms around Clare, and she collapsed into me. Jeff held her hand on the other side.

"What's happening, love?" My voice cradled Clare, her bony shoulder jabbing me in the ribs. Tears drowned her deep-brown eyes and flowed across her hollow cheeks.

"I feel sad, scared, and embarrassed all the time. I don't know what to do," she said.

"I promise I'm going to figure it out," I whispered.

A week later, I drew my feet into my chair in our dark living room. I hugged my knees and called Clare's seventh-grade counselor at nine o'clock on a Tuesday night. "Hi, Kathryn. Sorry to call so late." I tried to sound calm, but my voice cracked.

"Let me get to a private place."

My tears fell as I recounted the last several hours. How Clare had sobbed as she stumbled from her room, *Thirteen Reasons Why* in her hand. How she had said the book gave her the answer to her pain. She planned to kill herself in one week. She had calmed as she explained it, logical and coherent. As we walked our neighborhood, she never wavered. She listened to my arguments and said, no, suicide was the answer.

"Is she safe now?" Kathryn asked.

"Yes. With Jeff." He had her in our bed. He'd stroke her arm like when she was little until she fell asleep.

"Lynn, what has to happen for you to know you're not enough? That you don't have what she needs to be okay?"

I felt the truth click inside me, like the final right number on a lock that springs it. I rocked as I registered the knowing. "This. I cannot keep her safe." I slipped off the edge of my relentless striving into a chasm. I tumbled, breathless, terrified, and relieved. When I hit bottom, it would either hold me or destroy me—both felt like better options than what I'd been experiencing for so long.

"What do I do now?"

The Chasm

Psych patients in the Children's Medical Center ER had small, cold rooms with a glass wall that faced the nurse's station. Like old-school zoo enclosures that let you watch the caged animals. Self-harm watch. Clare huddled under a blanket on the bed, Jeff sat on a dusky blue hard-plastic chair, and I leaned against the counter that ran along one wall. Every hour or two, a doctor or nurse came in to "chat" or evaluate and then left us alone again. The fluorescent lights buzzed and glowered; the gray-and-cream color scheme drained any hints of vivacity away. But we laughed a lot in that room. We all felt safe for the first time in a long while tucked away there together.

When I had rubbed Clare's back to wake her that morning at home, she'd turned over and shifted her legs like a grasshopper under the covers. After a minute, she'd cracked open her eyes—swollen slits from her sobs the day before.

"I talked with Kathryn last night," I'd begun. "We agree you shouldn't have to fight to make it through the day at school today." Clare had exhaled as if she'd been holding her breath for weeks.

At the hospital, she narrated stories about people who passed by the glass wall, and Jeff told dad jokes. They ate a vending machine lunch, and I pulled almonds out of my purse—my food-allergy-safe sustenance.

"Sure you don't need more than that, Mom?"

"I'm okay as long as I have my almonds."

Clare repeated that line again and again, hilarious that I just needed those little brown teardrops. A private joke in the making.

The biting smell of disinfectants kept us awake as the day wore on. I fidgeted and flitted like a hummingbird from counter to chair to bed. Checked the time and realized our friend Avis Strong had already picked Anna and Lucy up from school. We watched other kids through their glass walls curled up on their gray beds. And other parents' faces—wrinkled foreheads, tight jaws, heads rested in hands. *How could we be in this story?*

Late afternoon, our favorite nurse slid open the glass door. "How are you guys?"

"Cold and hungry but okay," I said.

"Wish we could change that. *Hospitals.*" After a pause, he continued, "The doctors believe Clare is a danger to herself." He looked regretful, sheepish even, but I relaxed. Clare excelled at camouflage; she covered her struggles with charisma. Jeff and I called it *Happy Clare*, the mask she wore for the world. But I *wasn't* crazy in believing she needed help. "We have an open bed on floor eight—the psychiatric unit. Typically, a seven-to-ten-day stay."

Jeff and I exchanged relieved glances: Clare would be safe, and they would tell us how to help her. We gathered our things and followed him onto the elevator.

When a *ding* announced our floor, he slid his key card to unlock the door to the unit. Clare grabbed my hand, and we took an instinctive step back. But he led us inside.

A young man approached, and the nurse said, "This is the girl for room twelve. Clare." His face softened as he turned to us. "Wish you the best. Hang in there, kiddo." He slid his key card again, and the door clicked shut behind him.

"I'm Jack, a milieu therapist. I hang out on the floor with you. Need anything, just ask." Clare nodded. "A quick tour, then time for goodbye. You'll have an hour visit each day while you're here." Clare's and my hands grasped tighter; Jeff's face paled, and the wrinkles around his eyes deepened.

Jack walked us down the hall, pointing out cameras that linked to the nurse's station—everyone monitored at all times. He gestured toward a room with an open door, and we all four walked in. "This is Clare's."

A single bed with no sheets sat against one wall with a desk built in the opposite one. A camera hung in the corner, and a secured, translucent square covered a fluorescent light in the center of the ceiling. Jack said it stayed on 24/7 the first several days to ensure safety.

My heart hammered: *But she'll be terrified, won't be able to sleep, needs her music and blanket.*

No pencils or pens—self-harm—ditto paper clips, underwire bras, shoelaces, and drawstrings because of hangings. Bathroom only when staff was present to unlock and stand outside the door. Jack listed these things like tedious details of everyday life. "Clare, you have to sing or say the ABC's, so we know you're not drowning yourself. We had a patient try a few days ago."

Wave after wave pushed against me as if I stood way out of my depth in an ocean. *But our daughter doesn't need this . . . does she?*

Jack turned to go, and Clare turned to me, her face inches from mine. Her eyes filled her face; her mouth twisted in fear; tears ran down her cheeks. "Please, Mom. Please don't leave me here. Please. Please. I promise I'll be good."

My face mirrored hers. My hands on her shoulders, I looked deep into her. "It's not about good or bad, love. It is so scary." I choked on the words. "I don't want to leave you here, but we have to keep you safe. I promise you'll be okay."

All emotion and life drained from her face.

Jack spoke from behind us, "While your parents sign papers, come with me to the common room and meet some kids." Clare took a deep breath, turned, and followed. Never looked back.

After Jeff and I zombie-signed releases and promises to pay, the administrator unlocked the door and said good night. When the elevator opened on the ground floor, I walked a few steps and sank to the floor against a wall. Jeff held me as my body shuddered. His tears fell on my cheek and merged with mine.

"It feels like we're abandoning her." He looked at the ceiling as if to the universe and moaned, "I *can't* leave my child in this place." I slid up the wall and held him. As I stroked his hair, he cried harder. "How did we get here?" I had no response.

In the days that followed, we visited Clare for an hour each evening while various friends stayed with Anna and Lucy. Sometimes we played cards and talked; sometimes she turned her back and played with her new friends. A psychologist diagnosed reactive attachment disorder. It both made sense of our life and devastated us. Clare first lost her Haitian mother, then her family; I'd left her in Haiti, Karen in Waco: dominoes teaching her attachments weren't safe as they fell. Clare was a poster child for RAD: dysregulated emotions, the push/pull, the crawl up inside me and claw her way out I'd described to my therapist in Vancouver. We read handouts that said Clare would likely never have real relationships. She excelled, though, in the predictability and smallness of the hospital ward away from us. She participated in groups, did schoolwork, and earned points for meeting goals.

Our insurance ran out ten days in. Her team advised Jeff and me to lock up knives, tools, scissors—every possible weapon—at home and drop her at day treatment from eight to four for two weeks. Our insides twisted as we loaded toolboxes with sharp objects and clicked locks on. We filled out goal sheets, met with psychiatrists and family therapists, and picked up new medications. At home, Clare resisted the points-for-privileges game and the structure she'd thrived on at the hospital. Rage simmered under her skin and fear under Jeff's and mine, but she didn't mention suicide again. As day treatment ended, Clare turned thirteen. She stepped down to weekly sessions with a psychiatrist and a therapist over the summer.

Summer relieved the social and academic squeeze Clare felt at school, but unstructured time undid her as well. Jeff occupied her as a helper at the Well. He noticed striking similarities between Clare and the community members. Her stories matched her feelings rather than the facts, and she spun chaos and confusion. She didn't consider how her behavior impacted herself or others: a youth pastor called us after she accused an unsuspecting boy of sexting her; our distressed pastor sought us out after he had found Clare crying one Sunday morning, and she had told him Jeff and I fought at home, I was violent, and we had filed for divorce. People ricocheted from heroes to enemies for Clare, especially me. And, as always, consequences had no effect.

One night as Jeff and I read in bed, I asked how he was doing. He took off his glasses and massaged his eyes. "I want to crawl in a hole. Disappear." He replaced his glasses and rubbed his shoulders. "She is defiant, disobedient, and manipulative. *Why* is she doing this to us?"

"I hate her sometimes," I said, and Jeff winced.

"What mother says that about her child?" I admitted. "Terrible and true." It wasn't the first time I'd said it.

He nodded, "She told me things would be okay if I divorced you and we bought a big house and lived without you."

My nose stung as my eyes began to fill. "She told me she needed to get away from us and live somewhere else—a group home, foster care, anywhere."

"I sit at the Well sometimes and imagine her like some of our community members: relationships damaged beyond repair, struggling to function in society in any healthy, meaningful way." Jeff picked up our books and laid them on the bedside table. "My stomach hurts all the time. I'm terrified, Lynn."

I touched his cheek then slid down under the covers and buried my head under my pillow.

He turned out the light. "What are you doing with her tomorrow?"

I often dropped her with our friends for the day as life at home became unbearable again. She was helpful, respectful, all smiles and laughs with them; then she walked into her shadows at home. "She's helping Courtney with the kids."

My friend Courtney knew our reality. She had come over for tea one night and then sat alone in our living room as Clare melted down. Jeff had contained Clare on the attic stairs as she marred the door, while I'd lain with Anna and Lucy in Lucy's bed, one girl in each arm with my hands over their ears to block out Clare's screams and moans. I whispered, *Daddy is safe* and *Clare will be okay* and sang songs to drown out the growls and excavation in the stairwell. I'd gotten Lucy and Anna settled as Clare fell asleep, exhaustion shutting her body down. She'd wake up in the morning back in her right mind for a while.

Courtney had sat, stunned, as I returned and I'd nodded. "Unbelievable, I know. And our life. We'll be okay now." I tried to smile.

"I don't know what to say." She shook her head. "I'm sorry. I love you."

I had walked her out then, carrying our half-full teacups to the kitchen sink.

When school started in August, we feared the added pressure. The first week I picked up my phone, saw North Hills Preparatory on the screen, and held my breath. *What now?*

"Lynn Alsup? This is the middle-school nurse from NHP."

"Yes?"

"Clare is fine, but I wanted to talk to you about something."

"Okay?"

"Clare needs a real breakfast and lunch to do well in school."

"I agree."

"But you don't send lunch. She comes to my office with a stomachache. I give her crackers, but I don't keep much food."

I must have sighed audibly. "I offer Clare breakfast, and she refuses to eat."

"Really?"

"When I send her with lunch, she brings it home untouched. I have to throw it away."

"Oh."

"I put peanut butter crackers and Clif Bars in her backpack. At least then I don't have to waste organic turkey and bread."

"I assumed. . .."

"She's convincing. Please talk to her counselor when she comes to you," I sighed and ended the call.

Then I yelled at Clare; she said nothing.

On Friday, she left school with the Strongs on a weekend road trip to San Antonio because we knew she'd erupt at home. They dropped her off on Sunday afternoon. Within fifteen minutes, she had climbed out our bathroom window. As she stomped away in her red high tops, her black basketball shorts hanging to her knees, Jeff followed her. I took Anna and Lucy to Courtney's in anticipation of a multi-hour saga. When she hugged me at the front door, my I-can-handle-anything exterior cracked.

"Can I hide in your room a minute?" I asked, hurried down the blond hardwoods, and shut the door. I had to get it together to face the storm. But my legs folded to the floor between the bed and the wall. I curled into a ball. *Why? Oh God. Why? Help. Help. Help*—my only prayers.

Courtney knocked. "Sorry, but it's Jeff. He needs you." She handed me their phone and a box of tissues.

"Coming," I said into the mouthpiece.

"I need you now. The police are here."

I heard terror. Shock catapulted me into gear. "On my way." Courtney didn't ask questions. I drove ten minutes home primal, desperate.

"Oh, God. Oh, God. Oh, God. Oh, God." As I pulled in our drive-way, Clare, Jeff and two police officers walked out our front door. One a tall, male officer, red-faced and sweat-drenched. A female officer stood near Clare with a clipboard. Clare's eyes darted from side to side, ready to launch herself in escape.

The tall officer bellowed, "What the hell is going on?" The other scribbled notes.

My brain switched into crisis mode: crystal clear. "Can I help? I'm Clare's mom."

"Don't know what y'all have going on, but it doesn't look good. A neighbor reports a Black girl knocking on doors asking for help. We find a White man following her around, and she's terrified. Her bedroom is a two-hundred-degree attic. What the hell?"

Jeff's anger erupted. "I told you she'd run if I got too close. I was following her to keep her safe." The office sneered at him, but Jeff continued, "All I've ever done is try to help her."

"Let's go inside and I'll explain." I walked in at a clip and sifted papers on my desk in the living room. "She's been out of town, so we turned off her air conditioner." I spoke over my shoulder. "She just got home and ran away before we could cool it down. She's under the care of Dr. Manesh at Children's outpatient psychiatry." I handed the sweating officer the Children's discharge summary and psychiatrist's notes. He took an audible breath and ran fingers through his wet hair, scanning the papers. Jeff sat on the edge of the couch ready to fight. The officers looked at each other and then Clare, who was now crouching on the living room floor like a cat. All nerves and fear, paranoid and dissociated.

"Makes sense." The officer exhaled loudly and turned to Jeff. "Sorry to accuse. It looked bad, and we have to be careful with kids. Let's talk on the front porch." They had two options: take Clare to a psychiatric facility or follow us to one if she agreed to ride safely in our car. Inside he repeated the choices to Clare. She was terrified of the squad car but refused to ride with us. She ducked into their back seat, and Jeff and I followed.

"I can't do this again." I wept as Jeff drove. He held my hand while I called Wayne and Avis Strong. After a snapshot of the situation, I said, "We can't do this alone. Please meet us there?"

"Of course. We'll be right there."

We pulled into the circle drive of Timberlawn Psychiatric Hospital at the same time. Clare's eyes flickered with recognition when she saw the Strongs, but she kept scanning for danger or escape. She sat down between Wayne and Avis in the waiting room, and they drew her out talking about the weekend they'd just spent together. Jeff and I sat rigid on chairs across the room.

Clare came back to herself bit by bit. She looked less animal, more human over the hour we waited to be interviewed by the intake staff. Another hour passed after the interview. Clare, exhausted and herself again, stood without a word. She crossed the room, sat beside me and laid her head in my lap—transformed back into the girl who needed me above all else. I stroked her arm. The admission staff reemerged to find Clare asleep. She woke, clearly not a present danger to herself or others, so they sent us home.

The next day we had an appointment with Clare's therapist, Annie. Clare asked her to send her back to the inpatient unit at Children's. She felt safe there.

"Doesn't work that way, Clare. You can't go back whenever you want. We've been working on living *with* your feelings by paying attention to them but not holding on to them."

Determination slid over Clare. "If you make me go home, I'll hurt myself." She held Annie's gaze, then slouched in her chair. Her ever-present basketball shorts and T-shirt made her look like an athlete or an urban kid on the courts. She was neither. She tapped the toes of her black, clunky high tops together. Annie sighed. She and Clare both knew the law required Clare to be evaluated at the ER after she said she'd harm herself. Annie made the call; Clare and I met Jeff at Children's for another round in the little glass-fronted room. But we didn't laugh or hope this time, just waited. At the doctor's request, Annie arranged for Clare's admission to Hickory Trail Hospital, a much rougher unit at the edge of town, hoping to convince Clare that hospitals were not solutions.

After I emailed my closest friends a plea for prayers, my dear college friend Christine searched for options. She'd cried with me through our infertility, welcomed me to Vancouver, and caught me when baby Patrick disappeared. She scoured every resource she had and emailed me a list of contacts for parents of kids with RAD, depression, or anxiety. I sat at my desk and looked up each option. Made phone calls. Prayed. Briefed Jeff each night in bed.

Residential placements for attachment disorders averaged twelve to eighteen months. I couldn't fathom Clare away that long. After all the chaos and pain, the chord that had stretched across Commercial Drive in Vancouver ten years before still held strong. The astronomical costs staggered us. "You can take out a loan," said admissions directors from several long-term placements. "Like for college. If you don't do this, she may never go to college. Might as well spend it now." I called an Appalachian wilderness program named Footsteps at Second Nature Blue Ridge, tucked in the list between therapeutic boarding schools and residential treatment centers. The program focused on strengths and support and had a therapist who specialized in attachment. Six weeks and six thousand dollars—an astronomically expensive summer camp. But I felt a twinge of clarity run through my core; a familiar guiding pull. I hid the recognition in my heart and continued down my list.

After ten days inpatient at Hickory Trail, Clare spent nights at home and attended the day treatment program. The second day, I listened to her stories on the way home. Mean, cussing, fighting kids teased her, she said, and she wouldn't go back. I said she would. She refused to enter our house: a protest. She sat in the middle of the street in front of our house and waited for a car to hit her. I pleaded and threatened; she lay down; I called Jeff and the police. The officer who'd found her broiling attic room a few weeks before talked with her until she agreed to come inside. A seemingly inevitable future ran through my mind—runaway, rape, kidnapping, juvenile detention. I begged Clare not to run and promised to find her a safe place away from us. She agreed.

While Jeff dropped her off the next morning, I dropped Anna and Lucy at North Hills and came back to sit in silence in my grandmother's gold chair. As I sat, my insides quickened: I knew it was Footsteps. Clare hated the outdoors; maybe her magic ability to morph into new environments and pretend equanimity would fail at a wilderness program. And that might save her. I called Footsteps at Second Nature Blue Ridge back. They said we could bring her two days later. We made plans with my sister Kim for my brother-in-law to pick Anna and Lucy up from school the next day. The girls would stay with them while we took Clare to North Carolina. My mom would come help.

The next day, Jeff, with a packed duffle in the car, signed Clare out of Hickory Trail while I met my brother-in-law at North Hills. We stood outside the tall metal gate to the elementary building as a teacher called student numbers on a bull horn, and I smiled at Anna and Lucy as they walked out in their matching plaid jumpers and big backpacks. Lucy's forehead wrinkled and eyes scanned the crowd of parents, like every day. When she saw me, she broke into her gap-toothed, first grader smile and ran. Anna smiled and hugged me but looked confused. I led them to stand under the shade of a tree.

"Weird to have your uncle here, right?" I asked.

They both nodded and he laughed, "Best surprise ever."

"You get to sleep over with Aunt Kim, Annie, Ben, and Kate tonight." Lucy smiled big, and Anna squinted at me. "Daddy and I are taking Clare to a camp for a while to work on her big feelings. We'll be back tomorrow to pick you up."

"Where?" Anna asked.

"North Carolina in the Appalachian Mountains. It's beautiful, and the people are nice. She'll do lots of cool stuff. Hopefully feel better."

"How long?" Anna needed information.

"About a month. Like a summer camp." I put my arms around them. "Love you both so much. I have to meet Dad and Clare at the airport now. Have fun with the Altizers. See you tomorrow."

Lucy's eyes widened. She unzipped her backpack to hold her blankie that she still took to school every day. She reached out her pinky to hook it with mine.

"Pinky promise you'll be back tomorrow. And I'll be okay while you're gone? And I won't throw up?"

I hooked my pinky around hers and whispered, "Pinky promise all of it the whole time." I squeezed her close.

"Who wants a snack on the way home?" To a chorus of *Me!* my brother-in-law led them to his car. Used to the turbulence of our life, Anna and Lucy trotted along behind him.

I met Jeff and Clare at Dallas/Fort Worth International Airport not far from where Clare and I had landed with Karen and my dad twelve years earlier. Again, we inhabited a surreal space of intimacy and relief, Jeff, Clare, and I. Someone would help us, and Clare would be safe. Three hours later, we drove north from Atlanta and crossed into North Carolina in the dark. The full moon rose over the towering loblolly pines of the Appalachian Trail. The next morning, we went to the Second Nature office. It felt like walking into the REI catalog when they showed us their storeroom of gear, Clare's pack already stuffed full. She smiled goodbye like she was beginning a grand adventure—a mask for every occasion.

Each night back in Dallas, I stood on our back deck with our dog, Charlie, watching the moon wane and wax day by day. I imagined Clare under the same moon. It went dark, filled out, went dark, and filled out again without her return home.

Lost

In my dream, I sit at the far side of a ballroom. An enormous floral arrangement sprouts from the middle of a round table covered in white linens. Maybe it's a wedding, but I don't see a bride or groom. People chatter and laugh, watching a toddler twirl on the blond wood dance floor in the center of the room, enchanted. The band takes a break. Still the girl flits like a butterfly trapped inside. Glasses clink like cymbals as people cheer. The child skips to my table; I smile and scoop her into my lap.

People begin to filter out as light fades outside. *Who do I give the child to? Where is her mother?* Looking around, I see most everyone has left. *I guess that makes* me *her mother now.* The child starts to wriggle, cry, and rub her face into my chest, smearing tears and snot across my dress. Food will make it better. Standing, I place her in the chair on her own. "Stay here. Be right back."

On a buffet table now in the middle of what was the dance floor, deep red, white, and golden gladiolas reach toward the ceiling surrounded by daisies, greenery, and roses. I look for something a baby could eat. It seems now the toddler is a baby. Polished silver laid to dry covers the table. *There must be hummus and a teaspoon.* Two friends from high school appear, and I tell them I've adopted a child. But I've left the baby in the chair alone, a terrible idea. When a teaspoon and silver bowl of hummus materialize, I take them back to my table. She is gone.

My stomach drops. *What have I done?* Lost her after only twenty minutes. My heels clack as I rush around. I hike my dress up and squat, looking under tables; I scan the expansive room, dash around the perimeter, call her name. *But what is her name?* I find no one but see a stairwell like one that leads into the hull of a boat. Families sit around a dining room below. Teenagers play pool and watch TV, and adult conversation and laughter overlay the bangs and clicks of billiard balls. Frantic, I ask if anyone has seen the baby/toddler. This concerns no one. I rush across a lawn that stretches to a sidewalk sea-wall. Looking, calling, I run along it until it transforms into a path through the woods. I've flung my shoes off somewhere, and branches tear my dress, but I have one focus: *find the baby.* A group of cabins in a clearing stops me—no way could she have gotten this far. I have no idea where I am or how to get back. But a rope stretches taut between a tree and the ballroom somehow. Relief floods me; maybe I will still find her. Hand over hand, I head back.

Water rises around me in the middle of a city street at night. Red and white lights reflect off the surface. I pull myself by the rope—so grateful for it—and search for the child underwater. My arms never waver. The fecund, unpolluted smell of a country river surprises me. Its current carries me. Then Jeff's voice is in my ear saying it will be okay; he holds me and the rope. I rest into Jeff as he and the water buoy me, release one hand and hold the rope lightly with the other. Together we reach the end of the rope at a few cement steps leading back to the ballroom. As we stand on the top step, the water recedes, the expanse of lawn and sea wall visible again.

I begin to cry. "I've searched for our child. I foolishly lost her. Searched but didn't find her."

He is nonchalant. "She wasn't really ours. It's just as well."

I can't speak.

∾

I slipped from dream to Dallas as our air conditioner kicked on and woke me. A moment of relief washed over me as I reached for Jeff beside me. It was just a dream. But then my hand felt the warmth of his arm, and I remembered: Clare was in the forest somewhere in North Carolina. A tear slid onto my pillow. How had I lost her? Light creeped in through the curtain. If only I could stay in bed and not face another day.

Wilderness

We emailed letters to Clare via her therapist Annette every Sunday night, some guided by the program, some by our hearts. I sat at our dining room table one morning with my hands around a warm cup of tea and read Jeff's *Impact Letter*, describing the effects of Clare's behavior on us all. He'd followed Footsteps' instructions: be specific, don't be gentle, include emotional impacts, expectations, and the positive.

> *Dearest Clare,*
>
> *Leaving you at Footsteps was perhaps the most difficult thing I have ever done. But I believe it is absolutely the right thing. I love you too much to watch you spiral down into the lies that dominate your thoughts and emotions. You are safe. You are loved. You are welcome. But something inside you has kept you from experiencing those truths.*
>
> *I feel sad and hurt by your rejection and fear of us. I feel angry when you spin the truth to make us out to be bad parents, unloving or unkind. I hurt for Mom when you say she is a terrible mother. I feel angry about how your behavior and choices affect Anna and Lucy. I am confused because you can be loving and kind, and then so quickly become hateful and mean. I am exhausted by the ups and downs.*
>
> *You are a strong young woman and can use your strength to confront the lies. You are an amazing person. Friendly, kindhearted, intelligent, and charming. You make others feel good*

about themselves. You love people well. You include outsiders and embrace strangers. You work hard to make others feel welcome. Now is the time to work hard to experience the truth that you are welcome, too.

I love you so much. From the first moment I saw you until the moment I said goodbye, I have never stopped loving you. I love camping with you, listening to you sing, reading your writing, going on daddy–daughter dates, and watching you grow. I cherish our talking about real things. I'm grateful that you trust me enough to come to me and talk. I'm filled with pride and wonder at seeing you act on stage and work hard to achieve your goals. You are a gift to me. Footsteps will help us be the family God created us to be, but it's going to take a lot of work. Please, please open up, do the work, and come home.

Love, Dad

I blew my nose, wiped my face, and breathed in the bergamot of my Earl Grey tea.

Annette scanned and emailed Clare's letters to us once a week. Her first letter undid us, begging to come home. But after that, she recounted funny stories about staff, hiking, digging latrines, making fires and new friends. Happy Clare in the wilderness. She sent an apology to Anna for her meanness and excluding.

Anna dictated a letter to me in response. (Anna's first had been three pain-filled lines: Dear Clare/ How can I help you?/ Love, Anna.)

Dear BFF,

I forgive you. You are the best writer on EARTH!!! I love you. I love, love, love you. God is with you. You are the best sister. Charlie is very, very sad. He still sleeps in his kennel at night. He is missing you. Sometimes I cry at night, too, because I miss you. Can we have sleepovers in your room upstairs on Saturdays when you get

home? I love how you laugh, play, and have fun with people. Have
you met new people? Are you friends with them? Is it scary to sleep
in a tent?

　　Love, your pal Anna

After Clare's birthday letter to Lucy, she dictated a response:

Dear Clare,

　　I wish that I was living with you. I had a great birthday at
Pump It Up. I got Hello Kitty toys and an American Girl dog with
a pillow, two food bowls, and a book. I got Legos. I wish you were
here to see all of my wonderful stuff. School is scary without you.
I hope you can see me all tall and grown-up now that I am seven.
You are a great dancer. I will not go to sleep because I will think
about you the whole night. I'll sit and look at the moon and I hope
you will, too. 'Cause guess what? Whenever you're not with some-
one, you still look at the same moon. It is beautiful. I'll blow the
moon a kiss, and I hope you do, too. I bet you will be back soon. I'll
give you lots and lots of presents, and I'll kiss you, too, one hundred
times. I love you. We love you. Good night. I love you.

　　Love, Lucy

Anna and Lucy both started meeting with a counselor at school,
and on Tuesday mornings, I went to Jeff's office for our weekly call
with Annette.

"How are things at home?" Annette jumped in. Jeff described
Anna's angry outbursts and Lucy's daily meltdowns. "I'm sorry you
guys aren't getting a break while Clare's away. That can be one of the
gifts of a wilderness program."

"It's exhausting," I said. "Clare used up all the energy and oxygen
in our home. With her gone, we thought we'd catch our breath." A
peaceful house, a break with Anna and Lucy had sounded amazing.

But the extra oxygen had stoked embers in Anna and Lucy: the wounds of adoption, years of volatility and violence in our home. Our choice to send Clare away threw tinder on the pile. They believed they were next. A fireball had exploded.

~

Only two weeks after Clare left, I had asked Anna—eight years old and capable—to pick up her room while I made an afterschool snack. Turning to the cutting board and apple, I paused to drink in an unseasonably cool breeze whispering through the open window. Anna had walked over with hands on hips, tipped her chin up just beside my shoulder to look me in the eye and refused.

I stretched my five feet, four inches and held her stare. "There will be a consequence if you disobey."

"You are so mean. I hate you!" Her ponytail grazed her shoulders as she turned to run.

I had grabbed her hand and corralled her onto the front porch away from Lucy. Anna yelled, red-faced; she swung at me. Her fist hit my shoulder, and I grabbed that hand, too.

"You make me do everything. Lucy never has to do anything." Sweat beaded up on her forehead, and spit flew from her mouth. *Where was Lucy? Was she watching?* Anna had always been the one looking out for Lucy while Clare raged.

"Calm down, Anna. You can't go back inside until you do." I let go and held my hands up, don't-shoot-me style. As I sat on the top step to wait out the fury, a loud pop and crackle jolted me. My head jerked around to see Anna's fist clenched at the small window in the top of the front door. Her shocked face. She had punched and shattered the glass. And with it, all the internal restraints that had held her together.

Desperate to contain her, I made her do jumping jacks for daily disrespect or disobedience. Movement knocked her out of stubbornness and anger for a bit. When she refused and yelled, I sent her to her room. She'd plant herself—strong, solid, and immovable—like a mountain. My parenting hadn't worked for Clare; now it didn't for Anna.

"You can walk to your room, or I will help you," I said one day. My code for *I'm about to use my body. Last chance.* She stared up from where she sat on the floor, daring me. I knelt down, grabbed her ankles and dragged her down the hall on her back, Lucy watching from her doorway.

"You're hurting me!" Anna screamed. I deposited her in her room, slipped out the door and held it closed, my heart thumping like I'd been in a boxing match.

"Let me out! Let me out!"

"When you are calm, we can talk." I tried to slow my breath and calm myself.

Her screams turned to whines, "Mommy, please. I'm hungry. I need food. You have to feed me." She stomped her feet and banged on the door. Then pleaded, "I have to go to the bathroom." Her voice defiant: "I'll pee on the floor if you don't let me out."

"Anna, I'm going to open the door. Go immediately to the bathroom." I opened the door; her need disappeared. Defeated, I walked away.

Later that evening, I sat on her bed. "I'm sorry about today, Anna. It's wrong for me to use my body against you."

"It's okay." She played with her stuffed horse.

I tucked a strand of hair behind her ear. "It's not. I want to live peacefully and respectfully together." She just nodded. My yoga, prayers, and mindfulness did not make me the mom I wanted to be. For Clare, Anna, or Lucy.

Lucy's sobs began at *brush teeth and put pajamas on* every night. "I can't, I can't, I can't," she'd moan. Her big, almond eyes squinched up. Her mouth turned down like a Greek tragedy mask. One night I knelt on the tiles of the bathroom floor—my pale face turned red—grabbed her shoulders, not even as high as the pedestal sink, and my voice rose. *Get it together!* A growl through my clenched teeth. And she cried harder.

Each morning, I woke them for school at six thirty. While Jeff showered for work, Anna got dressed and ate breakfast. Lucy lay under the covers as I wrangled her into white tights, pulled off her nightgown, and buttoned up her white Peter Pan collar blouse. Her fingers couldn't manage tights or buttons. Fine motor skills were still a challenge.

Her voice came out a tiny, whiny squeak. "I'm *tired*. I can't go to school."

"I know, love. But you are an important piece of the puzzle of your class. They won't be whole without you." It had worked in kindergarten when she loved her teacher and got to sing and dance in class. First grade, not so much. I sat her up to wrestle a plaid jumper over her head.

"I'm scared, and my stomach hurts."

"You are strong; you can do it. School is your work." I put on her saddle oxfords, and Jeff carried her and her breakfast to the car.

"Time to go, love," I called to Anna. She hugged Jeff's legs from behind as he leaned in the car to buckle a writhing Lucy.

He knelt to Anna and hugged her. "Love you, babe. Have a good day."

"Love you, too." She hopped in.

His eyes met mine as I opened my driver's side door. Weariness, sadness between us. "Good luck," he said.

"Thanks. Hope I make it to my session intact." I'd started Year Three of HeartPaths, meeting with people as a spiritual director intern.

"I'll say a prayer for you."

I tried to smile, but it felt more like a grimace.

Lucy worked to silence herself, but as we crossed the bridge over the Trinity River onto I-35, her wails began.

Anna held her ears. "Shut up! Shut up! Shut up!"

I reached behind to hold Lucy's hand.

Anna darted from the car as we pulled up to the curb at school—embarrassed by her sister's tears and red, swollen eyes. Lucy swallowed her sobs and wiped her face with the tissue I handed her. She stuck out her pinky. "Pinky promise I won't throw up, and you'll be here when school's out, and I'm not sick?"

"Pinky promise, love. All of it the whole time." She climbed out and hoisted her backpack onto both shoulders; almost disappearing in front of its bulk. Lucy reminded me so much of Clare. That terrified me. I cried as I pulled away.

~

After six weeks, Annette talked to us about what came next for Clare. "She's doing great work, off watch now, participates fully. Becoming a strong leader on the trail. She notices who's struggling and encourages them along."

I smiled at the speakerphone on Jeff's desk, remembering Clare's beauty. "Definitely one of her strengths, watching out for people on the fringes. She has amazing empathy sometimes."

"She's talked about adoption and fears of being abandoned," Annette continued. "It's deep in her, like many adopted kids. Have you heard of the book *Twenty-Five Things Adopted Kids Wish Their Adoptive Parents Knew*?"

Jeff and I looked at each other and shook our heads. "No." I scribbled the title down in my notebook.

"Good to read sometime."

"I'm glad Clare's talking about real things," Jeff said, encouraged.

"She's taking off her masks."

That sounded good. But Annette said Clare needed a few more weeks to get all she could from the program. Then she might begin deeper healing. *Begin.* "Honestly, if she transitions *home* from

Footsteps, I don't think she'll stay open and heal. Not alongside her stressors in normal life. She holds deep pain and no true identity. It's big, long work."

I laid my cheek on the desk, sighed at the *Happy Family* pictures framed there. Jeff rested his hand on my back. I felt its warmth as my tears dropped onto the desk.

"I imagine this is hard to hear."

"Incredibly disappointing," Jeff said. My body had become lead. *This journey* begins *not* ends *here?*

As Jeff and I talked, cried, and prayed over the next week, we came to believe Annette.

Through an educational consultant, we found New Leaf Academy, a therapeutic boarding school in the high desert of Oregon. On the eastern edge of the Cascade Mountains, it was 1,898 miles northwest of our home. For girls ages ten to fourteen with no history of substance abuse, sexually acting out, or legal issues. Average stay: twelve to eighteen months. We ignored the staggering cost; somehow we'd figure it out. We surrendered completely.

On October 29, my parents stayed with Anna and Lucy while Jeff and I flew to Atlanta like we had ten weeks before with Clare. We hadn't seen her face or heard her voice since. My whole body vibrated with anticipation. And fear that our relationship was broken beyond repair. At ten in the morning, unknown to Clare, Jeff and I stood in hiking boots and Gore-Tex jackets in an ancient grove in Nantahala National Forest—base camp. Staff radioed Clare to come help unload supplies. She rounded the giant pines, froze, and then broke into a run.

I hadn't lost her.

I scanned through misty eyes as she raced toward us. Extensions long gone, her russet hair stood on end six inches in every direction, a few sticks and leaves nested there. Khaki hiking pants with dirt smears across the knees. She'd gained some needed weight. Her eyes were clear, shining. Smile enormous like she'd spotted an oasis in the desert. We engulfed her in our arms, all three clutching each other. Giggles, snorts, and sobs bounced off old-growth trees. I held her face and gazed at her—eyes speaking beyond words. Hand in hand, Clare led us to the campsite, and we joined the backpacking-grubby group gathering firewood. Clare shape-shifted into Wilderness Girl, her expert survival skill of adaptation on display. She built a fire and started it with a bow drill as snow flurries began to fall. Jeff and I pulled out gloves and hats.

Later, we sat on fallen logs for a first and final family session with Annette and Clare. Clare said, "During our last session, Annette rustled leaves and asked if I knew any sayings about living in a new way. I was clueless." She laughed. "She gave up and told me she was talking about turning over a new leaf and my next placement—New Leaf Academy." Happy Clare smiled.

We'd written to her about our decision; Annette had told us about their conversation. I reached for strength. "I bet that was hard to hear, love."

"Yeah. But it's best." She studied the decaying forest floor under her boots.

"We're in it together, no matter what." Jeff reached over and took her hand. She held it but didn't look up.

At dusk, Clare cooked group dinner over the fire. Solid. Clearheaded. Strong. She strung our "bear bags" high on a branch and pounded sticks in the ground to create Jeff's and my shelters for the night—blue tarps stretched taut. Her capacity and centeredness gave us hope. We left together the next morning after a restless, freezing night. Trying to sleep on an incline in the open, I had been too cold to crawl out from under the tarp and pee behind a tree until I thought my bladder would explode. We drove to Atlanta together, grateful for the warmth of the car, and stopped at a Black hair salon. I had no idea how we'd take care of Clare's hair in uber White Oregon but keeping her alive and healing trumped that in my mind. For a brief respite, we inhabited that intimate space of the three of us heading toward a solution. The gentle rain of Portland, Oregon welcomed us the next day. Red and yellow leaves cascaded over our rental car as we wound our way up Mt. Hood. Evergreens reached up on either side of us like centurions lining the road. We sang to the radio, told stories, laughed and snacked in our small, safe world.

When we emerged from the pass, Clare fell silent. I looked over the seat. She'd shrunken from a petite thirteen-year-old into a scared child. I unbuckled my seatbelt and scrambled into the back; she laid her head in my lap. Farmhouses replaced evergreens. The landscape flattened into long brown swaths. We'd climbed onto the high desert. I stroked Clare's arm as Jeff drove on. A prairie falcon hunted alone in the bright-blue sky. For the last hour of our trip, we all cried silently.

Finally, we turned on a long, pine tree-lined drive into a parking lot surrounded by a grassy lawn. A two-story playhouse, complete with firefighter's pole and swings, butted up against the first of three buildings with peaked metal roofs. Clare sat up; we steeled ourselves. Cold, dry air hit us as we opened the car doors.

While Jeff and I met with Clare's new therapist, Cathryn, and the program director, Clare toured the facility and met the other eighteen girls. I stuttered through my sobs, so Jeff told our story. *School and relationships are hard. Clare tells stories from a kernel of truth until she seems to not know what is real and what is not. She gets out of control so that we can't even talk to her. She's violent. And we love her desperately.* They nodded compassionately and assured us she was in good hands.

Cathryn brushed her long blond hair over her shoulder as she led us to Clare in her new bedroom. Three sets of white metal bunk beds with colorful bedding and stuffed animals stood alongside three dressers, two with framed pictures and knickknacks on top. Clare's still empty. Cathryn asked us to say a quick goodbye.

Clare let Jeff side-hug her, then pleaded with me with her eyes. *Please, Mom. Please.*

I held her shoulders. "I love you, Clare. We are forever no matter what." I cried as she turned away. No hug. No more words. A rerun of leaving her at Children's six months before.

This love was the desperate kind. Wounding to heal. Like surgery. I prayed it would be the strongest, truest love somehow. Jeff and I recrossed Mt. Hood Pass at twilight, colorless evergreens enshrouding the road, and boarded a plane back to Anna and Lucy in Dallas. We chose to believe New Leaf gave Clare the best chance to have a real relationship one day—knowing it might never be with us—and stay alive in the meantime: our highest goals.

Still, disbelief, anger, and resentment crashed over us; we hated the story we were living. People asked, *How are you?* I answered, *Okay; hanging in there; believing good will come.* But I felt like I was dying. My belief in God—stripped to questions in Waco, mystery in Dallas—distilled into a cry: "Please, please, Mother of all, birther, healer, comforter. Hold and heal my baby. Don't let this choice be foolishness. May this story have a happy ending. Somehow."

I poured it all into researching attachment and trauma and their effects on thinking, behaviors, and bodies. I chafed at some attachment therapies: swaddling people of all ages, rocking and bottle-feeding to relive preverbal ages and attachments. Others advocated rigid schedules and consequences to control behaviors and create safety within impermeable boundaries. Then I discovered Heather Forbes, LCSW. Her book *Beyond Consequences, Logic, and Control* described the neurological effects of trauma, explaining why positive and negative consequences might fail. *Why yes, they did.* She said purposeful love and support could regulate and rewire the brain. We signed up for her January workshop in Austin and tried to keep walking.

Jeff, depressed and unmotivated since Clare was first hospitalized six months earlier, lost his job. The Well board wanted a new director who'd fundraise more effectively. Jeff mourned the loss of the community, Clare's absence, and the chaos at home, angry he couldn't fix any of it. Without time or energy to fear unemployment, we packed his office as we packed our family to spend Christmas in Bend, Oregon—our first visit after leaving Clare seven weeks before. We'd created visit guidelines during weekly Skype family therapy sessions with Clare and Cathryn. A daily schedule: meals, chores, an outing (we'd each choose one), physical activity, and "my time." Limited sweets and TV. A designated "healing hearts" chair for calming down. Thirty minutes of extra chores as consequence for direct disobedience or disrespect. Lose a privilege for full-on tantrum. Just like at New Leaf.

Our nerves buzzed as we flew to Seattle to catch a plane to the small Redmond/Bend airport. Crowds, noise, and unknowns scared Anna and Lucy. Clare scared them. My loud, authoritarian coping scared them. And we were all eager to be together anyway—the power of family. *Could a weight, a person, a boulder hold down the fear, anger, and resentment side of the seesaw I rode and suspend me in excitement and joy? For a little while? Could I just feel happy to be with my baby?* In Seattle, the sign at our gate said *Delayed, boards in one hour.* Anna clutched Jeff's hand and Lucy mine as we walked the crowded concourse to a restaurant. Anna's pink-and-purple horse backpack bumped Jeff's leg as she walked. Lucy looked straight ahead, gripping her blankie. A cacophony of voices, music, announcements, and beeps accosted us until we tucked ourselves inside the refuge of La Pisa Café. We returned to the gate thirty minutes later.

A jumpy airline attendant said, "Alsup?" We nodded and dropped our backpacks on the ground. He continued, defensive, "We called and called you over the loudspeaker. The flight just pulled away."

I stared at him. I wavered under the weight of containing the chaos of our life. I crumpled to the floor. Anna gulped—embarrassed. Lucy knelt down beside me, her long blue skirt draping over my blue jeans. She bit her bottom lip and fought back tears.

Jeff's soft eyes grew hard. "The board said delayed. We took that as truth." He used his you-are-incompetent-and-its-not-okay voice. Anna sidled up, leaned into him, shoulders hunched, and dug her toe at the floor.

The agent took a step back. "It's always subject to change, sir. We called you."

"We couldn't hear in the restaurant. You have to do something."

I stood up with Lucy and swept her braids over her shoulder. "We have to get to our daughter." My flat voice somehow sounded shrill.

"That was the last open flight. You'll have to wait until tomorrow afternoon."

"We can't." My voice rose. Failure to get to Clare the next morning felt like the final failure of motherhood.

A navy-blue Alaska Airlines uniform approached from across the walkway. "Can I help?" She must have seen me collapse moments before. We explained. Moving the man aside, she took his place at the computer. "There must be something we can do." She tapped the keys like a woodpecker. They could offer vouchers to free four seats on the next Redmond/Bend flight: eleven that night. I almost kissed her; I cried instead. When we boarded an hour later, Lucy laid her head in my lap and slept.

We settled into our Airbnb after midnight. It was perfect—a family's home with toys for Lucy, prayer flags over the door, and a short picket fence around the front yard. Sleds in the garage; a sweet, small, stocked kitchen; wood-burning stove in the living room. All we needed was Clare.

We pulled into New Leaf the next morning to a pack of girls out front, craning their necks for families' arrivals. When our rental car got close enough for Clare to see us, she broke away from the group and ran toward the small parking lot. I jumped out and squeezed her to me. She still fit under my arms. We clung to each other until she peeled off and hugged Jeff. Then Lucy and Anna. I stood back a bit to drink her in: blue jeans, royal-blue Texas Rangers T-shirt Jeff's mom had sent her, the red shadow of the T, the deep brown of her skin—all beautiful, even her unkempt Afro. Anna and Lucy stuck close to Jeff and me as Clare showed them around, not seeming to trust this new, steady version of their sister—four months gone, unseen, unheard. After an hour, we checked Clare out and went to our rented house: a family of five together again.

Christmas morning, Clare gave each of us gifts for the first time. I cried. She'd beaded the handles of a bottle opener and butter knife for Jeff and me. She'd made Anna and Lucy big graffiti-style cutouts of their names. The little girls glowed. After we cleaned up paper and boxes, they pulled on bright pink and blue ski bibs. Anna led Lucy to the alley with sleds in hand, face already squinched up, shoulders shaking with her giggling. Jeff and Clare read with hot chocolate by the fire. I collaged in my art journal. I made a shiny red tree out of strips of wrapping paper and big white snowflakes cut from a Christmas card. A red bird cut from a paperboard gift tag sat in the branches like the one I watched out the window. Silver, white-dotted wrap made the snow flurries; glittery silver stars with green and red circles and snowflakes made my snowdrift. I sat back, looked at the pages, and felt a hope and joy I didn't recognize. We all went to bed excited to ski on Mt. Bachelor the next day.

But I woke with a raging fever. Assuring everyone I'd be okay, I told them to go on and sank under three comforters with a cup of tea. I burned up, threw the covers off, then gathered them back when chills returned. I slogged through hours of fevered dreams until my eyes opened, registered darkness, and I bolted upright. They weren't home yet.

Jeff answered on the first ring. "We're okay." Tense. Short. "Should be there in thirty minutes."

"You're just *now* leaving?"

Clare bawled, and Jeff continued, "Anna, Lucy, and I were the last ones off the mountain. Clare needs you."

"Mom?"

"Breathe, baby." I counted aloud to five and back again, but she cried harder, gulping for air.

She squeaked out, "It was so scary, Mom. I was at the bottom of the mountain." I wriggled up the pillows to sitting.

"Breathe, love. You're okay now. I'm sorry it scared you."

She took a deep breath. "I didn't know what had happened. Everyone left but me and my instructor, and I stood there looking and looking up the hill." I imagined her terrified face. She started to cry again. "I thought they were dead."

"That must have been scary. Take another belly breath." I heard her inhale and exhale. "Have you eaten?"

"No." The tears abated a bit and she sniffed.

"Dad brought beef jerky and Clif Bars; ask him for them. It's late and you've worked hard. I bet you're starving. I promise it'll make you feel better."

"Okay." She sounded two years old.

"I did snowboard, though. I loved it." I heard a small smile.

"I'm so glad. Please give Dad the phone, and I'll see you soon." I told Jeff to make sure she actually ate, checked in about Anna and Lucy, silent in the back seat, and we hung up.

When they walked in the door, I jumped out of bed. Anna yelled, "It wasn't my fault!" and began pulling off boots and bibs. Her eyes welled up when I knelt down to help her. I wiped one tear from her red cheek as Lucy burst into sobs. I made sure Lucy had eaten, then took her to the warm bath I'd drawn. Once Lucy settled, I found Clare bundled on the couch with iPod headphones dangling from her ears and Anna snuggled in front of *How to Train Your Dragon*. Jeff poured pasta into boiling water as I sat down.

"What happened?"

"A whiteout at the top of the mountain as Anna, Lucy, and I took our last run." His shoulders slumped. *When did he get deep lines on his cheeks?* I reached for his hand and propped my head up on my own.

"Oh, no."

"Somehow, I got in front of Anna. I guess she got scared and sat down."

"I wasn't scared," Anna yelled from the living room. "I was cold, tired, and couldn't see."

Jeff rolled his eyes and lowered his already soft voice. "She didn't answer when I called, and I couldn't see her. . .."

"I couldn't hear you," Anna yelled and stomped to her room.

"So, I ditched my skis and started climbing."

I sat up. "You left Lucy *alone?*"

He grimaced. "And it took me a while to convince Anna to come down the mountain."

"Lucy just sat in the snow?" My eyes widened with each question.

"Like I told her."

"She must have been terrified."

"The place looked abandoned by the time we made it to Clare and her instructor through the whiteout."

I shook my head, and pain pinged as if a clapper had struck a bell. "I'm relieved you're okay."

He dumped pasta into a colander. "I'm so sorry."

I stood and hugged him. "I have to go back to bed; I feel like I'm dying."

"Just another day." He sighed and kissed my forehead.

I ducked into the bathroom on my way. "You okay, Lu?"

She looked up through red-brimmed eyes. "Mommy, I thought an avalanche would *kill* Anna and Daddy, and I'd be all alone." Her eyes filled and overflowed as I sat on the floor next to the tub and wiped her cheeks. "And Clare was at the bottom, but *I* didn't know how to get there. People skiing by offered help, but I just shook my head and cried."

"That sounds so scary, babe. You did just the right thing waiting on Dad. I bet you were relieved when he got back to you."

"I was so mad at Anna for stopping. She's so mean."

"You're safe now. I hope your bath made you feel better." I picked up a lavender towel and held it out for her. "I have to lie down, babe. Your jammies are on the cabinet, and Dad has pasta ready. I love you." Water dripped down her legs like rain on a windowpane as she stood.

"I love you, too, Mommy." She wrapped the towel around her. "Can we go home now?"

"Tomorrow, baby. Tomorrow."

The next day I miraculously woke up fever free. I got up and made pancakes with Anna. Clare packed as Jeff washed dishes. At New Leaf, we said a quick goodbye as the staff had instructed and drove away in silence, all lost in our own thoughts and feelings.

Beyond Consequences

After New Year's, we met Jeff's parents at their weekend farm in Central Texas. Anna and Lucy loved them. And the donkeys, goats, longhorn cattle, and a sorrel quarter horse Jeff's dad had gotten Anna. When the girls were in bed, we sat down with his parents and thanked them for their generosity. Our dads had gone to lunch together and decided to split the cost of Clare's tuition and our travels to see her, never wavering in their generosity and commitment to us from the moment Dad helped us bring Clare home. We were overwhelmed. And knew everyone wasn't so lucky.

Jeff and I woke early on Saturday and drove an hour and a half into Austin to the Beyond Consequences seminar with Heather Forbes we'd been waiting for since November. We found seats at the back of the church hosting the workshop—relieved not to be wrestling Anna and Lucy for a day. A tall, thin woman with long blond hair and a bright, toothy smile walked on stage, radiating enthusiasm. She introduced herself: Heather Forbes—clinical social worker and adoptive mother of two Russian children. When they had spiraled out, she'd researched explanations and solutions. I crisscrossed my feet underneath me and held Jeff's hand. *I'm with you, Heather.* Sticker charts and consistent consequences hadn't worked. I leaned forward. She'd felt like she lived in Crazy Town. Heather bounced between laughter and seriousness. *Maybe we weren't the only ones? We didn't create Crazy Town with our bad parenting?* One of my deepest fears. I squeezed Jeff's hand and let myself drop into a new country with a landscape I recognized as my own.

As the morning unfolded, Heather introduced us to two theoretical boys—Billy and Andy. Andy had been loved and provided for from the beginning. He felt safe. He responded to sticker charts and consequences, followed directions, had friends at school and in his neighborhood. Teachers loved him. But Billy struggled at school, at home. Maybe he'd moved a lot, experienced violence or addiction at home, a physical injury to himself or someone he loved: trauma. Maybe he was adopted. Changes in routines could make Billy rage; a substitute teacher or a morning without Cheerios, and World War III broke out. I looked around the nodding room. They knew Billy; lived in Crazy Town, too. I wanted to raise my hand and shout, "Yes, Heather! I live with Billy, too!" Three Billys.

After a coffee break, she clicked up a slide of two bar graphs. The one labeled Billy was filled in almost to the top. Andy's was mostly empty. The blank areas showed daily capacity to manage stressors: stress tolerance windows. Andy had space for lots. But because he carried trauma, Billy woke up almost at his limit. So an unexpected change—no Cheerios—might put him over the edge. That and the meaning it held for him. Maybe past neglect had left Billy with a light-touch trigger. Either way, overwhelm or fear caused his response, not brattiness. It made so much sense.

I leaned over and whispered to Jeff, "Our girls have zero stress tolerance."

"Right?!"

Clare *had* experienced incredible disruption her first year of life. But Anna and Lucy? No abuse or neglect. Anna came home at six days and Lucy at three months. Shouldn't they be Andys?

Heather led us through brain anatomy 101. The frontal lobe handled logic, planning, consequential thinking. The midbrain, the limbic system, housed emotional responses. The brain stem she called the "lizard brain," reptilian seat of automatic fight, flight, freeze responses. *Okay. I'm with you, Heather.* Click. A lizard appeared on the screen.

The audience chuckled. I looked at Jeff and smiled. He returned it and squeezed my hand. She introduced us to the lizard, smiled her bright smile, then said when people's stress tolerance window closed, their frontal lobe shut down, leaving them no access to logic or reason.

"At that point you are essentially talking to a lizard. Why would you reason with a lizard?" We all laughed. Talking about our intense, confounding, heartbreaking children, she had us smiling and giggling. Was she magic? A profound shift began in me. I'd searched since Clare came home to make sense of her; this time things lined up. Heather said to focus on connection and a sense of security during a meltdown rather than controlling or consequencing behaviors. Especially since that didn't work anyway. Creating connection brought the frontal lobe back online. In time, unconditional love and acceptance could widen the window of stress tolerance.

"Love wins," she said.

Jeff leaned to me and whispered, "Does that mean it's a free-for-all? Talk about Crazy Town."

It seemed Heather heard him from the back of the room. She clicked again, and Mr. Rogers split the screen with General Patton. We all laughed again. She said love didn't mean no boundaries or authority: keep everyone safe; be in charge; no violence allowed. It took wisdom to know when to be Mr. Rogers and when General Patton. *Ah, makes perfect sense, Heather.*

"Guess she's been critiqued before," Jeff said.

"Always ask what will strengthen relationship," Heather said. "And what unmet need lies under the behavior."

Before we broke for lunch, Heather made a statement that engraved itself in me as she spoke.

"Adoption is trauma."

Even in the best circumstances, adopted children began life losing their biological families. Severed from the people meant to provide for them and keep them safe. No matter how often we told the story as loving choice and our deep desire for them. How many times we read *On the Night You Were Born* and other books celebrating adoption. Before our girls had words or understanding, they felt given up, and the subtext was they were not good enough to keep. They held the experience in their bodies if not their minds. Some called it the "primal wound."

Jeff and I walked in silence across the street to Central Market for lunch. Once we sat, I asked, "What do you think?"

"Makes a lot of sense. But it turns our parenting on its head. No consequences? Won't it reward and increase their misbehavior if they get our loving attention for it?" He took a bite of pizza, and I nodded. Wrapping our heads around this new paradigm felt like contortion. It wasn't about making kids behave; it was about seeing behavior as communicating needs and meeting them.

"She did talk about circling back once the wise mind is back online to address behavior and make a plan for next time," I said.

"It's hard to imagine."

I agreed. "It's uncanny how she described the lizard brain. We've always said it's like Clare becomes an animal and then has to crash and sleep to become human again." We fell into silence. We were so very tired.

Back at the workshop, Jeff jutted his arm up when Heather asked for a volunteer to role play. I raised an eyebrow at him.

He shrugged. "I need to understand what happens in our home."

Heather pointed at Jeff. "You near the back. Thanks for being brave." I smiled and shook my head as my introverted husband walked to the stage. How many people sat in that room? Two hundred? He climbed the steps and sat next to Heather on stage. She asked his name, a bit about his story and gave him her full attention.

"That's my wife, Lynn." He pointed and I waved. "We have three adopted daughters. One is in therapeutic boarding school after spending last summer in and out of psychiatric hospitals and autumn in a wilderness program. As soon as she left home, the other two fell apart." As he described life in our home, heads turned to me; people sucked in their breath and groaned. I held my hands tightly around my belly and looked straight ahead. My eyes stung as I listened to our story. And I felt validated by a room *full* of experienced parents and professionals reacting to our situation as extraordinary. Maybe we *should* be weary.

"That's a lot." Heather reached over and touched Jeff's shoulder. "Clearly you love your girls. And you haven't given up." She smiled. "And I have to say, if Lucy can't even brush her teeth at night, she can't handle school."

Jeff nodded. "We've decided to homeschool after spring break. Make their world small."

"Good. It doesn't matter how much school gets done; she'll catch up later. Lucy's showing you she's overwhelmed. She needs connection and compassion right now."

They agreed to role play a typical scene with Jeff as daughter. He chose to be Anna. They'd begin together in her bedroom. Heather—as parent—stood open and loose. Her arms hung at her sides instead of crossed over her chest or with hands on hips as mine often were.

Jeff, sitting, harangued her. "You're so mean. You never give me anything. And you never do what you say. You only care about your iPad. Get out!" Jeff's body had morphed into the hunched shoulders and stricken face that lived on Anna.

Heather's face stayed soft, compassionate. She stepped back, outside an imaginary bedroom door, and pulled her phone out of her back pocket. As her fingers tapped the screen, she narrated texts. "It sounds like you're hurting, honey. I hope I can help. Heart emoji. *Ding.*" We chuckled at her sound effects and took a collective breath. Except Jeff.

He'd sunk deep into Anna. He looked young, angry, and scared. Surprised by the text, he pulled his phone from his pocket. Back and forth went his attacks and Heather's empathy. Anna never softened fast or easily, and he wasn't going to either. Finally, his shoulders relaxed a bit. He received the invitation Heather offered—instead of condemnation. Connection in any way possible. Texting knocked the wind out of Jeff's fight, the surprise of intimacy not beyond what he could bear. And Jeff as Anna revealed her vulnerability.

"Promise not to tell anyone something? I'm crying. I don't know why I can't stop fighting. I'm sad so I want to hurt you. I'm sorry I'm so bad."

Heather responded, "I can tell you're sad. I wonder if part of you needs to keep me far away. And if you feel like you don't have everything you need. Can you hear me when I say I love you, and I'm on your side?"

"It's easier like this. I'm sorry."

"I love you, babe. Can I come back in and sit with you?"

I'd hugged myself into a ball, watching, and as I connected to the feelings underneath Anna's rage, tears flooded my face and dripped onto my knees where my chin rested. My anger fell away.

"I guess." Jeff's body continued to relax as Heather walked through the imagined door, sat, and put her arm around him. The connection between them was palpable. I tried to cry silently in the room full of people who knew I was the other parent, but my sobs escaped as gasps. Others' weeping popcorned up around the room. Long moments passed as streams flowed down Jeff's cheeks. Heather held the space for us all. Little by little, light seemed to return like at the end of a movie in a theater.

As Anna faded and Jeff emerged, Heather asked, "May I hug you?"

He nodded and let out a nervous laugh. I let go of my legs and let my feet touch the carpet as Jeff and Heather talked about what the experience had been like for him. He'd seen inside Anna, shone a lantern in the cracks behind her attacks and rage. I took a big breath as Jeff walked down the aisle back to our seats. He sat down, and I put my arm around him; he rested his head on my shoulder and grasped my other hand.

We had dinner at Mother's Café—our favorite vegetarian restaurant in our Austin neighborhood from graduate school twenty years before. As we drove back to the farm, we committed to practicing Heather's philosophy for six months. Long enough to see if it made a difference.

Our understanding of trauma and attachment deepened a month later. My mom, Jeff, Anna, Lucy, and I stepped onto a tarmac in Bend one February afternoon and swerved around puddles left by recent rains on our way into the terminal. The fresh smell of juniper and sage in the crisp air enveloped us. We'd rented a house by the Deschutes River in town. Mom would hang out with Anna and Lucy while Jeff and I attended a two-day New Leaf Academy workshop. She'd get to see Clare, then fly home, and our family of five would spend the weekend together.

Jeff and I hugged Anna and Lucy goodbye and showered thanks on Mom the first morning. We drove to the edge of town to a lodge surrounded by pine trees and mulched gardens. The snowcapped Three Sisters Mountains stood off in the distance. In a conference room full of parents, we took our customary seats at the back. When we broke into small groups, Jeff and I joined a husband and wife also new to NLA by a wall of windows where the high desert sun filtered through the pines. We shifted in our seats. Clare's coach, Autumn, pulled up a chair and asked us to remind each other to which kid we belonged.

She had us picture five empty buckets. "Everyone is born with these buckets. The first one is red. It represents physical needs. The next four are silver: social, emotional, cognitive needs, and a developed conscience bucket on the end. They fill in that order."

I imagined buckets in vertical descent, water flowing from above into the first bucket. When it overflowed, number two started filling up. Three and four reminded me of Heather Forbes. "So, reasoning with our kids is cognitive, and that won't work if they aren't emotionally connected?" I asked.

"Exactly. Ideally, you parent to your kid's first empty bucket. The tricky bit is that water levels always change. If I notice a New Leaf kiddo feeling anxious, first I make sure she's fed, watered, and rested." We laughed. Basic like a horse. "The red bucket has to fill before the others can. Physiology first. How do you guys act when you're tired and hungry?"

Jeff looked at me. "Lynn hits a tired wall and shuts down; she has an off switch."

"True. He stops talking, I turn over wherever I am and go to sleep."

"Great example," Autumn said. "We all get out of sorts when tired or hungry. And scared when we think our physical needs won't be met." The other parents nodded but didn't chime in. "Then I might ask if I can braid her hair or something else that offers physical connection." I took some notes. Safety, predictability, and pleasure filled the red bucket. "Trauma drills a hole in the red bucket, so we have to keep refilling as we try to patch the hole."

Jeff shook his head. "Do our girls *ever* have holes in their buckets." I wrote down *fill the red bucket.*

"I have another metaphor for you from a professor of psychiatry at UCLA med school named Dan Siegel. Maybe you've seen his books, *Parenting from the Inside Out* or *Whole-Brain Child*?" We hadn't.

Autumn held up her right hand like she wanted to high-five. "The wrist is the spinal cord. It comes up and then you have the brain stem and the limbic area. Take your thumb and put it in your palm." She pointed to her thumb crossed over her palm. "Arousal, emotions, and the fight/flight/freeze responses happen here. Also, memory and attachment." She curled her fingers over her thumb and tapped her knuckles. "This top part is the cortex behind your forehead, allowing you to perceive the outside world, think, and reason. It regulates all the other areas. When we get tired, stressed, or triggered, we can flip our lid." She snapped her fingers straight up so the cortex of the hand-brain disappeared. "Emotions rise up from the brain stem and limbic system and override the frontal cortex. The connection to it is lost. Instead of being regulated, connected, balanced, and flexible, we lose moral reasoning. Behave terribly." Once we flipped our lids, we couldn't access reasoning or consequential thinking. Like Heather Forbes's lizard brain. Why talk to a lizard?

I asked questions and scribbled notes—*frontal lobe off-line equals no reasoning*—until our lunch break. Jeff and I walked down a hill and crossed over the Deschutes, the clean smell of pine thick in the air. On the bridge, I felt the power of the water that churned beneath us. The sunlight threw warmth and shimmers as the river rushed, smoothing rocks and changing the landscape day by day by year by year with its twists and turns. I let my heart hope.

After lunch at Café Yumm on the river, we trudged uphill to our circle of five chairs by the big window. I noticed the forest shadows kept icy snow patches on the path. The man of the other couple slumped; his wife's shoulders were raised tight to her ears. I knew those feelings. Autumn invited us to talk about having a child at therapeutic boarding school, then we'd touch on coping tools to close out the day. Everyone's eyes hit the floor.

Into the long silence I murmured, "I feel relieved to not live with Clare. Also, ashamed. Like a failure." Tears stung my nose and eyes.

The other mom nodded; her face filled with empathy. She got it. "It's awful running into people. They ask how the kids are. I don't admit we've brought her here. It's too embarrassing. And the look on people's faces."

Jeff said, "You see on their faces, 'how could you get rid of your child?' or 'it can't have been *that* bad.' It feels like giving up." I sighed and nodded.

The man straightened a bit. "As if we haven't tried absolutely everything else first. They can't even imagine what we've been through." His wife reached for his hand.

Clare had been away for five months, at NLA three, but this was our first connection with parents who understood. Maybe the first since she'd come home from Haiti. Here, no explanation was needed. We *all* loved our children deeply, fiercely. We hadn't sent them away because we'd given up—just the opposite.

My words tumbled out. "I defend our choice at church, on the phone, at school. To people who love Clare and question us." The circle held the raw pain. For the first time in a long time, I didn't feel alone, misunderstood, judged. I didn't want to be in this club, but if we had to live this journey, I felt grateful for companions.

Jeff spoke up. "It's the hardest thing we've ever done. Harder even than being together." He fell silent. I took his hand as he wiped the corner of his eye with his other. "All I ever wanted was to be a dad." Almost a whisper. Autumn let us sit in the silence, a lake we swam in together. The other mother's face mirrored my pain. *How many times could our hearts break and we still manage to get up and keep walking?*

We were spent but picked up Mom, Anna, and Lucy and drove on to meet Clare at New Leaf for dinner. The girls crowded the drive, and Clare raced up to greet us just like at Christmas. She gave my mom a tour, ending in the dining room where she told us she'd filled all the vases with flowers for the families. Other girls had hung colorful, papier-mâché masks from art therapy across one wall. Anna stuck close to Jeff and Lucy to Mom as Clare introduced me to the cook. The room buzzed with families as Clare checked on my allergen-free meals. Like at Christmas, she had considered our needs and made things special. My mom, amazed and hopeful, commented on it all back at the rental house. Before sleep, I read my list of goals Cathryn had asked us to write: acknowledge Clare's feelings instead of telling her to feel differently; choose what's best for all of us, not just to avoid

Clare's meltdowns; have confidence in my decisions; shift away from consequences and control toward connection and compassion. We all had big work to do.

The next day, Clare joined Jeff and me at the lodge. First, we made art projects to introduce ourselves. Clare cut a big, white heart, wrote *Alsup* in the middle and *the heart of our family* along the side. In sky-blue, neon-green, purple, orange, pink, and brown script, she scattered our values: respect, prayer, creativity, uniqueness, music, kindness. Jeff included acceptance and compassion. I added laughter, peace, welcome, and service. At the top, Clare's final touch: *special is putting it mildly.* She hammed for laughs when she introduced us to the circle; we all obliged.

Separated into families again, the girls read aloud to each parent. Clare turned to me with bullet-pointed paper in hand: *I love it when you raise your hands up in the air and do your happy dance. I love it when you bring our puppy Charlie on my phone calls. I love it when you rub my arm at night. I love it when you cook me dinner every night. I love it when you forget your almonds. I love it when you sing the "Clare" song. I love it when you go shopping with me, even when you don't want to. I love it when you wear your vegetarian shirt. I love it when you wake me up in the morning. I love it when you jump on the trampoline with me.*

Tears ran down my cheeks. It reminded me of the collaged Valentines cards I made for the girls and Jeff every year filled with the things I loved most about them. But Clare had never expressed any of that before; I didn't know she'd noticed. Feeling seen and loved, I hugged her to me and thanked her. I kept crying while she read to Jeff: *I love it when you wake me up like a steamroller. I love it when you call me your brown-eyed girl. I love it when you take me to Wing Stop on the weekends. I love it when you break out in song at almost anything. I love how you are so compassionate about helping your dad. I love it when you call me a doofus. I love it when you say "Opah!" at random moments. I love it when you and*

Mom take the time to talk to me even when I disengage. I love it when you do your happy dance. I love it when you cook meat for us.

Jeff wiped the tears from his face. At New Leaf, Clare remembered more than pain.

The next morning, Jeff and I took Anna and Lucy to Clare to play with the NLA living room doll house while my mom took a cab to the airport, and we met with Clare's therapist. That weekend we followed our schedule, swam at the indoor rec center, and went to a sledding hill halfway up the mountain, laughing and screaming as we careened down the hill. We climbed back up and made snow angels under the evergreens, then sledded down again and warmed ourselves by the bonfire at the bottom. We tasted freedom and joy.

The day of our departure, Clare was already back at New Leaf. I woke to the bedroom door belching open as the wood rubbed against the frame. A chill of morning breeze slipped in the cracked-open window, and the river tap danced against stones. I startled as I remembered Clare was gone; fresh grief blanketed me. I kept my eyes closed. Maybe whoever had opened the door would go away. Instead, she crawled into bed beside me. Lucy. I turned to face her and opened my eyes.

"Good morning, love. Did you sleep sweet?" The corners of her mouth turned up as she brought her blankie to her nose, sniffed it and sucked her tongue like a pacifier. Her eyes twinkled, and she nodded, pleased with herself for finding her way into my bed alone. She made me smile. We lay there and chatted about Bend: racing down the mountain, the ducks on the river, and a deer so tame it let her pet it after it sniffed her hand.

"Wouldn't it be cool if I had one as a pet? I'd walk it on a leash."

I smiled and nodded. Voices rose in the living room—the familiar fuss and fight of Anna with Jeff. The peace broken. I couldn't make out the words, but it didn't matter. The subject changed, but the conversation stayed the same. Anna didn't have what she wanted or needed, and no one cared about her enough to give it to her.

"Anna's mad." Lucy scrunched up her face.

"Sounds like it." I rubbed her arm.

But the tone changed, and the bedroom door opened again. "Mommy, you're awake! Dad is taking me for pancakes before we go to the airport." Anna smiled and leaned over Lucy to me.

Lucy growled as Anna inadvertently trapped her. "A-nna!" The *A* high pitched and *nna* low with an audible exclamation point: the way we all said her name in frustration.

"Good morning, love. That's nice of him. Give Lucy some space?"

"I wanna go," Lucy chimed.

"Me, too." I imagined—fantasized—a peaceful walk to the café listening to the river sing.

Jeff called from the living room, "Why don't you brush your hair before we go, Anna?"

Personal hygiene escaped our girls. *When had she last brushed her hair? Her teeth?* Anna went to Jeff, and I pulled on olive pants, a gray bamboo T-shirt, and a fleece on top. From the bathroom, I heard Jeff quarrel with Anna about her hair. He gave up and moved on to teeth. Anna brought her toothbrush and toothpaste to the bedroom. She'd put on the horse charm necklace we'd given her a couple weeks before for her ninth birthday. "Help me, Mama."

You're perfectly capable of putting toothpaste on your toothbrush, I sneered in my mind, but then I remembered the red bucket. Physical gestures filled it and gave a sense of safety. I took a deep breath and squeezed Crest onto her toothbrush: *I'm here; you matter; I love you.*

As Anna walked into the bathroom, I dug the hair brush out of my bag. I wanted to help her obey Jeff for once. When she came back, I said, "Sit down, babe."

She snapped. "You're not brushing my hair with that. It hurts!"

"I'll be gentle, love."

I took her ponytail in my hand and drew the brush through. Anna wrapped a hand around her ponytail, stopping me. And just like that, my goal blocked, *I* snapped. "A-nna, let me brush it. I *heard* Dad tell you to."

"Nu-uh. He said, 'Why *don't* you?'"

"Let me brush it." I pushed her hands away. *I'm going to brush her damn hair. She's going to obey this once.* She moved them back. A distant voice inside me said, *Take a breath. Think relationship.* But I couldn't stop the steamroller; I'd flipped my lid. Maybe fueled by grief. Weariness. My stress tolerance window slammed shut.

"Fine. You don't let me; you don't go." I reverted to consequences.

Anna ran to Jeff. "Why does she care anyway; it's not her hair. She ruins everything."

I followed, grabbing her ponytail again as she sat on the arm of the couch. Her hands flew back, and she yanked the ponytail holder out. I moved the brush to the front.

"Not *that* part. You have to brush the middle first."

"Your hand is in my way. I can't brush the middle, so I'll brush the front." I'd softened my voice but spoke through clenched teeth. My body vibrated.

"Fine. I won't go."

"Fine." The burn of adrenaline. The taste of bile. *Why can't she once do what we say?* As I walked away, Jeff told Anna he'd stay with her, and Lucy and I could go.

"Please come, Jeff. It's not fair. One of us always has to stay with her when she bails on our plans because she can't cope. Lucy and I want to be with you."

Jeff relented. He, Lucy, and I walked out the door as Anna walked into her room alone. Proof she was unloved, unwanted. I walked along the river shaking.

A couple weeks later in Dallas, I released balloons at NHP with Anna and Lucy, their counselor, teachers and best friends to mark their last day at North Hills, and we started homeschooling. We bartered work for groceries at the organic food co-op since we were still unemployed and focused on connection instead of consequences. Tried not to talk to the lizard. The wailing and fighting abated a bit, but fear overcame me. *What if I get it all wrong and no healing comes?*

As irises wilted and lantana bloomed for the butterflies and bees, Jeff's dad approached him. Why not submit a résumé to the Nonprofit Management Center in his West Texas hometown—where our parents all lived? When he did, I stammered, "*Midland?*" I'd vowed never to move our Black children or myself there. To me it was the frontier. Ultraconservative, racially segregated, the flat Southern Plains. Actual tumbleweeds blew across the highway. But one of Midland's many foundations (Midland: also, an incredibly generous community) needed an executive director. Jeff's dream job—giving away other people's money to help children and families. Being a bridge between wealth and poverty, resources and needs.

As I struggled with the idea, I found a quote from a retreat with Christine Valters Paintner: "The Sacred is the quickening force animating and enlivening the whole world, including our own beings." The best definition of God I had. If I believed all of God was everywhere, then Beauty and Life lived in Midland, too. And we needed our parents' support with the girls. I agreed to go.

Clare spent her thirteenth birthday with us in Dallas in June: a weekend rendezvous in a ten-month, long-distance relationship. She packed her room for the move and said a few goodbyes. On our flight back to Oregon, she laid her head in my lap, and we both shook with tears. It was excruciating. And she didn't recover quickly.

Birdwings

On July 13—our first Saturday living in Midland—we went to the farmers' market with Jeff's mom and dad. They introduced us to Sarah, a striking White woman with jet-black hair. She sold hand-crafted jewelry, textiles, and toys from her nonprofit in Uganda, her husband's homeland. Her children invited Anna and Lucy to play behind their table, and Jeff and I got cups of Big Bend Coffee Roasters dark roast and wandered the small market. We chatted with Teffanie, a Black woman with a quick smile and long dreadlocks—a few dyed red and blond for her recent wedding to the founder of the market. Her daughter sold homemade hula hoops. Anna and Lucy joined us for an impromptu lesson in the middle of the market. Music streamed from an amp as we all giggled, trying to rock our hips just right to keep the hoops spinning. Teffanie introduced me to the Children's Museum director/market potter, a massage therapist and Reiki master, a family of organic farmers, and a new-to-town Montessori guide named Natalie. *This is Lynn. She just moved here. She's one of us.* On repeat. Faces lit up; people hugged and welcomed me. I imagined an expat community in a foreign country. We stayed long after Jeff's parents left. I thought, *I might make it in this town after all.*

I spent the first hour of weekday mornings blessedly alone. While Jeff showered, I ventured out on walking meditations. I wandered past purple sagebrush and brushed my hand along knee-high foun-tain grass that looked like my childhood troll dolls' hair, as if they'd been buried with just their hair left swaying aboveground. I practiced centering prayer at a picnic table behind the Lutheran church on the corner while birds sang, and wind blew. I'd return to our small house as Jeff finished breakfast with the girls, ready to begin again.

Before we'd left Dallas, I'd told Jeff, "We need a grandma house. Someone has moved his mom into assisted living—sad—and needs us to rent her house—happy". A few days later, the man passing his job on to Jeff emailed. He'd just moved his mom; did we want to rent her two-bedroom house? *Why yes, thank you.* That's how the alpacas became our neighbors. One white as a cloud, one beige, one dark russet brown in the two-acre yard across the road. They batted long eyelashes at Anna, Lucy, and me. "Hello, lovelies," I'd say on our way to visit horses, cats, and barn owl babies at the polo field a few blocks away.

We walked between paddocks saying good morning, petting noses and necks. While Lucy sat with a blue heeler dog who belonged to Molly, the riding instructor, Anna stood under a tree grooming a sorrel horse. Beside Anna, Molly—trim and fit from working horses— cleaned reins. Dirt covered her ball cap and deeply tanned face.

"I'm hot." Lucy looked like a wilting plant as she stroked the dog. Her brown face had taken on a red undertone, and Anna's had gotten pinker and pinker. The summer heat rose here near the edge of the Chihuahuan desert by ten each morning.

Lucy and I left Anna with Molly, whom she idolized, and headed to the field behind the barn. Water spewed from a fifteen-foot reel sprinkler crawling across the giant field. We stopped just outside its range and watched the stream peak and fall into golden drops in the sunshine, ran through the freezing cascade, and chased rainbows on the ground. I cringed at thousands of gallons of water poured onto the field to supplement Midland's fourteen inches of annual rain. And I loved the joy and life we found there. By eleven, the girls and I had tucked ourselves back into our small, enclosed courtyard along with Anna's black-and-white Dutch rabbit, our dog Charlie Brown, and a turtle that Lucy—with a bit of Doolittle in her—had discovered. She brought it into her blue-and-purple pyramid tent for the one math sheet and thirty minutes of reading to which our formal schooling had dwindled. I chose to believe that a focus on attachment and healing trauma mattered more than five subjects a day, public-school style. Though some moments, I feared they might be unhoused and uneducated as adults because of it.

Lucy lay in my lap one morning on our ruby-red futon after Jeff had left for work. Six months of his not working made the adjustment a challenge for us all. Lucy had clung to his legs and wailed, "Don't leave!" Every. Single. Day. For a month. He'd peeled her off and handed her to me writhing like an octopus. Then driven fifteen minutes across town to his office. The whole town of 130,000 was smaller than our neighborhood in Dallas. No more packed highways and hurried people. And his job had zero stress and 100 percent flexibility. A great gift.

I held Lucy as the howls tapered off. But then they hit a curve and ramped up again. She spoke and, though I usually understood even the words her tongue tangled, the sobs blurred them more.

"Slow down, babe. I can't understand. Take a breath."

She heaved, "I'm. So. Sorry." *Gulp.* "I. Knew." *Gulp.* "It. Was. Wrong."

"You're sorry?"

She took a deep breath. "Don't be mad. At me." Her eyes shone. I held a tissue to her nose and said *blow*. As I dropped the mucky mess to the floor, she buried herself under my arm.

"Mad at you?" I evened out my breath and relaxed my muscles to coax Lucy's body to do the same. Rubbing her back, I heard Anna rustle with her bunny in the bedroom. Lucy mumbled.

"Unbury your head so I can hear you, love."

She looked up at me. "At North Hills, I copied off my friends' work." It came out small and serious. "I know it's wrong, but I couldn't help it."

I rocked us as she began to cry again. "Shh. Okay."

"I'm bad. I've wanted to tell you for so long."

"People are not good or bad. They're precious." My mantra. "You're precious. You did your best. North Hills wasn't the right place for you."

"I need you to know in case you die." Her lament swelled, and I struggled to catch the fast-flowing words. "First grade work was *hard*. The teacher went so fast, and when I raised my hand to ask a question, she just said the same thing again. I couldn't keep up." My heart cracked. Again.

"I'm so sorry." A familiar knot rose to my throat. My eyes overflowed, and we held each other. So much I hadn't understood. So much to mourn.

We reached out to a parenting coach who worked with Heather Forbes. Once a week, the girls had dinner at my parents' while Jeff and I climbed onto bar stools at our kitchen counter to Skype with her. The familiar ring sounded, and Mona popped onto the screen. She had short brown hair, a round face, and a kind voice. I told her about Lucy's confession and, also, that I'd helped the girls write letters to their birth moms that week. They talked about them often. We'd mailed the notes to Hope Cottage to file in case either woman asked after them. Running my fingers across my short hair, I noticed wrinkles around my eyes and mouth. My forehead seemed permanently furrowed. I quieted to give Jeff a chance to talk.

"We're exhausted. They want us with them every moment. Anna's meltdowns are less frequent and less severe, but Lucy loses her mind every morning, and they're in our bed every night. Even though they share a room."

Mona started with the positive. "Great that Anna tolerates stress better."

He grimaced. "But I hate leaving Lynn with a wild-animal Lucy every morning. I feel guilty that I get to go to work. And I want my bed back." Dark circles hung under his green eyes. "I want to sleep with Lynn, not my children."

"That makes sense. And it might not happen yet." Jeff's jaw tensed, and Mona continued, "Their behavior communicates they don't feel safe."

I nodded and told Mona about their frequent nightmares where Jeff and I disappeared in the night, or someone stole them.

Mona posed a question: "What if they're showing you their need? And meeting the need is how you ultimately get more peace? Think of the last year's changes: Clare leaving, Jeff's unemployment, withdrawing from school, homeschooling, moving, and now Jeff back at work."

Jeff sighed and nodded. I cocked my head. "What do you suggest?"

"Push your beds together in one room? Big enough for everyone to sleep. Just for a time. If you give them a felt sense of safety, after a while they might not need you in the night."

Jeff and I looked at each other, weary and wrung out. It was the exact opposite of the break we wanted. Some days it seemed Anna's anger and Lucy's fear might tear us to bits. But we'd committed to this way of parenting beyond our six-month trial in Dallas. Because life did feel better. Crazy, but better. And Clare's absence showed where our alternatives led. We agreed to try.

Before the call ended, I broached a subject I'd been nursing. "The girls take everything I've got. Clare's care in Oregon, being teacher, mom, problem solver here. I can't also keep our marriage alive." I looked at Jeff. "For twenty years I've made sure we had dates, stayed connected, got away. But I can't now. I need you to." Jeff's face froze, wrinkled and in pain.

We sat in silence until Mona spoke. "How do you feel about that, Jeff?"

"Defensive."

I touched his arm. "I'm not trying to accuse you."

He softened. "It's an accurate read. I feel guilty. And ashamed, I guess."

I pulled one knee up and rested my chin there as he dropped his hands into his lap and looked at Mona, continuing. "It's not my personality to take charge, make decisions, lead out like that." When he turned to me, I agreed. He looked back at Mona. "Lynn shoulders the weight of the girls. I'll try." I imagined our marriage in my cupped hands, offering it to Jeff. He picked it up by his fingertips like a teacup he might break.

Having a family bedroom thrilled Anna and Lucy. We put Clare's double bed between their twins and pushed them together like a big raft. The bunny's hutch and litter box sat in the corner of the room and Charlie Brown lay at the foot of the bed. Miraculously, we all slept.

We got a break from the family bed and menagerie during our second NLA workshop in Bend in September, our parents caring for Anna and Lucy at home. The river, mountains, and trees breathed life into us, but Clare was mopey and belligerent like the four months since her weekend in Dallas. I returned to Bend two weeks later for an equine intensive. Still, we kept leaving her, like re-stabbing an unhealed wound. At home, her anger, fear and sadness had hung on pegs labeled school, friends, food. At New Leaf, they hung on the truth—being left. But Clare trusted her therapist Cathryn more than she'd ever trusted anyone; she consciously explored her scariest emotions in the intimacy of that relationship. She began EMDR: eye movement desensitization and reprocessing. Cathryn told us it was bilateral brain stimulation to process memories and release trauma. EMDR exhausted Clare and pried her loose; she turned a corner.

At the same time in Midland, Anna's anger and aggression diminished; her delightful quirkiness and tenderness resurfaced more often. Lucy's funny, aware, articulate self emerged again. Mornings, she hugged Jeff goodbye and told me our life was great. We cruised a well-worn circuit that fall: polo barn for riding lessons, library, Petroleum Museum science classes, Art Museum of the Southwest, duck pond—a sacred, to me, collection of runoff and a rare source of natural water in our dusty town—and parks in old Midland where we threw a blanket down under trees watered by playas and read books.

I highlighted four blocks on a map near the duck pond and our favorite park: Midland's most racially and socioeconomically diverse-ish neighborhood within walking distance of the farmers' market and downtown. Our realtor laughed. "Midland oil booms leave few houses for sale. You jump on one the day it comes on the market. Would you consider not being quite that specific?"

"We'll see," I said, and the hunt began.

Back in the kitchen in our little house, Jeff and I had our now monthly call with Mona. I mentioned being triggered by Anna's occasional flares. "I breathe and stay calm as she escalates until all of a sudden, I can't. She yells in a certain way or threatens to hit me, and I snap out of mindfulness and into fight-or-flight."

"Can you give me an example?"

My eyes drifted to the kitchen counter where Anna had laid her whole body in defiance. I described the terrible night—including me physically restraining Anna—and her on edge the next day, mean and defiant. She had reached out to hit me with a ruler as math spun out. I had snatched it and thwacked her bottom with it. As hard as I could. Lucy had shrunk in her chair and tried to disappear.

Anna ran to the bedroom. "You are so mean! I hate you!"

I turned to Lucy. "I'm so sorry. I'm going to the other bedroom to calm down. Everything will be okay." I left her there and breathed until anger dissipated and reason returned.

"May I open the door please?" I asked Anna.

"Whatever."

I pushed it open but stayed in the hall. "May I come in?"

"I guess." Anna studied the floor.

"Please forgive me, Anna. I was wrong to hit you. I'm very sorry." She wiped her nose on her hand and sniffed. I asked, "Are you *ready* to forgive me?"

"I guess." Her chin rose a millimeter from her chest.

"Thank you. I do love you. I want us to be able to live peacefully together."

She had barely nodded as she tucked her hair behind her ear.

My hands shook as my eyes met Mona's again. Adrenaline raced through me.

"Lynn, you meditate, exercise, eat well, take time alone. You are *resilient*. But you have trauma in your body that hijacks you. Like your children." She described secondary trauma, caregiver fatigue, and PTSD. "Some modalities release trauma. Ever heard of EMDR?"

Miraculously, I found an EMDR-trained therapist in Midland and made a standing appointment for a time my mom could watch the girls. I would have tried anything to stay in compassion and kindness. To be the mom I wanted to be. To be free.

At my first appointment, the therapist, Elizabeth, guided me to choose symbols to anchor me in peace, protection, wisdom, and nurture. A colorful string hammock in the Far West Texas high desert—my new sacred place; the mastiff we'd rescued from the streets in Dallas; my spiritual director, Eunice; and the Sea Spirit from a picture book who was an image of God for me. Then I described a recent incident that had stolen my mindfulness. I'd just come in from a walk and could feel tension filling the house. I closed my eyes and saw Jeff's face—his features distorted, shadows around his eyes.

"I have to leave," he said. I nodded and he walked out. I discovered Lucy in a ball on the floor, rocking back and forth. Anna had locked herself in the bathroom.

"I'd never seen him like that," I told Elizabeth.

"What did you feel?"

I closed my eyes again. "Sad. Scared." I started to cry.

"Where in your body?"

"My chest—a burning." I fought the dissociation that still numbed me out when I felt threatened.

"What did you think?"

"I was on my own to take care of the storm."

She led me deeper, "What did you believe about yourself?" Elizabeth let the silence hang.

"I might not be strong enough to face the danger."

"Good work, Lynn." She handed me what looked like two small, gray, plastic river rocks plugged into a controller she held. "I'll turn the tappers on, and you choose the most comfortable strength and tempo." They pulsed in my hands; vibrated my palms and up my arms. "Now close your eyes and imagine the scene again."

Instead of our home, I was inside the *Wizard of Oz* tornado. But my funnel was whirling Jeff, Anna, Lucy, and me instead of the house, the cow, Dorothy, and Toto. Then Clare, too. Faces I loved fiercely, trapped in the violent rotation. *Where would we be hurled out? Would we survive?* Rivers streamed down my cheeks as my small, cracked voice narrated it all.

"The danger and out of control is an electric expansion in my chest. No matter what I say, do, or want, the storm will carry us away. I'm powerless. *I* don't matter."

Elizabeth guided me on. "Have you felt or thought those things before?"

I opened to memories, searched. I heard my dad call a family meeting—we were moving again, just like every few years. He told my third-grade self we were driving west after three years in Chicago. To the Rocky Mountains. Denver, Colorado. The scene sank to a deeper, truer root: my sexual assault.

"Four-year-old Lynn crouched beside a chair. My best friend's house in Houston."

"You're doing great, Lynn. A bit longer?" I nodded. She asked, "What do you feel?"

"Anger. Fear. I'm all alone. A black hole in my belly—an empty void. A burning in my chest and pelvis." The tears poured. I couldn't speak. Elizabeth directed me to open my eyes and list three things I saw in the room. Ground myself. Once I had calmed, she asked me to imagine my symbol of protection in the scene with me.

I closed my eyes and saw Bowen the mastiff, as big as an island, gigantic russet head, slobbery mouth. My ferocious protector and gentle love. A sense of safety and calm filled me. "No way it could happen now," I said. In my mind's eye, I lay on the floor with Bowen and rested in the room that had just held violation, fear, and fury. He stiffened his leg and rested his paw on my shoulder, as he often had before he passed away. I reached out and rested my hand on his soft red hair. The warmth of his breath, the gentle, steady up and down of his inhale and exhale, his musky smell all present with me.

She led me back to the original memory: Jeff's tortured face, Anna locked in the bathroom, Lucy crouched, rocking. I realized Lucy looked just as I had on the floor of my friend's house before Bowen entered the memory. But I felt strong and connected to Jeff and the girls. The tornado vanquished.

"I believe we have what we need to make it through," I said.

The image shifted, and we came together like a Mayan Circle of Friends sculpture: interlocked arms—strong, stable, unified, unbreakable—with a flame in the middle, dancing shadows. When I opened my eyes, the tears gathered there overflowed. The neuropathways in my brain had connected all my trauma and compounded it; EMDR had released some of it.

I drove spacey and spent to pick up Anna and Lucy at my parents' house. My eyes stung and my head ached. I wanted to shut out light and sound. But laughter welcomed me as I opened the front door. Anna sat on the blue sofa, weaving a bracelet of Rainbow Loom plastic bands in her lap—always creating. She flicked long brown strands of hair out of her face, smiled, and called out, *Mama!* Lucy, on a stool at the edge of the coffee table, picked up a tortilla chip from a blue plastic bowl and dipped it into a pink one of salsa. She said hi with her mouth full. My mom's white slacks and nice blouse seemed dangerously near Lucy when she was eating—she sat in her taupe chair just behind Lucy, watching *Reba* with them. *Should an eight-year-old and nine-year-old watch Reba?* They turned back to the TV, so I walked to the dark guest bedroom and rested. My mom filled my red bucket that day. And little by little, with EMDR, I became freer, more able to love myself and others well.

Anna and Lucy began to see Elizabeth, too. They sat in my lap, rocked, held the tappers, and told stories about their big feelings and the big fights they had. I sprinkled our life with anything that might make us more whole, healthier: vision therapy for Anna's reading, vestibular therapy, counseling, animals, playgrounds, laughs, and snuggles. Jeff and I even jumped in a swim lane right next to Anna and Lucy to give them confidence for lessons. We giggled, splashed each other, and worked our asses off, swimming to the end of the pool and back. I thrived in the underwater world. It muted my senses and suspended me. Fine-tuning my technique propelled me through the water, sliding silky over my skin. Anna loved it, too—always happiest working hard, once she got started. And so strong. Lucy jumped and splashed, but translating directions into movements seemed impossible. She persisted, though, and we all improved. At the end of our first month, Jeff begged off, but the girls and I kept at it. Anna and I even joined teams. In practice—bonus, a break from the girls—as my mind focused on strokes and breath, endorphins surged through my body. It gave me strength for each day.

Wet from the pool one day, we met Jeff at a yellow adobe house in the Grafaland neighborhood two blocks from the neon rectangle on my map. It had four trees (a small miracle for Midland), a big backyard, three bedrooms, and a breakfast room that could become a fourth. I'd given up my value of small and simple; our girls needed their own corners for resets. We made an offer on the spot; a day later the owners accepted. We took Clare to see it over Christmas on her first visit to Midland, pacing out where her room would be. Showing her I was working hard to create a space for her at home with us. She ran through the rooms with exuberance. On Christmas morning, we gave them bright sensory beanbag chairs like the one in our therapist's office. Clare's red, Anna's blue, Lucy's purple. We all squeezed onto Clare's, and she took a selfie of us: five different shapes, sizes, colors, hair—all smiling.

A few weeks later, we left Anna and Lucy with Jeff's parents for my mom's seventieth birthday dinner in Dallas. In the intimate restaurant, the waiter touched my shoulder to lean over me and refill water, and I didn't flinch. I *always* flinched when strangers touched me. It felt like magic. But it was EMDR. And back in Midland, when everyone moved into their own bedroom on Illinois Ave, it worked. Jeff and I had regular visitors in the night but not *two every* night.

When Clare came back for Easter, we walked around the corner to First Christian Church. We hadn't found a church home but wanted to go to an Easter service. We entered through big, wooden doors and followed red carpet into a pew. Jeff slid in first, Anna close behind. She wore a rainbow-colored slip dress and seemed to be tipping toward teenager, even though she'd just turned ten. She sat next to Lucy, still little in a short purple dress with a silk sash tied around the waist. Clare followed her into the pew and sat between us. She had long braids again and a young woman's body at almost fifteen, but she still fit under my arm when I put it around her as I sat. "I'm so happy you're here," I whispered as the organ played the first hymn. She laid her head on my shoulder, smiling. Jeff leaned over, a finger to his lips, shushing us with a twinkle in his eye. I winked.

The pastor began a sermon about love and life winning over death and hate. Not by fighting but by staying true to its nature, even when that meant crucifixion. Love wins, like Heather Forbes said. Like Jeff and I tried to live out with our kids—the Jesus way. The hardest road we'd ever walked. I cried from beginning to end. It felt like resurrection sat between us on that pew. As the service ended, we all stood and sang:

In Christ alone my hope is found/ He is my light, my strength, my song.

This cornerstone, this solid ground/ Firm through the fiercest drought and storm.

What heights of love, what depths of peace/ When fears are stilled, when strivings cease!

My comforter, my all in all—/ Here in the love of Christ I stand.

Clare and I skipped home. Anna held Jeff's hand, chattering. Lucy raced to prepare for the crowd we'd invited to celebrate new life: our parents, my ninety-year-old granddad, Jeff's brother with his boys, my best friend Deidra and her family from down the street, and our friends from the farmers' market—Sarah and Meddie with three kids, Natalie and her husband Tom with their new baby. Lucy grabbed a bowl of eggs we'd dyed with beet juice, purple cabbage, and onion peels and made a centerpiece along with a bird's nest she'd found under a tree. The sun shone warm and bright in a clear blue sky onto our sun porch where Anna took drink orders. Izze sparkling juice, lemon water, or bloody Marys. Jeff made eggs Benedict to order; I poured bloody Marys. We used Mexican cascarones—confetti-filled, bright blue, pink, green, and purple eggs—for an Easter Egg hunt and then for their primary function: cracking over unsuspecting heads. The yard reverberated with squeals as kids raced around and jumped on the trampoline. Confetti carpeted the back sidewalk. Clare sat in Jeff's lap in an armchair on the sun porch and laughed as my granddaddy told stories. Resurrection, indeed.

At summer's height, Clare graduated from New Leaf Academy. My parents, Jeff's parents, and Kim all traveled to Bend with us for the ceremony. The night before, I stayed up to write cards to Clare and Cathryn at the long, pine table we'd had since Clare came home from Haiti. Natalie knocked at the door. She knew my fears: *Could I possibly absorb Clare back into our daily life when Anna and Lucy took all my energy? Could we maintain the growth we'd all experienced over the last two years?* We'd try to recreate the safety, consistency, and predictability of New Leaf at home, but we were a family, not a therapeutic boarding school. Two parents, not a staff. Natalie kissed my cheek and handed me a poem written in flowing cursive on ecru paper.

Birdwings *Rumi* Your grief for what you've lost lifts a mirror up/ To where you're bravely working/ Expecting the worst, you look and instead/ Here's the joyful face you've been wanting to see/ Your hand opens and closes and opens and closes/ If it were always a fist or always stretched open, you would be paralyzed/ Your deepest presence is in every small/ Contracting and expanding/ The two as beautifully balanced and coordinated as birdwings.

At graduation, I blubbered. *Thank you, Cathryn, for saving Clare's life and giving our family another chance.* Then I sobbed Clare's card to her. "To one of the bravest, strongest people I know. You are my hero. You have led me deeper into God and into my truest self, been my spiritual director. I am closer to who I'm meant to be because you are my daughter."

Clare read a poem she'd written. "Where does my beauty come from? Where does your beauty come from? Where does my beauty come from?/ Though I come from places of hurting, despair; I recognize it gives me the power to empathize; Like nobody's business, it's a gift./ Where does my beauty come from? I know it *doesn't* come from pretending; Putting on loads of makeup; Wearing the cutest clothes/ The word beauty doesn't mean anything unless you Actually live it./ Once you know you've got it, *declare it*! Tell the whole world! Nobody can declare your beauty like you can./ Empathy, honesty, deep inside; That's where my beauty comes from/ Where does yours come from?"

Her voice didn't waver. She stood straight and tall, strong and wise. She seemed whole.

The Purple Book

Clare had watched *High School Musical* for years; she wanted to experience that fantasy "normal." She begged us for a "typical" high school experience, so we enrolled her with special education accommodations at the two-thousand-plus-student Midland High School, Jeff's alma mater, a few blocks from our house. With trepidation but no good alternatives. Clare started her sophomore year at MHS, and Anna and Lucy took first steps back toward school. They joined Deidra, Sarah, and Natalie at their fledgling Montessori co-op two days per week. And I watched for the bottom to drop out. But it didn't. Not right away. Instead, Clare started to dance.

She had always wanted dance lessons but hadn't been able to manage anything outside of school. *Maybe now?* Twice a week she hip-hopped and jazzed. When I peeked through the window into her classroom, she glowed. Her body pumped, punched, crouched, and kicked. Braids sailed around her nonstop. She laughed and sweated to the thumping beats I felt in my body from my side of the wall. She was *alive*.

I kept myself present and resilient. I sat still and silent in my grandmother's gold chair by my bed and filled my art journal, savoring the solitude. I dove underwater and fought my way across the Olympic size pool. A friend loaned me her office to meet with two new spiritual direction clients referred by my Christian mystics reading group. A familiar voice in my head said, *You're not doing enough. Not working hard enough.* I tried to say nicely that I didn't need its help just then. It could have a rest.

After school one day, I sat on Deidra's front step, snuggling her baby, Zoey. Anna rode up on her bike, parked it in the driveway, and scooped Zoey out of my arms.

"I've got her, Mom. How are you, sweet girl?" Anna singsonged. "Wet diaper! Let's fix that, baby Zoey." Anna touched her nose to Zoey's and gave her a butterfly kiss. Two heads, dirty blond hair, pale skin, blue eyes. They looked like sisters. Anna carried her inside to change her.

I turned to Deidra. "Lucy wants dinosaurs, Duplo blocks, and a Fisher-Price Little People farmyard for her birthday." My head drooped. Deidra put her hand on my back. "I *cannot* buy more toddler toys. She's almost *nine. Third grade.* When will she grow up and act her age?"

Deidra's forehead wrinkled. "I don't know, friend. But I know you're a great mom." I sank into her and sighed. Deidra's three-year-old twins often seemed like Lucy's peers.

Lucy stole into the preschool classroom with them at the co-op, struggling with the chaos of elementary school kids and separation from me. While Anna happily packed a backpack and went, Lucy felt ambivalent. She shone with friends and at organizing games—still the police officer from preschool days. But she often retreated to the calm down/reading closet with the black therapy dog named Jet. She'd always gravitated toward younger children and animals.

She and Anna both still took riding lessons at the polo barn. Lucy basically did gymnastics and dance on a horse—equestrian vaulting. She could do things on a horse she couldn't otherwise like tell right from left, balance and calm herself. Anna rode jumping horses and practiced polo. She cleaned tack, mucked stalls, hauled hay bales, and dumped them in paddocks at feed time with her instructor, Molly. She loved it all. Her new mantra: horses are better than people. Except maybe Zoey, Jeff, and Clare.

As the weather cooled, Clare brought a handful of new friends home for lunch in our backyard a couple times a week. Jeff joined me on the sun porch to feed them and hang out.

"Hi, babe. How's your day?" I hugged Clare in her stretchy jeans and long Vans T-shirt. She shrugged and smiled. "Hey, Mom."

Jeff joked with the kids as I invited them into the kitchen to a counter spread with bread, mayonnaise, turkey slices, peanut butter and jelly, and potato chips. Some days I got fancy with spaghetti and salad.

"Thank you, miss." The girls smiled and chatted with us at the table. "How's *your* day?"

Soon the dark-haired kids—all Latinx—filtered into the backyard and catapulted each other on the trampoline. The few MHS Black kids said Clare wasn't Black enough. She "talked White." She *wasn't* White so didn't fit with White kids either. Latinx kids formed a middle ground. Outside, Clare's laughter rang loudest. After thirty minutes, the boys muttered, "Thank you," looking at their Converse sneakers as they shuffled out the gate back to school.

After the holidays, Lucy's anxiety spiked again returning to co-op. I called our pediatrician. In the exam room, my leg bounced as I studied the mural: orange basketballs, white soccer balls, and brown footballs. Cartoon fans shouting, "Yea, team!" A child's cry leaked in as Dr. Nabulsi opened the door and sat down on the round stool my girls liked to spin on.

He turned dark, compassionate eyes on me. "How can I help you, Ms. Alsup?" I described Lucy's incapacitating anxiety and nightmares.

"Anything else?" He encouraged me to continue, so I unspooled her bed-wetting, struggle to connect verbal instructions to physical actions, her almost illegible handwriting, her speech evaluations at three years old and again at five. He knew about her allergies, chronic sinus infections, and asthma, but it hadn't occurred to me to mention these other issues earlier. He prescribed occupational and speech therapy at Midland Children's Rehabilitation Center. And Prozac. I mistrusted medication. But I knew my antidepressants were vital for clear-ish thinking and level-ish emotions. I'd try anything to help her.

After two weeks on a half dose, Lucy woke up one morning in her own dry bed. Jeff and I woke up alone in ours. For the first time in the fourteen years since Clare had climbed in at St. Andrews Hall in Vancouver. Hallelujah. After two more weeks, Dr. Nabulsi increased it to a therapeutic level. A week later, Lucy came into the kitchen after dinner and got a butcher knife.

"Whatcha doing, love?" I asked.

"I need this." She walked back toward her room.

"You don't." I dropped a soapy dish rag in the sink and hurried after her, wiping my hand on my jeans. "Lucy?"

"I do." She sat down on her bed with the knife.

"Let me hold it, love." I moved slowly and took it from her hand. "Why do you need it?"

"He told me to. I have to die now."

A chill went through me. "Who?"

"The man in my head."

I kept my voice level, calm. "What else did he say?"

"To use a knife."

Biting my cheek, I nodded. "Well, I'm your mom. I'm in charge, and I say no."

Lucy argued, but I repeated my mom line.

"Jeff," I called down the hall. His footsteps padded to the door. A look at the knife in my hand and Lucy fuming, his eyes questioned: *What the hell is going on?*

"A man in Lucy's head told her to kill herself, but *I* told her I'm mom and in charge." I handed him the knife. "I'm sleeping here tonight." I laid us both down and spooned with Lucy until the sun came up.

I kept her by my side for the next week as Dr. Nabulsi tapered the medication and sent us to a psychiatrist. When I told Lucy that chemicals can affect our brains and make us hear unreal things, she believed me; she enfolded that into her amazing self-awareness and ignored the voice in her head. The psychiatrist scheduled a neuro-psychological evaluation. Then I ran away with Anna and Lucy to the family farm for a week. We slept late, rode bikes, and read books. Lucy hung out with the donkey. The voices dissipated. She picked yellow wildflowers while Anna trained her new horse. (She'd harangued us for a horse since kindergarten. By eight years old, the bulldog-child had worn Jeff down. He'd made her a deal: save five hundred dollars, and he'd buy a horse. At nine, Anna handed him the cash. April, a sweet black-and-white pinto leased onto the farm, had joined our family.) During our week in Central Texas, Anna worked with the trainer every day.

Anna climbed into the car in her cowgirl boots as I sat on an old church pew bench on the front porch, tying my shoes, and Lucy took one last running jump onto the wooden porch swing. We drove the caliche farm road and turned onto the paved county road at our gate.

"Ready to see April, babe?"

"My sweetie-girl!" Anna balled herself up and rocked in excite-ment. She schooled me in Parelli Natural Horsemanship for five minutes, then pointed to April in her paddock and squealed. April trotted toward the car; Anna said because she knew us—her people—and loved Anna. She was right. The trainer, Tracy, met us at the car, and Anna loped off with her to groom and saddle April. They spent the morning in the covered arena while Lucy and I wandered, petting barn cats and horses until some kids came, and Lucy ran off to play. I climbed the arena fence and sat on the top rail.

"You're doing great, Anna. Relieve the pressure right away when she does what you've asked," Tracy said.

Anna, rapt, nodded. Connected to trainer and horse. Her focus and self-control surfaced in an arena like nowhere else. She lifted up the four-foot-long carrot stick: an extension of her arm, it guided and supported April while she learned the Parelli fundamentals. Anna clicked her tongue and moved April toward the fence without touching her. As soon as April stood within inches of the fence, Anna stroked April's neck with the stick—her reward. As Tracy praised girl and horse, Anna and April stood relaxed and confident. I balanced on the rail, and my heart relaxed, too. She was amazing, that one.

As we waited on Lucy's evaluation to begin that spring, Angelle— who'd become family after ten years raising our Hope Cottage babies in Dallas together—called me. Isabelle, Anna's baby-buddy, had focus and self-control issues like Anna, anxiety rivaling Lucy's, and melt-downs like Clare: three in one. Angelle had tried yoga, occupational therapy, ADHD medication, homeschooling. But Isabelle pulled out handfuls of her hair and bit her fingernails to bleeding. She also ran like the wind, was a star on the soccer field, and loved babies and animals. They loved her, too. But nothing abated the chaos Matt and Angelle experienced. She told me Isabelle had spun out during a family friend's visit to their new home in Little Rock, Arkansas. Angelle had said to her friend, "I can't fix this." Her friend went home and goo-gled "behavioral conditions that can't be fixed," dug deep and hit fetal alcohol spectrum disorder, FASD. *Never heard of it.* She suspected it caused Isabelle's hurricanes.

I loaded Anna and Lucy up and headed east. My turn driving the 650 miles of I-20 that lay between Midland and Little Rock. After a morning French press of dark roast coffee, Matt, Angelle, and I corralled our five kids for a hike. Greening woods. Flowing water. Chosen family. Relief. Back at their home, we did living room yoga, then gave the kids screen time. I padded across a ruby-red carpet in Angelle's office off the kitchen to begin my own research for their family. A flagging cartoon octopus sighed at me from the cover of *Foetal Alcohol Spectrum Disorders: Parenting a child with an invisible disability.* I tucked my feet underneath me in a big, brown chair by the window. The authors, Julia Brown—an adoptive mom—and Mary

Mather, MD, began with "The unpredictable impact of alcohol on the developing brain." No safe amount for alcohol during pregnancy; FASD wasn't just about alcoholics. The possible effects astounded me: sensory processing, sleep, communication, maturity. Also, "the major problems of time, money, and mathematics." Near the end of the short book they said, "Nearly 80 percent of adults with FASD do not live independently."

The kids raced into the kitchen, and I looked up. Their movie had already ended. And I'd been holding my breath, my muscles clenched. I stood, stretched, and met Angelle in the kitchen. The kids grabbed clementines and clambered into the backyard.

"Super intense." I stared at Angelle. "Never live independently?"

"No shit." She bundled long, dark hair on top of her head and stuck a pencil through it.

"Mind if I keep reading?" I rubbed my eyes.

She handed me the lotus blossom green tea she'd made and began paying bills. Back by the window, I picked up a slim, lavender book with a floral mandala on the cover: *Trying Differently Rather Than Harder* by Diane Malbin, a social worker. She also wrote about the effects of alcohol on a developing brain. How alcohol—a little or a lot—killed brain cells and could change brain development. She quoted people with FASD: *If someone opened the top of my head and looked in, you know what they'd see? They'd see a whole bunch of black holes; There's a wall in my brain. I know what's behind it, but I can't always get over there; It's like the wiring is scrambled. Sometimes things just don't connect.* I turned my gaze out the window and breathed in the steaming, light floral scent of my tea. A bird squawked and flapped in a massive pine in the backyard. The kids' fort-building backyard fights added to the cacophony. I turned back to the book.

Brain changes caused behavioral symptoms. Sometimes inspiring: creativity, athleticism, nurturing, perseverance, and more. Sometimes challenging: dysmaturity, dysregulated sensory systems, processing delays, lack of executive function, spotty memory, disrupted sleep and nutrition. She described Isabelle. And Lucy. Trying harder—parents *or* kids—couldn't rewire faulty memory or create impulse control. Couldn't reverse the damage. It just increased frustration and acting out. Diane advocated trying differently: accommodate the invisible, physical disability (just like providing a wheelchair, ramp, or book in braille) to allow more peace, success, and joy.

We knew Lucy had been exposed to amphetamines in utero but not alcohol. Would that explain her missing connections? Toddler toys? Years of learning letters, numbers, math facts? Why hadn't a doctor, therapist, *anyone* ever mentioned this to *one* of us? My face grew hot with anger and fear. I took a deep breath. Ran my fingers through my hair. Stretched my neck. And turned a new phrase over in my mind: *neuro*behavioral paradigm. Hadn't I embraced a new paradigm, Beyond Consequences, two years before? And yet, we still often lived in confusion and chaos. Was this what we'd been missing?

In the kitchen, Angelle danced as she punched down pizza dough on a cookie sheet to "The Girl from Ipanema" bouncing around the room. She looked up as I walked in.

"You look wrecked."

"I think Isabelle and Lucy *both* have FASD."

"Really? Oh, shit."

"It makes so much sense. What do we do?"

"I've been thinking a lot about that. First, get a diagnosis. No, first eat pizza." She wiped a white smudge of flour from her cheek.

Back in Midland, I ordered the purple book *Trying Differently Rather Than Harder* and the octopus book. I poured over them and ordered copies for Jeff and our parents. I had a brief conversation with my mom about how Diane's descriptions reminded us of Clare, too. But in Clare I saw that for which I looked: disordered attachment and trauma. My mantra for Lucy became "can't, not won't." It wasn't that she *wouldn't* act her age, try harder, think clearly. She *couldn't*. I told our psychiatrist I thought Lucy had FASD. He looked right and left at her face and said no. She didn't. But I *knew* at least 90 percent of people affected by alcohol in utero didn't have the facial features associated with fetal alcohol syndrome. The spectrum of disorders reached much wider. I never went back.

As Jeff and I sat in bed at night, I gave mini lectures on my FASD discoveries, updates on Clare's escapades and appointments to attend. After I'd handed our relationship to him two years before, I'd stopped initiating, arranging dates and babysitters. Our marriage had devolved into a Prepare Children for Life partnership with Jeff as my executive assistant. I grieved that with any leftover drops of energy and forged ahead.

When Clare broke up with a lunch bunch boy who'd been her boyfriend for a few months, my alarms went off. They'd had fun. She was happy: dancing, working as a swim instructor. At school she even had A's and B's with the support of Ms. LaCaze, her special ed counselor. I thought Sam had gotten too close. We talked about how she pushed people away. *Maybe give him another chance?* But she'd already turned her back. Severed and moved on in a day.

The next week, she called Angelle—who'd always offered to talk anytime Clare didn't want to talk to me. Clare announced she was ready to be sexually active. Angelle said sex was a very adult choice for a 15-year-old, tried to convince her to wait. But Clare had decided. So Angelle told her she needed to be adult responsible. Birth control beyond condoms. And she could tell me, or Angelle would have to. After school the next day, Clare asked me to take a walk with her. We passed a neighbor's garden of prickly pear cactus, agave, sage, and creamy yucca blossoms, hanging their heads dramatically ten feet in the air. Rounding the corner, chatting, we crossed to the duck pond and stepped onto the oval path that led around the water.

"I talked with Angelle, Mom, and she told me to talk to you."

I paused to inhale. . . exhale. "What about?"

"I'm ready to have sex." Clare watched her feet.

I slowed but kept my voice level. "What makes you think so?"

"It sounds fun." She smiled at the ground.

I stopped and looked at her. "You're fifteen, love. And just broke up with your boyfriend."

"Sixteen next month. And I'm not having sex with *Sam*."

"Is there someone else?"

"Don't know yet." She met my gaze. "I know we disagree about this, but I'm ready."

My stomach clenched like a fist. "Every single time you have sex you can get pregnant." I repeated the warning I'd chanted for years.

"That's why I wanted to talk. I need birth control." Clare walked on.

"You know you can still get pregnant?"

"I won't."

"And when you give yourself to another person, you connect. Deeply. You could get hurt."

"I want connection. And it sounds fun. Like dancing." The girl in her body. I'd cried at her dance recital a week before. An extracurricular activity with friends that had *worked*.

"Sex is best in marriage," I said as we completed the loop around the pond.

She stepped off the curb toward home. "I disagree. I'm ready."

I flashed to three years before when killing herself had been the answer as we walked our Dallas neighborhood. I knew I couldn't sway her. I surrendered and agreed to get her birth control.

Turning back to Lucy's FASD, my vision narrowed. Angelle and I exchanged a flurry of emails as we researched. We read dismal statistics for criminality, substance abuse, homelessness, school failure, and suicide. I gasped awake at night, dreaming of Lucy dependent forever, in jail, dead. Angelle found a geneticist in Little Rock who diagnosed Isabelle with alcohol related neurodevelopmental disorder, ARND, one diagnosis under the umbrella of FASD. He said we could do nothing, change nothing. We were devastated. I found a developmental pediatrician, Dr. Karen Rogers, who ran a FASD clinic two hours from Midland. A multidisciplinary team—speech language pathologist, occupational therapist, psychologist, and Dr. Rogers—that used the University of Washington's protocol I had read about. Our pediatrician referred me, and I waited for a call.

I dove deeper online and discovered the Canadian FASD Research Network and the Minnesota Organization on Fetal Alcohol Syndrome. They said with support and accommodations, people with FASD could thrive. Maybe there *was* hope.

In June, my phone rang as I cooked dinner. I turned down the stovetop. The administrator at the developmental pediatrician's office offered a July 17 appointment—*hooray!*—for Lucy's evaluation for anxiety—*what?*

"I thought it was an FASD evaluation."

I heard papers shuffle. "Dr. Nabulsi wrote anxiety as the presenting problem. The FASD clinic is only two Fridays per month, so those appointments are six months out."

"Wow. So long." I looked out the window. I could talk FASD at the appointment. Maybe we'd slide into the clinic sooner if we were already in the practice. "I'll take July seventeenth."

While Lucy, Jeff, and I drove 117 miles of flat, open prairie, we listened to *Wonder* on Audible. Auggie's courage and wisdom inspired me. I felt his mother's fear and pain. A flock of birds rose up into the wide, blue sky. One took the lead, and I watched them fly in formation until they became black dots far away. I prayed we'd get a diagnosis under the FASD umbrella. A framework for understanding and accommodating Lucy. She fell asleep halfway there. I woke her as we pulled up to a long, squat building alone at the edge of a mostly empty parking lot in Lubbock.

Dr. Rogers asked Lucy questions. I recognized checklists for anxiety, depression, and ADHD. Maybe autism spectrum disorder.

Unhurried, she smiled at Lucy with focused attention. Many questions I rephrased when Lucy turned to me blank-faced.

Dr. Rogers looked at me. "You translate for Lucy. Do you do that a lot?"

"When things don't make sense. I guess I've learned how to decode for her."

She made a note and turned back to Lucy. "What do you love most, Lucy?"

Lucy looked beyond her at the wall. "My mom, dad, sisters, and our dog and cat. We found her on our car engine when she was tiny."

"Awesome. She's lucky. What do you like to do?"

Lucy turned to me, and I smiled but didn't offer suggestions. After a few beats, she answered, "Gymnastics and dance." She concentrated on the floor. "I love music and building blocks. I hate math."

"What do you hate about it?"

"It doesn't make sense; it's hard to remember what things mean."

Lucy didn't look up, but Dr. Rogers nodded. "What are you good at?"

"Being a friend. And I Spy. And talking to animals." Lucy met her eyes. "My cat listens."

"Those are wonderful things."

Lucy smiled and looked away.

As Dr. Rogers left, she said, "You take care, Lucy. And keep smiling. Your smile lights up the room."

Lucy leaned over. "Mom, I thought electricity lit up the room."

I smiled. "It does, babe." I made a mental note to introduce the words *literal* and *figurative* to her.

Our full evaluation came in the mail six weeks later: sleep disturbance, speech disturbance, fetal drug exposure, generalized anxiety disorder, fine motor impairment, and at the very bottom of page four, FASD-ARND.

Paradigm Shift

When school started in August, Clare lit up about a new boy each week. Week one: Javier. Week two: Darius. Week three: Rafael. Week four: Anthony. Anthony stuck. She brought him home for lunch one day along with her one true friend, Miranda, and a couple tagalongs—new friends who appeared when Clare had gotten her driver's license in June. She bartered rides and loans for a version of friendship. I chatted with them at our table and stole Whataburger french fries from Clare's orange-and-white-striped bag. Anthony smiled a big, toothy smile and didn't say a word. Just sat and looked cute in his tall Afro. He didn't often join the lunch crew; he had his own. Clare said he wasn't *really* in a gang, but he wore colors—red for the Bloods—and fought at school. Sometimes over Clare. Miranda didn't like him. But he charmed Clare and made her laugh. And he was Black. He opened a door for her into a small crowd of Black kids at MHS. They still mocked her for talking White but let her in. We saw less and less of her.

A month in, she came home before curfew and went straight to bed, saying her stomach hurt. I sat on the edge of her bed. And I knew it had begun.

"How are you, honey?" I touched her bony shoulder. She seemed to shrink day by day.

"Not good. Maybe I have a bladder infection?"

"Because you and Anthony had sex? That sometimes happens." I kept my face and voice gentle. I had to keep her talking.

She looked stunned. "You knew?"

"I'm your mom. I know things."

She sighed and turned over.

I stroked her hair. "Did it hurt?"

"A little." She turned back to me. "I think I bled. It was pretty quick."

"Was it what you wanted?"

"Yeah." She looked embarrassed. "I thought you'd be mad."

"Not mad, love. A little sad." I imagined where it might have happened. "It's not what I wanted for you. Sex is precious." I sighed. "Did you use a condom?" Then my voice rose and quickened before I could stop it: "Remember, two forms of protection. You can still get a disease on the pill."

"I know, Mom." She turned away and silence filled the space between us.

"I love you, Clare. No matter what." I rubbed her back.

"Love you, too."

"Remember, we're forever." I kissed her head and walked out.

Eventually, I told Jeff, and his heart broke a little. For her and for her rejecting our values. Would she never follow the rules we'd accepted as kids: obey and respect adults, especially your parents; when things get hard, work harder; and sex is for marriage? My nerves hummed—a steady supply of adrenaline flowed through me. I begged her to use protection. Every. Single. Time. *No babies* became my mantra. I picked up the foil packet by her sink and counted pills. She insisted on taking charge, which meant random remembering. She missed days; I researched options. I decided on an IUD because it meant no remembering pills, 99 percent effectiveness, five years of protection. But I had to convince Clare. She vacillated. I cried and gave her the exact time it took to take Anthony home and return, or I'd ground her: eight minutes. After fifteen, she'd walk in the door and hand over her keys without a word. As always, consequences changed nothing.

One grounded night after refusing dinner, she went to the backyard to "take some space." Ten minutes later, I called to her and peered through darkness, looking around the side of the house where she sometimes hid. She was gone. I panicked. Jeff stayed with Anna and Lucy while I searched the shadows of the neighborhood. I called Ms. LaCaze from Midland High—Clare's counselor/confidante—while I walked, but she hadn't heard from her. She called back as I hunted the duck pond. "She's at Miranda's. I convinced her to let you come get her." When I walked in our front door, Jeff walked out the back and drove to pick her up. Once she was asleep—her keys hidden in our closet—I put my book down and reached out, touching Jeff's arm across our bed.

He shook his head and sighed. "I'm so angry and confused." I kept my eyes on his. He sank in the pillows, and a tear crept down his face. "We rode home in silence. How can she treat us this way? I'm so afraid we're descending into the madness again."

"Me, too," I said. "Me, too."

Understanding FASD was helping us climb out of the madness with Lucy. She and Anna had joined fourth and sixth grades full time at the Montessori school Deidra, Natalie, and Sarah had opened in September. My first semester not homeschooling in two and a half years. I spent my free time diving deep into fetal alcohol, learning how Lucy's brain worked. Evenings, Jeff and I redefined "success" for Lucy and for us as her parents. Reevaluated dreams and goals. Whittled things down to what really mattered. I watched for clues each morning: was it an "on brain day" or "off brain day;" what "age" did she seem? If I met her at her daily—sometimes hourly—developmental level of functioning, it dissipated frustration.

One night, Lucy wiggled on her stool at the dinner table. She stood up, sat down.

"Lucy, put your bottom in the chair," I barked.

She popped up and bent over her stool; she studied the top, sides, legs, underneath. She did the opposite of what I asked. My instinct was to scold her. But my time on FASD sites had taught me to get curious rather than angry when things didn't make sense.

"What are you doing, Lu?"

"You told me to put my bottom *in* the chair, but it's made of wood. I can't."

I paused as my mind bent around her words then smiled. "I wasn't clear. Sit on top of the chair and don't get up until we've finished eating." She sat down and didn't get up. Amazing. Literal versus abstract was for real for Lucy. If I could communicate in a way she understood, we got peaceful dinnertime instead of a confused meltdown. At least with Lucy.

In November, Clare finally said, "I've decided I don't want to get pregnant, and an IUD is the best option." Relieved, I searched for someone in West Texas to put an IUD in my sixteen-year-old. The whole area touted abstinence and had shut down Planned Parenthood. But abstinence wasn't an option for Clare. Frantic, I took Clare out of school for a day and drove five hours southeast to the East Austin Planned Parenthood. Babies worried me way more than grades. Though those were an increasing concern, too.

On the day of our appointment, Clare rolled out of bed and into our blue Honda Civic. She pulled her hood over her head, stuck in her earbuds, and went back to sleep. Or at least pretended to. I turned on NPR. Scraggly, green mesquite grew out of dusty ground outside of town. Hills rose into vast mesas after a couple hours.

At the clinic, women came in and out—college students, professionals. Not sixteen-year-olds. Clare sank into a chair just like she had in the car. I took a seat beside her. After what seemed like forever, a nurse called Clare's name.

I stood up and the nurse said, "Just her, please."

"But I'm her mom."

"If she'd like, you can join her in a bit. It's up to her."

I sat back down. I had no control, and Clare's decisions and reasoning shifted like the weather. My foot tapping, I snapped the pages of a magazine front to back on a stupid, plastic chair as canned laughs rang from the TV that hung at the ceiling. One-word prayers wheezed from my heart to the universe. *Help. Please. Mercy.*

Clare emerged twenty minutes later, inviting me in. The nurse practitioner—a young, blond ponytail with a quick laugh who seemed like the newest Team Happy Clare recruit—said, "Clare's a delightful young woman." *If you only knew.* They'd agreed an IUD was best.

I held back tears. "How long will it take?"

"It's quick. We do it all the time, so it's no big deal."

"Great." I exhaled.

"The front desk will schedule it. Appointments are about a month out."

My face fell. "We live five hours away, and Clare is *very* sexually active. We need it inserted today."

"We never consult and do a procedure the same day." She laughed and picked up a handful of square, black packages covered in bold red, blue, and yellow graffiti art. "Aren't these great, Clare? An artist designs them. Condoms for you." She dropped them in a paper bag. "Nice to meet you both. See you in a month."

I drove toward blazes of orange at the horizon that turned deep blue, then black.

School unraveled in time with our relationship, two threads pulled in different directions that unwove our life together. Regular robot calls announced Clare's tardy or skipped classes. Teachers called about missing work or failed tests. Jeff met with the school counselor and vice principal. I joined him with Clare and Ms. LaCaze in the counselor's office one afternoon to clear up the latest conflicting stories, chaos, and confusion. Jeff and I sat across the desk from the counselor as Clare and Ms. LaCaze stood in the little space left. The faint smell of cleaning supplies and teenage sweat hung in the air. From behind a metal desk covered in papers, highlighters, and red pens, the counselor listed classes and assignments missed and teacher complaints. A worn album we'd started playing when Clare was in fifth grade at Rosemont Elementary in Dallas. She looked at the floor, stone-faced.

Fire burned in my belly. "This is serious, Clare."

"I know." She didn't look up.

"You say that but you don't change. How are you going to graduate next year?"

"Don't know."

"If you don't graduate, how will you get a job?"

"I'll figure it out."

"You say that. To trust your way. But it gets you here." My voice bounced off the walls as Clare shrank.

"Mom, stop yelling."

Jeff intervened. "Clare, we are doing all we know to help. What do you need?" She seemed to have disappeared into herself.

I took a breath. "Why are you not in class when you're supposed to be?"

Ms. LaCaze stepped closer to Clare and rested her hand on her shoulder. "We can't help if you won't tell us how."

Clare looked up at her. "Math is so hard; I hate going. It's embarrassing." She shifted and scuffed her white Converse while we waited. "Sometimes I feel like crying on my way, so I go into the bathroom. Sit on the floor and cry until class is over."

"Not a solution, Clare." My voice came out baritone through clenched teeth. "Solve your problems." The bell clanged over the loudspeaker for classes to change.

The counselor offered compassion. "We all want what's best for you, Clare. We're on the same team." Clare nodded and her counselor continued, "What are *your* goals?"

"I don't know."

She sighed, "Promise to at least go to class?"

"Yes."

"We'll keep working together. Remember, I'm here for you."

Clare went back to class, and Jeff and I walked home in silence. I sought a psychiatrist to sort out Clare's ADHD and anxiety meds. When he said we just needed more discipline at home, I turned to Lucy's developmental pediatrician, Dr. Rogers, in Lubbock for help. She evaluated Clare just before the holidays, and we waited for the results.

Clare drove herself and Anthony to dinner and a movie for her first New Year's Eve out with a boyfriend. She'd agreed to text us every time they changed locations. But didn't. *Point Break* ended at eleven fifteen; she didn't respond to our texts or calls. She and Anthony showed up at Deidra's where the rest of us were celebrating just before midnight. She smiled, laughed, and said hello as she shrugged off her coat. Anthony, eyes red and glazed, shuffled behind her. *Did I smell weed?*

"I haven't heard from you; you've clearly changed locations," I said.

"Sorry, Mom. I forgot. But we came to say hi right after the movie."

"It ended at eleven fifteen. It takes fifteen minutes," I scowled across the table strewn with board games and half-empty glasses. Anthony inched his way behind Clare.

"We're here now." Clare folded her arms across her chest.

"Take Anthony straight home. You have eight minutes."

"It's almost midnight. On New Year's Eve."

"And you didn't do what you said. You lost your privileges."

Clare morphed from sparkler to smoldering ember. Anthony followed her out the door. A bitter wind slipped in behind them.

She didn't come home.

Jeff hunted for her. I called Anthony's mom; she hadn't seen them. I paced. Jeff called AT&T to track Clare's phone, but they couldn't. We both paced. And paced. At four in the morning, a key turned the lock in the front door. I leaped from bed. The wood floor by Anna's bedroom squeaked as she emerged. I reached out to her, and she snuggled into me.

"Give me your keys." Jeff almost whispered from the couch. Clare said nothing, handed them over, went into her room, and shut the door.

Jeff smoothed Anna's hair after she climbed onto his lap. "Clare's home now. Safe. You can go back to sleep."

"I haven't been asleep. I've been waiting. Listening."

I took her hand. "Babe. It scares you, huh?" Anna had raged over Christmas, more aggressive than ever. *Was it fear?*

"I'm okay." Stoic. Like a mountain. Or a dormant volcano.

Jeff walked her to bed, tucked her in, then collapsed on ours. I lay on the couch, listening for Clare's escape. But there was silence. All day. She slept. And slept. Through a neighborhood kid revelry of snowballs and hot chocolate. And we were grateful for the pause.

At two in the morning, I found Anna on the couch, eyes on Clare's bedroom door.

"Love. You're worried about her?"

She nodded. "I'll make sure she's safe."

"That's not your job, sweetheart." I kissed her pink cheek. "I promise I'll watch."

She held my gaze for a long moment then reluctantly went to bed. Back in my own bed, middle-of-the-night demons plagued me. *Clare won't graduate. What life unfolds if Anthony gets her pregnant?* The house creaked. *She won't consider abortion or adoption. In seventeen months, she turns eighteen, and we lose any control.* My blanket couldn't keep out the cold. *Residential treatment is our only option.* I talked to Jeff when the sun came up. He feared it would destroy our relationship with Clare and couldn't imagine living through another placement—the anguish, cost, travel, therapy, Anna and Lucy undone.

I called the Change Academy Lake of the Ozarks, CALO, in Lake Ozark, Missouri. Three years before, the drugs, violence and sexual acting out that sent boys and girls to CALO had sent us to New Leaf Academy so Clare could remain a little girl with other little girls. A year and a half after her NLA graduation, CALO fit. They specialized in reactive attachment, now called complex developmental trauma, and golden retrievers for canine therapy. I talked to the admissions director and cried on my parents' couch—terrified Jeff wouldn't let me send her. But then he punched a hole in the wall.

The night had begun with Clare, still grounded, rocking and crying on the floor by the fire in our living room. "I need Anthony and Miranda. You're taking them away." A tear rolled down her cheek. "I can't live without them." The campfire smell of smoke wafted over us. We tried to reason with her, but she just wrapped herself into a ball and teetered back and forth, back and forth, back and forth. Jeff lost it.

"You want Anthony? Fine. I'll get Anthony."

Clare looked up, alarmed. Jeff stomped down the hall and came back with keys jangling in his hand. He left without a word. I mentally pivoted from challenger to supporter and sat beside Clare. My arm encircled her as the fire licked the air and warmed our backs. It popped and cracked. I turned and stared into the flames and let myself float away.

When Jeff and Anthony arrived, Clare tucked her head into her knees and swayed. Anthony sat in the corner, stupefied, and Jeff paced like an angry drill sergeant.

"This is what you wanted, Clare. Anthony. All better now? He's what you need to be okay?"

Clare seemed unbearably small, as if she might evaporate. "I don't know . . . I don't know."

"Jeff, why don't you take a break?" I saw him recognize he was out of control. He spun around and walked down the hall. Then his footsteps silenced a beat. *Crack.* The drywall gave way to his fist. Clare's cries amped up. We'd entered an alternate universe; Jeff's peace turned violent.

He came back rubbing his knuckles. "Come on, Anthony. You're going home."

I tucked Clare into bed while he was gone. Standing in her doorway, I imagined a hideous end—the suicide we'd avoided three years before. When Jeff returned, I held him until he slept then spent the night on my back, eyes at the ceiling. *Help, help, help* the drumbeat in my chest. When the weak winter sun spilled into our room, Jeff opened his eyes.

I said, "It's time."

His eyes brimmed with tears. "I know." We held each other and cried.

I called CALO and gathered papers for Clare's admissions application. Jeff hired a licensed transport company to take her. She wouldn't go willingly this time; she'd run for sure. By Friday, one week after New Year's Day, we had everything in place for Monday. We just had to make it through the weekend. Months before, Deidra and I had planned a Saturday night Mother Blessing for Natalie and Sarah. They'd both discovered they were pregnant at the end of spring. They were weeks away from delivering. I refused to cancel.

A few closest friends circled up, laughed, and shared stories as we prepared to welcome their surprise babies. People brought their favorite fabric to make banners infused with our love and prayers—a set for each family. We sat by the warmth of our fire as scissors shaped fabric, talking motherhood and hopes. One friend painted gorgeous mandalas on two taut-sphere bellies. The acidic smell overpowered the peppermint tea and orange chocolate except when we raised it to our lips. As the lovely night wore on, the sounds from Clare's adjacent room changed. Furniture scraped across wood and paper tore. Something clunked onto the floor. I got up to refill the tea pot and plate of dark chocolates and opened her door. She sat surrounded by papers, books, pictures. She'd moved her bed so that it blocked most of the room.

"What are you doing?" I closed her door to silence the echo of my irritation.

"Going through things." Her face electrified me: the unreachable version of Clare.

"Could you do it more quietly? We're trying to bless Sarah, Natalie, and their babies, and you're being so loud."

She threw things around as I talked, creating more and more chaos. She nodded.

I closed the door and walked back to my friends. The circle of them in the firelight. Faces, hearts wide open. Really seeing each other and being seen. Clare came out purposeful, in charge. Her adrenaline flushed the room as she walked through in baggy, black sweatpants and out the back door. She reappeared with black garbage bags and a few boxes from the garage.

"Hi, Clare," Deidra said. "Doing okay?"

Clare smiled her perfect, Happy Clare smile. "I'm good." She closed her bedroom door behind her.

Deidra turned to me. "Everything okay?"

"I don't think so."

I tried to keep my attention on Natalie and Sarah. A friend had sewn the top inch of our fabric squares over a cord one by one.

Natalie glowed. "Perfect."

Sarah said, "Now I'm ready."

Clare stomped from her room to my bedroom winding her braids on top of her head as she went. I followed her. "*Please* stay in your room quietly. For one night. So I can gift my friends? You're distracting and selfish, Clare."

"Okay, Mom." She sounded like a million other annoyed teenagers. "I just need something." She turned and elephant-walked back down the hall, back through my friends into her room and banged the door shut.

"I should get going." Sarah braced herself with a hand at her hip and heaved herself up.

"You don't have to go." My face held my pain.

"It's time. And Clare's not bothering us near as much as she's bothering you."

Books thudded into boxes and heavy trash bags rasped around Clare's room as Natalie walked to the front door with her fabric in her arms. "I love you all." She held my gaze as I put my hands on her head and looked deep into her eyes.

"I can't wait to meet this baby, love." I handed her a poem I'd read in our circle. "I wrote this on my piece of the banner."

Natalie read it aloud: "Our hands imbibe like roots/ So I place them on what is beautiful in this world/ And I fold them in prayer, and they/ Draw from the heavens/ Light. St. Francis." She squeezed me tight with her one free arm. "Thank you so much for tonight. It was perfect." I kissed her cheek, and she walked out the door.

Sarah gathered her things. "I love you, Lynn. I'll be praying for you and Clare tonight."

"Thanks. I think we need it."

I walked toward the sound of clanging dishes. Deidra ran water over plates and put mugs in the dishwasher. "How can I help you and Clare, friend?"

I fell apart. "I think she's running away. It's like she's packing up to move."

She turned off the water and stepped closer as I gulped back sobs. "Could she come home with you? There I think she'll just go to sleep."

"Of course."

Clare's closet door stood open. She'd emptied out the shelves. Two big trash bags sat next to her; hangers, books and CDs climbed out the tops.

"Looks like you're moving out, Clare," I said. She looked up at me and shrugged.

"You seem pretty stressed, babe," Deidra said. "Why not come with me. Sleep in our guest bed. Things will feel better in the morning."

Clare paused the deconstruction. Her face softened. "I am tired."

She stood and robot-walked passed the smoldering fire straight out the door. Deidra rushed after her into the night.

I walked to our bedroom and said to Jeff, "We can't wait."

"I know. I saw it in her face." Jeff called his mom and asked her to ride with him and Clare to Dallas the next day to deliver her to the transport agents. She didn't ask for an explanation, just said *of course*. Anything for Jeff. And Clare. He'd secure the child safety locks on his truck and hide Clare's bag under a tarp in the bed. Pick up his mom and then Clare from Deidra's in the morning.

We lay in bed sleepless and silent. Nothing left.

When dawn cast shadows in our room, I texted Deidra. She'd stayed up all night with Clare perched on the back of her couch at the window. A tiger scanning for danger. *It wasn't human. I finally get it. I'm so sorry.* She had seen—an incredible gift. She said Clare could stay there until Jeff and his mom picked her up. *I'll bring Anna and Lucy down with me in a bit,* I texted. They surely felt the waves of tension and sadness rolling off me.

The girls walked into Deidra's front door and flopped onto the couch with her kids. They enfolded themselves into their best friends. Anna kept one eye on Clare, Deidra's husband, Cliff, and me, sitting at the dining room table together. Cliff had scooped Clare up already that morning by the duck pond when she slipped out their back gate.

"Clare and I've been talking about how she's so lucky to have family like you. How we all love her, and she can't run from her problems." Cliff nodded at Clare. Her eyes sagged, empty, but she nodded. All the words over all the years—Clare lay beyond where words reached.

"How are you, Clare? You seem better." I touched her small, soft hand.

"Okay."

"You're hurting."

"Yeah."

"Dad's picking you up in a few minutes."

She nodded.

"Can I hug you?" I walked around the breakfast dishes still scattered about the table and held out my hand. She took it and stood. I held her to me. Breathed in the scent of her. *For the last time?* Jeff's brown GMC pickup truck pulled up.

I stretched out my arms and looked square at Clare. "I love you forever. No matter what."

"I love you, too, Mom." She turned and saw Jeff at the door. They got in the truck and drove away.

As I sat up against my pillow in bed the night after, Jeff described what happened next. Clare had said hi to her Gram. She hadn't asked why Gram was there or where they were going until they approached the edge of town.

Jeff had answered, "We're going to Dallas."

Clare, shut-down-angry, asked, "Can I at least call Anthony and say I'm leaving?" After she asked several times, Jeff handed her his phone.

Clare howled, "*Nooooooooooo!* You can't do this to me!"

"Do what?"

"Residential treatment," Clare screeched. "I read your text to Wayne!"

I reached for Jeff's hand and held on as he continued.

"I know it's hard to hear, Clare, but that's what we need to do."

"This can't be happening. You're ruining my life. I can't leave Anthony. My friends. You can't do this." Like a tape on repeat.

He tried to help her get back into her wise mind. "I know you don't want this to happen. It feels awful. And you're scared." They'd only made it forty-five minutes into the five-hour drive. He pulled over and slid into the back seat with Clare as his mom drove on.

Clare hugged the opposite door. "Don't touch me!"

My stomach caught fire as he talked. I wanted to stop him. But he needed to say it all. And I needed to know and be in it with him. He looked up from where he seemed to watch the scene. Adrenaline rushed through him, reliving it; shoulders clenched, face flushed, eyes full of dread, fear, disbelief. I met them and nodded; took a deep breath and stroked his hand.

She was as far gone as he'd ever seen her. She would have jumped out of the seventy-mile-an-hour car if she could have. His mom grasped for something to say to make it stop. He prayed, then texted me that Clare knew and asked me to pray.

He begged Clare, "Can I hold you?"

She let him lay his hand on her from the other side of the car. Then a switch flipped. She dropped to the floorboard, curled into a ball, and fell asleep.

I blinked and wagged my head. I felt the relief in my body there on the bed. Jeff flapped his hands. "I was super adrenaline filled. On high alert. All my senses vibrating. Like I'd been in a fight." Tears welled and his voice cracked. "It was the worst thing that ever happened to me."

We sat in silence a few minutes. Then he continued. "Four hours later, we parked in a hotel's dark parking lot. A flood lamp above the backdoor cast one circle of light." He stepped out to meet the strangers to whom he'd give our daughter, terrified we were making a mistake.

I shook my head. *How did he do that?*

"I'm Jeff," he said. "Matt and Breanna? Clare is asleep in the back seat."

A small, Black woman stepped forward. "We'll take care of your daughter. I know this is hard. But you're doing the right thing." Relief, sadness, heartbreak, terror washed over him.

Jeff stopped and started. His mouth in a small *O* as if he'd run out of breath for sound. His eyes filled, and his face reddened. He looked like the picture of Jesus in my meditation closet: face full of sorrow, a broken heart shining through his chest.

Clare clutched her teddy bear, Franklin, who had been with her in the Appalachian Mountains and the high desert in Oregon as she got out of the car. Breanna and Matt introduced themselves; Clare was polite and respectful. She let Jeff hug her.

"I love you, babe. We'll get through this."

"Love you too, Dad."

Breanna placed her hand on Clare's back. "Come on in with us." And she was gone.

Four streams of silent tears dropped onto our quilt. The intensity drained from Jeff's voice. "My mom and her lack of judgment. There for me, no questions asked. It was a gift." He turned his wedding ring on his finger as he spoke. "And here I am."

I wrapped my arms around him, and we lay intertwined into the night.

Three weeks later, an envelope arrived from Dr. Rogers. Clare's evaluation. ADHD, generalized anxiety disorder, and at the very bottom of page four: fetal alcohol spectrum disorder.

Clare had FASD. That changed everything.

New Ride

One snowy Missouri morning, exactly a year after Clare arrived at CALO, my boots clicked across the white tiled floor of the gathering room there. I opened the door and stepped into the large central room, looking for Clare. And gasped. She wore a royal-blue graduation gown. A black cap perched on the straight, chestnut hair that Samika, a Black staff person, had woven in for her as a gift. It flowed down Clare's shoulders and back. Black eyeliner and subtle, sandy eyeshadow made her dark eyes pop. She tiptoed in high heels and a short black dress she'd chosen for the day. Her lovely curves were back after a year of eating regularly again. She looked grown-up and elegant.

I choked on tears. "You're so beautiful."

"Trying hard not to fall down." She laughed and flashed her light-up-the-world smile.

I wrapped her in my arms. At seventeen, she was still a few inches shorter than my five feet four.

"You made it, love. We made it." I looked into her eyes.

A golden retriever trotted through the room with a lanky boy rushing after. "Hey, Clare. Congrats," he said as he grabbed the leash.

Clare petted the dog's head. "Thanks."

"I'm going back in, love. See you in a minute. I'm so very proud of you. Love you." She'd finished high school a semester early with the structure and support of the small school at CALO. Amazing. Samika walked up to wait with Clare for "Pomp and Circumstance" as I wiped my eyes, squeezed her, and turned back to the door. Jeff sat at the front of the gathering room with Anna, Lucy, and Simba—an almost one-year-old golden—facing Clare's teachers, CALO friends, the staff, and our families. I took my seat alongside them.

Clare's therapist, Heidi, peeked out the door and got a thumbs up from Clare and Samika. "Glad you're all here today to celebrate Clare's high school graduation, CALO graduation, and her adoption of Simba. So many milestones." Heidi turned to us. "We especially welcome Clare's family. Without your support, she wouldn't be here today." She nodded, and the graduation march began.

Clare stepped in, shining and full of life. Also, a bit shy in her dress and makeup. Simba jumped up from where he lay at Anna's feet when he saw Clare. Anna held on to his leash. Her long hair ran across his red-golden back as she pushed his bum to the ground. She wore a flowing blue shirt that matched her eyes; she looked grown-up, too. The CALO girls called out *Woohoo!* and whistled at Clare's transformation from her usual sweats and T-shirt. Jeff gulped—this moment unimaginable a year before. Clare beamed, walking down the center aisle to hoots and hollers. When she reached the front row, she stopped and hugged my mom and Jeff's mom, squeezed my sister Kim's hand; they all trembled with tears. Jeff embraced Clare as she sat beside him. He wiped his eyes and murmured a quiet *I love you* just for her to hear.

Clare's teacher, Ms. Allie, faced her. "You did it!" Clare laughed and pushed her long hair behind her shoulder. "It hasn't always been easy to keep you from wandering the halls or motivate you to finish algebra equations." Jeff and I nodded and laughed as Allie continued, "But you stuck with it; accomplished so much. We're proud of you." Allie motioned for Clare to stand and handed her a black folder. Clare opened it with wide, full eyes. "You are now a 2017 high school graduate. Congratulations." Clare held it up like a Super Bowl trophy to all our cheers.

The whole family cried, even our dads. Except her sisters, who were much more interested in Simba. Lucy had already slid off her chair onto the floor to pet him. Dog hair covered her red-and-blue Hannah Anderson dress and tights. I'd plaited the hair around her face in small braids and let the back stay curly and full. She was adorable.

Clare smoothed her gown under her and sat down while Heidi traded places with Ms. Allie. "It's my privilege to present your CALO gold coin." Cheers erupted, and Heidi asked Clare to stand again. "You've completed our program. Other girls look up to and learn from you. You have new self-control *and* self-awareness." I looked from Heidi to Clare in wonder. A tear slid down my cheek, and I squeezed Jeff's hand.

Heidi continued, "I've watched you begin to see yourself as beautiful, capable, and worthy. You are connected and committed to your family and confident in their love for you." Clare smiled at Jeff and me, the connection between us palpable. And astonishing.

"We'll miss your bright light, laughter, and dance parties," Heidi said, chuckling. "But you are ready. To be home and pursue your dreams." Clare sparkled as Heidi opened it up for staff members and girls to speak. It felt like listening to toasts at a wedding: lots of love, a little roasting, laughter, and happy tears. After a while, Clare stood, whispered *thank you,* and accepted the coin. She looked out, and a tear escaped her eye.

Heidi hugged her, and the dog trainer began the adoption ceremony. "My turn, Clare." Ariel talked about Clare training Simba from six weeks old. Being responsible for feeding, pottying, and teaching him. "Also, sneaking him into your bed at night." Ariel smirked, and we all laughed.

"That's a truth. I admit it." Clare smiled.

"You are his caregiver. We believe you're ready to adopt him. Is that your intention?"

"It is." Clare became serious.

"Jeff and Lynn, you commit to support Clare and provide for Simba's needs as well?"

"We do."

Ariel passed us adoption papers for our signatures. "Congratulations. Simba is officially an Alsup." Anna and Lucy applauded that one, and we all knelt around Simba for licks and pets.

"Thanks for coming, everyone." Heidi invited us to cookies and punch. And just like that, we were done.

Excitement, relief, and sadness washed in waves over Clare's face; she had loved CALO after a torturous first month. Together, we walked out the front door for the last time.

∼

Jeff and I had first walked through that door a year earlier. Two weeks after Clare arrived at CALO by transport. We'd flown to Dallas, handed Anna and Lucy to friends at the airport, caught the next flight to Springfield, Missouri and driven north to Lake Ozark. I had leaned my head against the window of our rental car and stared up at the slate-gray winter sky for the hour-and-a-half drive. Trees reached naked, gnarled arms up into the emptiness. CALO looked like a cross between a warehouse and conference center with a silver metal roof and cream-colored siding. We had sat in silence after Jeff killed the engine in the parking lot. Then took a deep breath in unison and opened our doors to the chill.

After walking down a few rock steps, Jeff held the front door for me to enter the lobby. No one in sight. We walked through double glass doors into the milieu. Empty groupings of black couches and chairs scattered about the huge room. A white picket fence marked off a dog training area in the middle of the room, enclosing a slide, tunnel, and bridge. A piano sat nearby, and a three-story climbing wall rose from a pit. A loft space with art tables overlooked it all.

"Where is everyone?" I asked. "And why can we just walk in and wander around?"

"What's that smell?" Jeff frowned. Maybe a pack of golden retrievers.

Eventually we found a staff person who then found Clare. She emerged from a door on the opposite side of the vast space and trudged as though through molasses toward us. She studied her feet; we waited. A few yards from us she looked up. The impenetrable Haitian expression.

"Hi, Clare. May I hug you?" I touched her shoulder, and Jeff took a step toward her, but she backed up. Jeff and I sat. The staffer said she'd return in a while, and I watched her walk away. Clare sank down across from us and dropped her chin to her chest. She looked imploded. *Underneath, did she smolder?* Silence weighed down on us all.

"Want to tell us what you're thinking and feeling?" I asked.

"Doesn't matter."

"Matters to me."

Jeff said, "Last time I saw you was hard. Want to talk about that?"

Clare shook her head, and the silence stretched on. I said we loved her and needed to keep her safe; were still in it together; would come back every month. To no response. A couple boys burst through the glass doors—cussing, bloody, explosive—with a staff member rushing in behind them. A fight had broken out on the blacktop. *What had we done?* That was our entire first visit. Jeff and I walked out into the frigid winter. But we kept showing up. And hoped one day she'd believe we hadn't abandoned her and never would.

Back in Midland, Clare's leaving hadn't rocked our world like it had three and a half years before. Maybe we had stronger muscles and support to withstand our stormy life: Beyond Consequences, attachment, and trauma knowledge, EMDR, a growing understanding of FASD, and trying differently. And a community of folks had begun gathering at our home on Sunday mornings for coffee and conversations about spirituality and living mindfully. The Barefoot Church one woman called it because some came in pajamas, shoeless. We all came just as we were. They held us as we cried.

I'd also reached out to our pediatrician about Anna's impulsivity, reading challenges, anger, and aggression. I'd answered yes to all but two of twenty questions on his ADHD questionnaire for her. He had suggested Ritalin. She'd swallowed one small, yellow pill the next day and read for me better than ever before. She played Monopoly with a friend—her first board game experience ever. She remembered to brush her teeth and didn't poke and bump into Lucy. She focused at swim practice. It felt miraculous. The Montessori elementary guide had moved on over the holidays, so Anna started the second semester of sixth grade at Hillcrest School—a hundred students with learning differences, especially dyslexia and ADHD, receiving individualized education. She thrived on the structure, teachers' attention, and built-in friends. Then she turned twelve and waded into adolescence.

Our power struggles grew toward the *I'll do whatever the hell I want* they would become. She resisted swim practice and meets. The exhausting tug-of-war began to outweigh the benefits to her mind and body; we let her quit. We dropped her gluten-free/dairy-free diet, even though it had helped regulate her emotions and digestive system over the years. She fought appointments with our family therapist; we found a young, hip therapist who specialized in intuitive eating as well as trauma and attachment. Anna started the slow process of building their relationship. Meanwhile, Lucy joined Bynum School for kids with developmental disabilities.

I walked into her fourth-grade classroom one day to pick her up early for occupational therapy: fine motor skills for handwriting and the trick of swallowing pills. My eyes adjusted to the soft light. A couple kids sat at a table, one in a wheelchair, and a few on beanbags on a large rug. Lucy lay on her belly next to a young boy wearing a helmet. Their fingers and heads danced together as her long braids swung from side to side. She didn't look up when I entered. Her thick, blue cotton dress had wriggled above her knees, and her turquoise leggings jigged in the air. I smiled at the teacher, then watched Lucy grin and laugh, conjuring both in her friend.

"Hi, Lucy," I called after a minute or two.

The dimple in her right cheek deepened. "Mommy!" She scrambled to her feet and swallowed me in a hug. "But it's not time to go!" School equaled fun. Victory.

When I asked to fill Lucy's teachers in on FASD, the director invited me to the upcoming staff meeting. I searched the internet and *Trying Differently Rather Than Harder* and put together my first training.

Six weeks into Clare's stay at CALO, Jeff and I sat at our dining room table for our weekly Skype family therapy session with Clare and Heidi. We planned to tell Clare she had FASD, making sense of her struggles, our struggles, over the years. She wasn't bad, lazy or stupid; she had brain differences. When I'd opened Clare's evaluation from Dr. Rogers, I'd initially felt shock, and then *of course*. It fit perfectly: her inability to organize and remember, her social and emotional differences, her overwhelm living a typical day, her embarrassment and sadness at not fitting in. Attachment and trauma affected her, but brain differences overarched everything.

Clare already had an image of FASD. We'd explained the summer before what it meant for Lucy. Lagging skills, a different developmental timeline, much more need for supervision than other kids her age. We'd told Clare that Lucy's brain had formed and functioned differently, and she might not ever live independently. Clare had preboarded an airplane with Lucy and me that fall at the call for people who needed extra time or assistance—her diagnosis validated her sensory overload and anxiety in crowds. Gate agents and passengers had looked Lucy up and down to find her disability and then sideways at us because it was invisible. But Clare had different effects, even if the overlap was clear.

I poured coffee from a French press into our Italian mugs. "Ready?"

Jeff shrugged. I sipped as Skype tones chimed on my laptop. He clicked ANSWER.

Heidi popped up on the screen. She sat in Clare's shared suite at CALO. She tucked back a loose strand of curly, brown hair and looked out at us with kind, blue eyes. A tan loveseat sat behind her with a canvas print of a lone tree full of red birds. "How're you guys doing?" Her Midwestern accent made me smile. I looked over at Jeff.

His quiet, Southern drawl answered, "Hanging in there, I guess."

"How's Clare?" I asked.

"Connecting with a few girls. She opened up in therapy group yesterday a bit. And she and Samika, her coach, seem to be bonding."

"That's good to hear."

"Ready for me to get Clare for our session?"

"I'm nervous to talk to her about FASD, but I guess it's time." I looked at Jeff; he nodded.

Heidi left in search of Clare, and I leaned my head on Jeff's shoulder. "I'm so tired."

"I know. Me, too." He stroked my cheek.

"It's right to tell her now?"

"Yeah, it is."

"What if she feels hopeless or labeled?" I was worried.

"Remember, no decisions based on fear."

"No decisions based on fear."

"It explains why things have been so hard. For her; for us. That it's not her fault." Jeff repeated what I'd said the night before.

"Right." I took a deep breath.

We sat there, eyes closed, breathing together in the pause.

After a few minutes, Heidi's door opened, and Clare's laugh faded when she saw us on screen. I searched her for clues of change: the hollow cheeks that had revealed her pain and desperation in the months before she left home were filling out; she wore a black headband, holding her long weave off her face. *We*

have to figure out a way to get her hair done in central Missouri,
I thought.

"Hi, love," I said, tentatively.

"Hi, Mom. Hi, Dad." She was speaking; that was good.

"Heidi said new puppies were born. That's exciting. How are the
dogs?" Jeff asked.

A glimmer of light flashed on her face. "They're good. I like one
named Nina a lot. I've gotten to hang out with her." Her face relaxed a
bit as she told a few stories about Nina.

"Clare, your parents have something to talk about if you're open."

Clare's eyes narrowed, but she said okay.

I took a breath and started in. "Honey, we got your evaluation
back from Dr. Rogers. Remember we went to see her for medication
in November?"

Clare nodded.

"She agreed with ADHD and anxiety. She also says you have
FASD."

Clare tilted her head. "Like Lucy?"

Heidi swiveled her chair to face Clare.

"Same diagnosis as Lucy, ARND. But it looks different for everyone. It doesn't mean it's the same for you as for Lucy."

Remnants of guardedness melted away; lines of fear replaced
them on Clare's face.

She leaned into me across the screen. "So, I have brain damage?"

"Well . . . yes. Your brain formed differently. That's one reason
things have been hard: math and remembering things and probably
much more." I focused all my energy and love at her. "You are still
exactly the same you, love. Beautiful, smart, and strong. We just have
new information to help us figure out what you need to make your life
work well."

Clare nodded and twisted her braids in her fingers. Heidi asked
how she was feeling, if she had any questions, but Clare's face was

blank. The news hovered at the surface; it would take a while to sink in.

"This must be a shock, babe." Jeff seemed to reach through the 793 miles across Texas, Oklahoma, and Missouri to her. "We're so sorry we didn't know before. We've made lots of mistakes and not understood what was going on for you. I'm so sorry." His voice cracked.

I reached over and took his hand. "We're going to figure this out," I said to them both.

"Okay." Clare's voice came out quiet, subdued.

Heidi offered, "How about you take some time on my computer to research FASD, and we'll talk about it again later?" Clare nodded.

"Be careful, though," I said. "Scary things pop up when you google FASD. But it doesn't have to be that way. Look at FASCETS, an organization that consults and educates around FASD, and the Minnesota Organization on Fetal Alcohol Syndrome, MOFAS, to start. They have great information." Heidi penciled down the sites, and Clare said okay. Suddenly, we were team Clare again, facing FASD together.

We continued weekly Skype family therapy, and Jeff and I visited Lake Ozark monthly. Our parents, miraculously, once again footed the bill. Clare settled in the predictable routine and controlled environment and the support of CALO's small school. Almost all CALO kids were adopted, many Black with White parents. She fit and leaned into the community. And she got an IUD, thank God. She'd moved to CALO before she could return to the clinic in Austin. I offered her FASD information bit by bit over the spring; she tried it on and came to own it.

By the end of the semester, Bynum had grown Lucy's joy and built her confidence, too; she was ready for more academic challenge. Also, she'd matured socially and emotionally to the point where typically developing kids began to separate—like a five-year-old, half her chronological age. She tried a friend's one-room schoolhouse over the fall, but it overloaded her senses and exhausted her. As Clare approached her January graduation, I decided Anna's school could meet all their needs.

I had a plan. Anna was furious. She liked her own space. Lucy and Clare's full-tilt exuberance embarrassed her. But the Monday after our trip to Missouri for graduation, we enacted it: Lucy and Clare joined Anna at Hillcrest School; Lucy in fifth grade, Anna in seventh, and Clare in a one-semester hybrid program with Midland College that the Hillcrest director and I had created. It offered Clare a consistent schedule and support transitioning to college, her goal.

Jeff's alarm went off at six forty-five each morning. He rolled over and kissed my cheek. As he started the shower, I stretched out and eased awake. By seven, I'd made our bed and opened Anna's bedroom door. She lay on her stomach with hair tangled around her and one pink foot stuck out from under her sunflower quilt. I rubbed her back. "Morning, babe. Time to wake up." Her head shifted on her pillow. Leaving her door open, I crossed the hall to Lucy's room.

The blue, gauzy fabric Clare and I had long ago danced on like a river in Vancouver hung over Lucy's loft bed, creating a safe cave for her underneath. I pulled back the fabric and singsonged, "Morning, honey." Moving her braids aside, I tickled up and down her back. She raised her blankie for a long sniff and sucked her tongue like a pacifier. Then she smiled her eyes open, rolled to her belly, and pulled the covers off, giving me full back-scratching access.

"Time to get up and get dressed for Hillcrest." I picked up the khaki pants and hunter-green polo she had laid out the night before. "Your clothes are on your bed."

She whimpered and returned my hand to her back.

"Got to put breakfast on the table, love. Meet me there when you're dressed." I turned on her music and crossed the living room to Clare. I paused after opening her door; she was really home. Simba clambered to his feet in the huge black metal kennel at the foot of her bed. He banged his tail from side to side in a full-hip wag. I swear he smiled. I smiled back. "Hi, Simba."

The top of a ruby-red scarf tied around Clare's long weave peeked out from a pile of covers. I sat on the edge of the bed and hunted for Clare's arm under the covers, then ran my fingers up and down it. "Hi, love. Hope you slept sweet." She exhumed her arm, and I kept scratching. "Time to get ready for Hillcrest and Midland College. Come eat and then walk Simba around the duck pond." I wanted to believe she'd get herself up—though her eyes hadn't opened—so I went to the kitchen. By seven forty-five, Jeff, Anna, Lucy, and three neighborhood kids were headed to Hillcrest in his truck. By eight o'clock, Clare had driven off to check in at Hillcrest before her first college class started at nine.

I drank up solitude from eight to three every day. Disoriented but gaining strength, like after a long bout of flu. Clare held it together. I waited with freefall nerves engaged as on a climbing rollercoaster—time slows down and pauses at the top, *things look beautiful*: ant-sized people walk clean-swept paths; swings spin into a sunburst, lifting, lifting, lifting. But I imagined the drop. Stillness and beauty swallowed up by a rush of adrenaline; stomach yanked into my throat; me clinging to the shiny, silver bar holding me in. But Clare embraced the reality of FASD and asked for help with money, time, and health—her biggest challenges. That was amazing. And enough. Still, bumps felt super scary to me: not caring for Simba—thirty minutes around the duck pond morphed into ten minutes out the back door into the alley; dating even though we'd agreed she needed stability first; complaining about Hillcrest and adding a YMCA afterschool job for cash. I tried to rest in the moment but scanned the horizon for lightning.

In April, I took a retreat, a break from my surveillance. Dry, dirty West Texas receded as I headed east (instead of my usual southwest path to solitude in Far West Texas). After a couple hours, the land greened and rose into mesas. I exhaled a bit, my body anticipating silence and beauty. Archbishop Desmond Tutu and His Holiness the Dalai Lama read *The Book of Joy* to me through my car stereo. I wound through oak groves, roadside bluebonnets, and pale pink buttercups, listening and laughing. They talked of meditation and centering prayer. I climbed the Texas hills, resonating with acceptance of inevitable suffering and possibility for joy. At St. Peter upon the Water—a center for spiritual direction and formation—I followed a creek, opening my windows to the trees and water's song.

Up at the limestone Quiet House, the smell of lemony rosemary greeted me as I unfolded myself from my car and shook the kinks out. The wind swayed long stalks of lavender, and I rubbed the leaves between my fingers to smell the sweetness. As I kicked off my shoes and rocked in a chair overlooking cottonwoods, a recent battle with Anna surfaced in my mind. She had yelled at Lucy when she'd caught Anna on the SnapChat app that Lucy knew I didn't allow. Anna had scared her. My stomach tightened, and I felt the invitation to breathe and look for life—my Easter experiment.

It had grown from a Lenten practice of praying with a life experience. Weeks before, I'd dropped into a memory of Jeff and Lucy at dinner: Lucy's quick smile, laugh, and silliness; her happiness, talking about Hillcrest, almond eyes deep and sparkling. My feeling the same awe I experienced at the sun's sparkle on a lake even knowing its shadowy depths. Gratefulness had welled up in me. The practice rooted the moment in me and brought my intention for the six weeks of Eastertide: only speak of joy, beauty, and life the girls and Jeff brought instead of my frustrations with them. I steered my mind toward Anna's tender heart and determination. Her funny, curious, creative self. A cool breeze swept over my skin at sunset as I wrote in my journal. I went inside and slept.

The next morning, I approached the Wounded Healers Conference name tag table. "I'm Lynn Alsup here for Wounded Healers."

"So glad you're joining us today." The smiling woman's name tag said Carol. She looked to be sixtyish—about fifteen years older than me with the same pale skin and greying hair. On a long silver chain hung a Celtic cross that shone on her navy-blue dress.

"I'm grateful to be here." I smiled back.

I found a seat, and Carol came to the front of the room. "Welcome to many old friends and some new." She smiled in my direction. "We hope today will nourish you, and you will share that with those you companion in spiritual direction." She invited the twenty-five participants to introduce ourselves and our hopes for the day. I relaxed into the familiar language of spiritual directors.

During morning talks about suffering in our world, I heard echoes of Desmond Tutu and the Dalai Lama and sensed the deep well my suffering had carved inside me. After a simple boxed lunch, I took a walk under a bright, blue sky until we gathered again. Carol told us to pair up and trust the Spirit to hold us gently as we shared with each other. I turned to a woman next to me whose wavy brown hair matched the warm tone of her skin and hung down past her shoulders. When she smiled, I felt her joy. She introduced herself as Felicia.

We chatted a bit as Carol shuffled papers, then began. "I'll ask some questions and offer a few minutes to write responses." Questions appeared on the screen behind her: What are the wounds for which you seek healing? How did they come? After five minutes of journaling, she put up another: How have you felt the Healer at work in your life? After the third—How might your life be different if your wounds were being healed?—I journaled until the pressure of the pen stung my middle finger. Carol asked partners to take turns sharing answers.

"You go ahead," Felicia said.

"I should warn you I've had some intense years. I feel pretty raw and probably can't censor myself." My face turned pink.

"If you can't be raw and honest among spiritual directors, where can you be?"

I nodded and let go as I read. "I seek continued healing from my childhood sexual abuse and the trauma I've experienced raising my children. And whatever makes transitions and chaos as hard for me as it is for my girls."

Felicia asked if I wanted to say more, and I gave her the nutshell version of my parenting experience. We continued: How have you felt the Healer at work in your life?

"Definitely through life with Clare beginning in Vancouver when I remembered my sexual abuse. Discovering HeartPaths and a universal sense of God. My spiritual director, Eunice, and counselors along the way. Also, returning to yoga a few months ago. I long to love my children and husband, Jeff, well, and I can't without release in my body, mind, and spirit." I read a quote I'd scribbled down that morning: "*Discovering the true self is essential because the false self cannot love,* by Susan Pitchford."

Felicia's eyes never left mine. She nodded and leaned toward me, receiving it all. She said that I had walked quite a journey and had many gifts of support. I agreed. As I talked about my healing, I felt its roots deepen and spread in me.

I finished my turn with, "How might my life be different if my wounds were being healed? I could love myself, the Sacred, and others more freely—release fear and self-protection. I could relate to myself and others as we/they truly are. My body would be healthier, freer. My marriage could heal and enliven." Longing and hope surfaced in me as I spoke.

"Sounds like deep pain and woundedness. And deep hope." Felicia asked if she could touch my shoulder and reached over to connect.

I paused to feel the warmth of her hand. "I believe suffering hollows out space in us to be filled with an equal measure of joy. Richard Rohr says both deep love and deep suffering lead us to the Sacred. My children have been the source of both."

Carol invited us to switch listeners when we were ready, and Felicia shared her woundedness and healing. We moved back and forth between her speaking and my responding like the gentle, steady rhythm of a seesaw. It offered strength and joy.

When we all finished, Carol put two quotes up: *The wound is the place where the Light enters you.* Rumi. *At the core of your most painful experiences, perhaps more than anywhere else, you will find the seeds of your awakening.* Pema Chodron. "Sacred wounds are the place where the light enters," Carol said. I liked that term: Sacred wounds. Suffering and the need to bear it *had* awakened me to healing, freedom, and intimacy with the Sacred.

I spent the night after the retreat on my own in the Quiet House. I called Jeff before bed, and he said he'd let the girls stay up late and zombie out on screens and junk food. There would be chaos when I returned—the price of going away. My frustration boiled.

In the morning, I turned to my intention for Eastertide. What did I celebrate about Jeff? I put pen to paper: *He accepts things as they are, likes alone and quiet, builds and fixes things, is curious, committed to being the best father, husband, son and brother he can, loves music and outdoors, goes along with my adventures, supports me following my path, is comfortable in any world, does dishes and bedtime, opens to new ideas, loves God, teaches others, reads, listens to NPR, loves me no matter what without stopping, understands new technology, has a strong body, loves my body, is conscious of healthy food and the earth, sings old songs, is faithful, quick to forgive, works hard even at things he doesn't enjoy, his coffee, openness to psychology and mystery, faith in me, deep respect for me, wants to snuggle even though I'm not snuggly, reads great books to Lucy, lives half his life at the barn with Anna, accepts and supports Clare's friends and passions, loves my friends, his good drinks, consents to no big TV, welcomes animals, takes walks with me, his kindness, loves lakes, rivers, and mountains, is real with people, loves hammocks, lives more simply than he has to, knows the bigness of the world, moved to Vancouver, his honesty even when it's slow in coming, humility, green eyes, he dances, listens, mourns. . . .* After eighty lines, I ended with: *Wow. And that's just this morning's list.*

I drove home thinking about my list, committing to focus on it. In my mind, I composed an email to people across our twenty-five years together, asking what they appreciated most about Jeff. Back home, I ordered handmade paper from Etsy, printed the lists as they dribbled into my inbox, cut and glued, sewed a binding. I remembered why I married him, that I liked him as well as loved him, and the beauty of our story woven through with so many people and places. After a month of work, I presented the Book of Jeff to him on his fiftieth birthday. He cried when he read it.

In June, Clare turned eighteen. As we celebrated her, I wept. We had gotten her to legal adulthood alive, with a high school diploma, without a baby, and in relationship with us. A miracle. Something began to uncoil in me. I had done everything I could. Now she would call the shots. We'd spent six months not plummeting over the peak of the rollercoaster; maybe we could move on to a new ride. From roller coaster to, say, bumper cars. Each behind our own wheel. I took off my seat belt, crawled out from under the shiny silver bar, and walked along the edge to the ladder to get my own feet back on the ground.

The Neurobehavioral Model

As I reoriented, I wondered, *What is my work to do?* Two things had fundamentally transformed me: education around FASD, especially the FASCETS Neurobehavioral Model, and contemplative practices—spiritual direction, centering prayer, art meditations. The latter felt like breathing to me; they flowed from my core. I began to offer group practices to my places and people: Yoga Sanctuary; Kamiposi Art Gallery, where I did kundalini yoga; Breaking Bread soup kitchen; Midland Unitarian Universalist Church where my friend was minister.

The social worker in me had been offering my FASD research in bits for a couple years: training first Bynum, then Hillcrest staff; to friends of friends afraid and overwhelmed by kids with challenging behaviors; to therapists and some of their adoptive families. Zealous to make FASD known and smooth the road for other families, I needed more training. Jeff booked a June flight for me to Portland, Oregon, for a FASCETS three-day training with my eye on the Training of Facilitators yearlong program, starting in November.

The bright-blue, early morning sky held an underlying threat of unusual heat as I walked out of my Airbnb in Portland. I passed the shuttered doors of a flower shop and tattoo parlor, glancing at a sexy cop costume in the window of a lingerie shop in the not-quite-gentrified neighborhood. I crossed Highway 405 on the pedestrian overpass and made my way through the definitely gentrified Pearl District past bike shops and sushi restaurants to the Mark Spencer hotel where FASCETS held trainings.

Julie, the workshop facilitator, and Wendy, who'd handled my reg-
istration, met me at the door to the basement conference room. They
stood side by side, petite White women with matching short, curly
hair—one blond, one brown. They welcomed me with a name tag,
binder, and smiles. I found a seat at one of the gray tables, smooth and
modular, set in a V like geese flying north for the summer. Small tran-
som windows at street level hinted at the world outside. I wanted to
take off my shoes and pull my feet crisscross in the chair, but I didn't
know these people. Instead, I crossed my legs at the knee and felt the
warmth of my thigh from my walk over. After a couple minutes waiting for the workshop to start, I stood up to get a cup of tea and avoid
the awkward *What do I do with my hands, eyes, words?* moments. I
grabbed a gluten-free breakfast bar from a tray outside the conference
room and thanked Wendy. Sitting again with my peppermint tea, I
licked sticky raspberry filling off my fingers. Pairs of people murmured. I deepened my breath and tried to relax my shoulders, release
my clenched jaw. *Can this really be all I hope: my home in the world of
FASD?*

I tuned into the chatter around me. Julie laughed in the hallway
with Wendy. Papers shuffled. The fluorescent lights buzzed. Each
table had blank white paper, markers, and a box of tissues. I scanned
the room, maybe thirty of us. Young couples and professionals, middle-aged folks and some who looked like grandparents. *What stories
lay behind those faces?* I could almost hear the weariness and fear of
the parents who'd come. I definitely felt it.

"Welcome." Julie stood at the front of the room. "I'm so glad you
are all here. It takes a lot to get away for three days, and some have
come far." Julie talked about confidentiality, where to find bathrooms,
and the agenda for the day, then invited us to introduce ourselves.
People shifted in their seats. I uncrossed and recrossed my legs and
took a breath.

A thin woman with straight black hair and pale skin spoke first.

"I'll go. I have a thirteen-year-old adopted son. Parenting him has always been a struggle. Last year we got an FASD diagnosis. The more I learn, the more I think my husband has it, too."

Julie nodded. "Many people learn about FASD and realize it's been part of their life for a long time. I realized my mother probably had it, too. It's very challenging. I'm so glad you're here."

Next, a woman with a broad stripe of turquoise in her gray, bobbed hair said, "I work in Canada at an FASD clinic and raise two grandchildren with FASD." My stomach clenched; I knew the Raising Grandchildren chapter could appear in my story one day.

When my turn came, I said, "I'm Lynn. A social worker and adoptive mother of three girls, two with FASD. My oldest was in therapeutic boarding school here in Oregon until about three years ago." My voice cracked, and I paused until I could speak without crying. I felt the heat and rush of an adrenaline dump, as if just introducing myself that way triggered the fight-or-flight response I'd lived on the edge of for so many years. "Sorry. It hit me landing in Portland last night— the first time since my husband and I brought her." As the plane had landed on the tarmac between the evergreens, my stomach had seized with echoes of dread, fear, and disbelief. "She's doing well now, I'm glad to say. I want to understand FASD better so I can help others understand it, too. I've offered trainings at my kids' schools and with their therapists, but if this is my work, I need more training myself."

"Thanks for your honesty. Everyone comes here from different experiences and seasons of life. We have a lot to learn from each other. Any feeling is welcome. Notice we have lots of tissues." Compassion shined in Julie's eyes. I smiled and worked to deepen my breath as introductions continued: foster parents, professionals from substance abuse treatment centers, parole officers, child protective service workers—places where people with FASD ended up without the support and understanding they needed. Sometimes even with it.

Near the end of the introductions, a young woman introduced

herself. "I'm Sunny and this is my husband, Doug. We have six kids." The room gasped. "I know, right? Four are adopted. Well, one almost but still in foster care. Then we have an older son with Down syndrome and one who's neurotypical. We're crazy, but we love it." She had loose curls like Lucy that rested on her shoulders, the same tan skin tone, and her eyes sparkled. She turned to her husband and asked, laughing, "Why are we here?"

"A few days away from the kids?" He shrugged and turned up a sly smile on his ruddy cheeks. We all chuckled, and the parents among us nodded. "No, seriously, we need to understand our kids better. And we are working with Child Protective Services to help train and support foster families, so we need to make sure we know what we're talking about."

I liked them. *Six kids and working, too? They are crazy, or I just feel lazy in comparison.*

We finished introductions and stopped for coffee, tea, and snacks. I smiled at the woman beside me; she kept her head down like me. I filled my mug with water and went outside to breathe a bit. The heat wave hitting Portland made me grumpy; I wanted to escape the Texas heat. But it was green and lush even in the basement atrium, so I drank in the moisture in the air and savored the bright pink and red flowers that grew in big pots around the courtyard. I lifted one arm up toward the sky and leaned over to stretch my side, then switched to the other. I bent over to touch my toes, glad no one spoke to me. I had no extra energy for that. We gathered back in the conference room after ten minutes. I slipped off my brown Birkenstock sandals and folded my legs underneath me in my chair.

Julie brushed a stray curl from her forehead and began. "Thanks again for your honest introductions. These three days can help us know we're not alone and feel the support community can offer." She introduced an exercise by asking us to grab a blank piece of paper. "Think about how your brain works." She paused. "Now draw a picture of it. No need for fine art, and there aren't any grades," she added to worried faces all around.

After five minutes of quiet punctuated by the rasp of hands sliding across paper and an occasional chuckle, she asked us to think about what our brains did for us every day and list some things beside our pictures. A slide popped up with examples: plan, organize, predict; use language; make decisions, manage money, plan time; manage emotions, adapt to changes; manage sensory systems. I'd never considered my brain. What it took to get me from the moment I woke up to right there in that chair. Afterward, a few people shared their work.

A woman in front raised her hand. "I'll go. This is my brain." She smiled and held up a picture of a circle with arrows pointing in every direction and stars bursting out around and in between the arrows. "The arrows show my thinking goes every which way, and sometimes my thoughts collide into great ideas—the starbursts. There's always a lot going on in here," she said, pointing to her head.

Julie handed the woman a piece of masking tape. "Mind hanging it on the wall behind you? That will be our brain wall." A few others described their brains—flow charts, precise and orderly; pictographs with different regions holding things they cared about. Mine was anatomical but crowded inside with storm clouds, lists, a calendar, and stars for inspiration. After five brains hung on the wall, Julie clicked to the next PowerPoint slide.

"This is a brain drawn by an eleven-year-old." The screen showed two rough, hand-drawn ovals. Straight lines made a tic-tac-toe symbol on one. Scratch marks squiggled across the other and marred its surface. "She said other people's brains were like CDs with clear, clean lines but hers was scratched up so the music skipped and got stuck sometimes. Notice the word *BAD!* in the middle?" Silence fell as we took it in. She clicked to the next image, a circle filled with dots, rectangles, roadways and what looked like jack-o-lantern teeth. "This is Jamie's drawing. He described it as gears. Some connect and some don't. Some get stuck and can't move at all." Looked like total chaos to me. *What did it feel like to try to understand or control yourself and hit a broken gear in your brain? What would Clare draw? Lucy?*

The last image was a faint outline of an oval with a two-inch hole burned through it and four other burn mark circles scattered around. A teenager had created it. She said her brain was full of holes. *Maybe her mom said, "Just think" like I had to Clare. Did people call her unmotivated, rebellious, or say she didn't try hard enough?* I felt my heart break in a new way—for my kids instead of because of them.

"It's a great exercise to do as a family. I've never seen two brain drawings exactly alike; we're *all* different when it comes to brain function. That's neurodiversity. What if we are all normal for ourselves?" Julie surveyed the room. "Everyone okay for about fifteen more minutes before lunch?" People stirred, took a collective breath, and nodded.

Julie introduced the reality that some brains functioned differently because prenatal alcohol exposure affected their formation and caused fetal alcohol spectrum disorder. That knowledge had compelled Diane Malbin to create FASCETS thirty years before. "Many other things physically change the brain, leading to other brain-based differences. So are FASD and other brain-based differences physical disabilities?" Silence.

"The foundation of the FASCETS Neurobehavioral Model is: *if* alcohol and other things damage brain cells, causing physical changes that affect brain structure and function, *then* FASD and other brain-based differences are invisible, physical disabilities/differences," she said, adding, "You'll hear me use the words disabilities and differences both during our time together. We prefer the language of difference instead of disability—we all have different abilities—and we also understand the word disability can help people acknowledge the physical nature of brain-based differences when behaviors are the only visible symptoms."

The weight of it hit me again. Like when I'd picked up the purple book in Angelle's study in Little Rock. People with FASD had physical differences just like a visual impairment or paralysis, except invisible. A memory flashed: me standing over Clare demanding she say her math facts. When she couldn't—maybe because the gears in her brain were stuck?—I had taken away gymnastics. It was as if I'd punished a blind child for not reading from the blackboard or a person in a wheelchair for not walking across the room. I untucked my legs and put both feet on the floor. I wanted to lay my head on the table and cry. I had made things much worse for Clare by constantly punishing her for things she couldn't control. Shame, grief, and regret filled me. And, in a way, relief to have time and space to feel it. I swam around in it as Julie looked out at us.

"Definitely time for lunch. You guys are a bit glazed over. Hearing these things can be hard. Please be gentle with yourselves. Take a walk, drink some water, stretch, breathe. Lunch is in the hallway. We'll meet back here in about an hour."

I ducked out of the room, grabbed a salad, and headed outside before I'd have to talk to anyone. After five minutes in the atrium gobbling strawberries, feta, and spinach, I put on my straw hat and climbed the stairs to street level. "Which way to the river?" I asked the guy behind the valet kiosk. He pointed east, and I started walking. I pounded the sidewalk past food trucks and coffee shops and home-less kids for fifteen long city blocks, wincing at the smell of urine in doorways. Pausing when I reached the river, I watched water flow and sparkle under the sun. A man sat on the bench behind me and fed pigeons. People jogged past with baby strollers. My heart beat like a drum; my mind cleared. Grateful, I received the river's calm and oxygen from the trees. Then I turned and hammered my way back uphill.

In the atrium, I called Jeff to check in. He picked up after one ring. "Hey, there. Glad to hear your voice." He sounded energized and happy to talk to me. Like always when I went out of town. "How's it going?"

"Good. Intense. I just walked to the river and back to burn off some energy. How are things there?"

"Smooth for now. Your mom's picking the littles up from art camp and hanging with them this afternoon. Clare's at work, I hope. I left her at home asleep this morning."

"Sounds good. Get any sleep last night without me?"

"Not a lot. You know I like it better with you in my bed."

"I know. Thanks for covering for me so I can be here. It's important. For me. And us."

"I'm proud of you, babe. You work hard for us all. All good here."

"You're the best. Love you." Man, was I glad we were friends again.

"Love you, too. Learn lots."

I arrived back in my seat in the air-conditioned room and drank the glass of ice water I'd poured on my way in while a trickle of sweat rolled down my back. When the woman next to me sat down, I asked how her lunch had been.

"Good." Strands of gray escaped the ponytail at her neck, and red, blue, and purple beads glimmered on the cord attached to her glasses. "Nice to have a break. I'm Trudy, by the way."

"I'm Lynn. I'm grateful, too. This is hard stuff."

Julie came in, and I turned and opened my notebook.

"I hope everyone got to relax a bit. Any questions about what we covered before lunch?"

A young, Latinx man in blue jeans and a starched white shirt raised his hand. "I work in juvenile detention, and my kids have so many labels plastered on them: delinquent, oppositional defiant, ADHD, addict. The list never ends. Isn't FASD just another label?"

"That's an important point. Labels can limit, for sure. But when we identify the underlying cause of behaviors, we can support in more helpful ways."

"That makes sense. It's maddening to build relationships and explain consequences but have no effect on kids' behavior. Offer interventions that work, and I'm all for it." People murmured agreement. I guessed we'd all tried lots of things that didn't work.

"Absolutely. If traditional methods don't work, we need a different approach. We will definitely brainstorm accommodations," Julie said. "First, another question. What if any brain change equals behavioral symptoms?" She clicked a new slide onto the screen. It said different sources, similar symptoms. I picked up my pen. The slide's image looked like an umbrella flipped inside out by a strong wind. At the top of each spoke was a word: Alcohol. Drugs. Tobacco. Traumatic brain injury. Genetics. Illness. Trauma. The handle of the inverted umbrella pointed to a box that said brain function, memory problems, executive functioning, processing. "In some ways, it doesn't matter *how* a brain was changed but *that* a brain was changed. Neuroscientists say a TBI can cause personality or behavioral changes. We know emotional trauma changes brain structure. As can a lack of oxygen at birth. The FASCETS Neurobehavioral Model addresses any brain-based condition with behavioral symptoms. That's why we say brain-based differences to encompass it all."

As a social worker, I knew about motorcycle crashes that caused TBIs and disability payments. I thought about a friend's son who had developmental disabilities after the umbilical cord wrapped around his neck in labor. Veterans with PTSD sometimes behaved like different people when they returned from war. My thoughts drifted to Anna's first therapist who suggested a PTSD diagnosis for her from life with Clare. And we knew she'd been exposed to diet pills in utero. Was this all about *Anna*, too? Trudy shifted, and I glanced over. She looked at her paper but didn't write; she grabbed a tissue. I scribbled in my notebook as Julie continued.

"We'll focus on fetal alcohol exposure as an example. Alcohol is a neurotoxin—meaning it kills brain cells—and a solvent, so whatever amount of alcohol a pregnant woman consumes passes directly to the fetus without any barrier. But the fetus is infinitesimally smaller and can't process it. Alcohol, though it is legal, is the most toxic substance known to the developing fetus and can lead to much worse outcomes than exposure to nicotine, crack, heroin, or methamphetamine." She paused in the silence that submerged us. "Some doctors say it's okay for a pregnant woman to have a drink, but the science doesn't back it up. Alcohol exposure doesn't affect every fetus severely, but we don't understand how the complex variables work together to make some fetuses vulnerable to a small amount of alcohol and others not. Genetics, environment, and developmental stage of the fetus all compound as factors. Drinking alcohol while pregnant is always a game of Russian roulette."

The air in the room thickened, dropping a heavy blanket over us all. Many women's faces had gone blank and steely. They were far away in their own minds and experiences.

"We also know low levels of paternal alcohol consumption lower sperm count, affect sperm quality, and can lead to trouble conceiving and miscarriages. Higher levels increase the risk as well as impact brain size, heart condition, and cognitive and motor abilities after birth."

"Wow," someone said with a sigh.

Julie plowed on. "Consider in America, eighty percent of people reportedly drink alcohol; fifty to seventy-five percent of pregnancies are unplanned." She let that sink in. I imagined college campuses, twenty-something bars, and young professionals with money to burn; people and places where alcohol and sex were braided together night after night. "FASD isn't a women's issue. Or an addiction issue. It is a public health issue."

Mercifully, she let us have a break. A hush swallowed the chatting that had filled the room and hall at lunch. It felt more like a wake: somber and subdued with tragedy and loss standing in the corners.

When I walked outside, heat smacked me in the face. I stretched my shoulders, bent over, took a few deep breaths. Back in the coolness inside, I rifled through the tea box to find a small, green envelope of mint tea. At my table, Trudy seemed as if she hadn't moved at all.

I looked over. "That was rough."

She turned her full attention to me and cocked her head as if deciding what to say. When she spoke, it echoed from deep places. "I drank when I was pregnant with my two girls."

I sat back, took a breath, and drew up compassion into my face.

"I didn't know. We all had wine or cocktails every night back then. No one told me. I would never have hurt my babies on purpose." A tear rolled down her cheek. "I don't know why I'm telling you this. I'm sorry."

I picked up a blue box of tissues and handed them to her. "Must be why these are here." I smiled. "No woman wants to hurt her child; we're all doing the best we can."

"Thanks." She pulled out a tissue and wiped her nose. "My youngest had a rough go but made it through school with lots of support. She just had her second child, a beautiful boy." She smiled a bit at the thought of him. "Her first son, Tommy, is three and already trouble. Can't sit still or follow directions. The preschool says he has ADHD. But I know she drank on weekends before she knew she was pregnant. As soon as she found out, she went all hippie-natural, but she was eight weeks along by then. Do you think that could have hurt him?"

It seemed like Julie somehow heard Trudy's question and clicked to the next slide: a wormy-looking sperm pointed to an egg that looked like a bullseye in the first column of a table. The next column showed differentiating cells in the middle of a circle. Then, an amoeba-like figure grew and took shape across the other columns until a body curled in the fetal position emerged and then stood to fill the last column. Underneath the pictures, scattered, shaded rectangles held names of body parts and systems. The graph was labeled Continuum of Effects and had a reference of Keith L. Moore at the bottom. I reached over and touched Trudy's arm.

"Maybe we'll find out," I whispered as Julie began.

"This graph helps us see how an embryo and then fetus might be affected across the span of development in utero and beyond. The gray horizontal bars show what develops at each stage. Alcohol exposure can affect anything developing at the time it's introduced as well as anything that develops after that. Notice the central nervous system develops from one to two weeks after conception through age four. By seven weeks, the heart, lungs, limbs, ears, and eyes are all well into development, and the fetus has two-thirds of its brain and central nervous system. This is the time when many people find out they are pregnant."

Silence, like in the moments between lightning and thunder, charged the room. I looked at Trudy and tried to fill my eyes with the sadness I felt for her.

"Many people know about fetal alcohol syndrome—FAS. It includes specific facial features from exposure between days eighteen and twenty-one of gestation. Right here." Julie pointed to a column with what looked like the bumpy arm of a prickly pear cactus at the top. I jotted down a note. "But more than ninety percent of people affected by fetal alcohol have no visible signs. Still, they may have many effects in other areas of development." *Click.*

She showed us two brothers sitting next to each other in front of a blue backdrop, Olan Mills Portrait Studio style. The first had been diagnosed with FAS as a baby because he had the facial features and had received many supports and accommodations along the way. The second, with no facial features, hadn't been diagnosed until he was in a psychiatric hospital as a suicidal teenager. The invisibility had made him much more vulnerable. The last slide looked like Hollywood Squares with a Black man, Asian girl, blond-haired White woman, a baby, and an old man. It said, *Remember that most often . . . there are no facial features.*

Julie looked out at most of us slumped in our chairs except for Sunny and Doug, whose pens hadn't stopped. I had one leg bent with my foot flat on my chair; my chin rested on my knee. We looked like a room full of people who had been traveling for days, stuck in an airport a long way from home. She said, "Let's finish up." I let my foot fall back to the floor and straightened in my chair. A few people nodded and pushed themselves back up to their full heights. "Our foundational premise is brain-based differences are invisible, physical differences. Brain changes equal behavior changes. One last question for today: Can you suspend your disbelief if you have any? Try on the FASCETS Neurobehavioral Model and see if, by the end of the workshop, it fits?"

Flashbacks

At the end of day one, I walked toward my apartment as if in a trance. So much information, grief, and pain. Climbing the steps, I unlocked the door, went inside, and fell onto the bed. But a swarm of bees buzzed inside me. I filled my water bottle and headed back out and up Burnside Road toward Washington Park. A friend had told me I had to see the park that was just up the street from my Airbnb. I realized before long that *up the street* meant *up a small mountain*. Buses and cars chugged past me, blowing out exhaust and honking. As the road steepened, I cussed my friend under my breath.

"Beautiful flowers," I panted, passing a woman watering and snipping in front of her flower shop. Fifteen minutes later, my GPS said turn left, and I ducked into a forest of giant evergreens. Coolness descended on me. The shelter of the forest. *Okay, it's worth it.* The path wound through the trees up and up and up. "Would have been nice to know the park was vertical. Up the side of a mountain," I mumbled as I trudged into an open space. I stood in the shade of a tall Douglas fir and looked around—a rose garden in full bloom studded with pink, red, white, orange, even deep-purple flowers. Then closed my eyes and took a deep breath, inhaling the sweet smell under the high, scorching sun. I pulled my water bottle from my backpack and sucked a long drink, letting water spill down my shirt. Teenagers, young families, older couples all laughed and chatted while they wandered the rows and rows. I strolled along, all my attention on petals, stems, and thorns around me. An overlook opened to Portland spread out below with Mt. Hood on the horizon. I had crossed that mountain to take Clare to New Leaf.

"Beautiful, isn't it?" a woman said a few feet away.

"Yes. It is," I said, nodding.

"The heat is weird. Makes it a bit hazy but still, the mountain is magnificent."

Magnificent and treacherous, yes. I held onto the metal barrier and looked out. She talked about roses, Mt. Hood, and all the people out and about. The conversation died down, and I turned away, grateful to recede back into my body, out of my mind. I walked uphill toward a map of the park alongside faded-green tennis courts.

"Whoa," I said out loud. "Hundreds of feet up to the Japanese garden?" *Not today.* I was spent. I turned myself downhill toward my apartment. Below the rose garden, a violin hummed slow and steady. A young man in the grass pulled his bow across the strings. It held me: the music, the green, the coolness of twilight coming on. I walked around a large rock a bit away from the musician and sat on the ground out of sight. I took off my backpack and felt the warmth of the rock against my back and took a deep breath.

"Thank you," I whispered, "for bringing music and beauty. For soft grass and a rock to lean against." I connected to the Mystery, without words, just breath and awareness. Then I got up and thanked the man and his violin. He nodded, smiled, and his notes followed me down the path through the trees.

I made it to the Mark Spencer the next morning in time for a cup of English breakfast tea and a blueberry muffin before Julie invited comments and questions that had arisen overnight. Then she directed us to the day's PowerPoint. "These 'red flags' increase the possibility that brain differences might underlie challenging behaviors. Some are complex risk factors, others outcomes. Not all people who experience these have brain-based differences, of course. But if a couple exist, and things aren't working, it's helpful to investigate." The list included adoption, foster care, involvement with the legal system, multiple mental health diagnoses, and school difficulties. I winced. Red. Red. Red. My kids had three out of five.

"The Neurobehavioral Exploration Tool helps us clarify how someone's brain functions because each person is unique." She clicked to the first of nine primary characteristics on the tool—developmental level of functioning—saying a person might function socially and emotionally more like a person half their chronological age but have advanced development in other areas like speaking, reading, or sports. That's when my flashbacks began.

I saw myself on Deidra's front step two years earlier. September Texas heat absorbed by the concrete had seeped into my legs and bottom as Deidra and I watched our kids scooter up and down the sidewalk. Weariness hunched my shoulders. I had said I couldn't bear to buy the Fisher-Price Little People toys Lucy wanted for her ninth birthday. Her toddlerhood seemed to have lasted seven years. When Julie moved on to sensory systems, I saw Clare on the floor of her Dallas bedroom, a hair dryer blowing full force, full heat inches from her face, calming her. I heard Anna yell at Lucy for chewing too loudly. Felt the tension that squeezed my body during battles with Anna over hair brushing. The same feeling I got walking into Cinergy movie theater. I raised my hand.

"I want to run and hide when I step inside one of the movie theaters in town. Music blares, and arcade machines beep, whistle, and click. Lights flash overhead in laser tag catwalks where kids run and scream." I looked past the turquoise-striped hair in front of me and up at the ceiling, squinted my eyes, and receded into myself as if I were there. "The smell of hotdogs, popcorn, and nachos blasts me." I covered my nose. "I always choose our other movie theater—old school with dirty blue carpet and an air hockey game with a faint *whoosh* and *clank* if someone plays." My shoulders relaxed, and I smiled. "Maybe *dunt, dunt, dunt* as Pac Man gobbles a fuzzy creature. I'm much happier there. That's about *my* sensory issues, yes?"

Julie's head bobbed along with mine. "Great example, Lynn. You're accommodating your own sensory needs. And avoiding overwhelm and meltdowns, I bet."

Maybe my brain works differently, too. Maybe everyone's does. I had to stand up and stretch. Give the bees buzzing in me again some space. I slid my chair back and shoes off and padded to the back of the room. I swayed a bit while Julie talked about number three: nutrition.

"Many people don't know they're hungry or full because of frayed connections in the brain. Also, many need more food than others because a disorganized, inefficient brain uses lots more energy for daily tasks. Think of a poorly insulated home leaking energy, so the a/c runs all the time." Every few minutes someone raised a hand and talked about experiencing exactly what she described with clients or family members. Heads nodded, people commiserated.

Julie pressed on to language and communication effects. I sat back down as she taught us the word *confabulation*. Stories grew from a kernel of truth but got twisted along the way when a brain filled in holes left by spotty memory or communication issues. In the end, the person didn't always know where fact and fiction diverged.

I raised my hand again. "I definitely experience confabulation in my family. I just told a teacher that my daughter wasn't a reliable source of information and to please let me clarify things." Sunny and Doug laughed and nodded. Julie smiled.

"I get that. Also, I want to point out the judgment in that statement. Unreliable sounds like a character flaw, and we're talking about can't not won't. What's a better way to say that?"

My face flushed and defenses rose. What I'd said was accurate; I *never* knew what was true. And I heard her challenge. Julie smiled—compassionate, funny, positive, and real. She'd told us the day before she had two adopted girls, one neurotypical and one neurodivergent. She was a physician's assistant. She lived this life, too; I trusted her. I needed to stretch into the Neurobehavioral Model.

"I hear you. I could use the word *confabulation* and describe her brain differences."

"That would be an amazing way to educate and advocate. Which falls on us often as parents who have educated ourselves about brain-based differences. We often know more than anyone in the room. Including providers."

I wrote *confabulate, educate, advocate* in my notes and gave myself a break. I was there to learn, after all.

Julie turned back to the slides. "To finish up language and communication differences—sometimes people can look or listen but not at the same time. Looking away might mean listening harder. Let's look at these PET scans."

My mind was doing flips. I fidgeted and leaned forward onto an elbow as she clicked through four images of brains lit up with red, blue, and yellow in distinct and distanced parts. They looked like weather maps of storms moving across a brain.

"These show brain centers at work when someone sees a word on the page, then hears it spoken, then generates a response, and finally answers it out loud."

In my mind, Lucy sat across the brown pine planks of our dining room table and stared after I asked her a question. Her face turned angry when I asked again in different words.

"I'm thinking," she growled. "Don't ask me another question."

"I thought saying it another way might help."

"Stop talking!" she yelled.

Was her brain processing the whole time? Slowly transitioning from one center to another? What about Clare's constant "I don't know" and "I don't remember"? Had I taught her to answer me that way because it was better than getting yelled at for "ignoring" me?

My mind stayed on Clare as Julie talked about memory. A brain might access memories sometimes, but at others, connections crackled like a stereo with frayed wires. *That explains knowing math facts one day and not the next.* "One of the complex brain functions necessary for learning from consequences—memory—might not work reliably for someone with brain-based differences," Julie said.

When she added, "Looks like time for tea," an audible sigh of relief escaped us.

"Hallelujah," one man said out loud.

I spoke again. "It's amazing to hear you describe my kids and explain the chaos and confusion of our life. And exhausting," I smiled.

"I'm so glad. For the amazing, not the exhausting part," she added, laughing.

I climbed the atrium stairs to take a quick walk before it got too hot. Turned right to make a square city block. At the corner, I turned left instead of right again, though. An old gray stone church with a tall steeple and red door drew me across the street. I sat on its smooth gray steps and watched a breeze bend and shake a yellow clump of daisies. Oak leaves above me danced in the wind. I breathed better on that step. My experience of what I called God had changed. I hadn't been to a church building in years. But the old symbols of connection still reached into the deepest parts of me. I pulled my phone out of my pocket and called Jeff. In a rush, he said all was well. When we hung up, I felt sad not to have connected.

I returned to the conference room, ready for more flashes of memory and insight: taping coins to envelopes to teach coin values, years attempting to make reading an analog clock tangible, Clare not anticipating outcomes or making wise choices. All these because of challenges with abstract thinking, not laziness, stubbornness, or meanness.

We landed on the eighth primary characteristic: executive functioning. "I think of executive function like the chief executive officer of an organization, the CEO. Organizing, planning, coordinating, making links. It's the highest-level brain function happening way up in the frontal lobe." Julie tapped her forehead, and I flashed to Dan

Seigel's hand model of the brain and the idea of "flipping your lid" we'd learned at New Leaf Academy. "It is almost always affected in FASD and other brain-based differences."

I leaned back and let my focus go soft on the floor. My heart and mind opened. Because of their brain differences, our kids needed support to think things through, plan, create or choose an environment that brought peace and success in life and relationships. Even *when* they could access their wise minds, they couldn't always function as their own CEO. I felt the surge of *Aha!* Parenting through an attachment and trauma lens had been vital but not *enough*. Not enough to keep our family together. To keep Clare out of residential placement number two. Because we still demanded she organize her life and act neurotypical; get out of her wheelchair and walk. Another wave of guilt, shame, and regret slammed me. My insides shrank, shoulders caved around my heart. I felt small and constricted.

"Is it even possible for our kids to make it in the real world?" Sunny questioned. I heard the ache in her voice.

"Yeah," Joseph, the juvenile probation guy, said. "You've described a person who doesn't fit. A train wreck waiting to happen."

"Maybe if we all still lived on and worked the land. More hands on, less complex," said the woman with the turquoise stripe.

"My friend says if the end of the world came, her daughter would be one of the survivors." I quoted Angelle's words. "She runs like the wind and sees everything—more instinctive than cerebral." *And Clare: adaptable like a chameleon, like a wild animal at times.*

Julie looked at us each in turn. "You're on an interesting track, and it's where we go next." *Click.* "Strengths are primary characteristics, too. Looking for strengths and accommodating brain function can lead to creative solutions. Like a young man with FASD who loved to build Lego and models, brilliant with his hands and spatial intelligence. His parents connected him with an architecture firm that hired him to build models of their projects. He thrived. It fit his strengths perfectly and didn't require things his brain couldn't do. People with brain-based differences can be amazing artists, musicians, forest rangers, mechanics, athletes, childcare workers, parents, salespeople, counselors, teachers. Anything that fits their unique strengths. It's all about fit between brain function, environment, and expectations. And accommodations, of course." Her words pumped more oxygen into the room. Some hope floated around as we broke for lunch. I ate at my seat, listening to a woman Julie had invited to tell her story.

Rhonda, a local college professor, looked a bit older than me with my same blue eyes. "I love FASCETS." She smoothed back her blond hair. "A three-day training a couple years ago changed my life. At this point in day two, I realized I had FASD." *She had FASD? This together, successful woman?* She said she'd come for one of her children but recognized herself. As a kid, she had struggled in school and with friends. Fought with her parents. Gotten into drugs and run away from home. Eventually, she lived with her grandmother in a rural town in Oregon. The small town saved her, and a special teacher helped her make it through high school. I pushed my food away and leaned onto both elbows on my table, holding my face in my hands. I stared at her as she continued.

"I somehow made it through college after six years. I wanted to be a teacher but couldn't pass the math part of the exam for the certificate. You know FASD and math." She laughed. "So I decided to get my master's; you don't have to do math for that. Then I could teach in college. And that's what I do now. As well as wrangle my three children and husband." Talk about knowing your strengths and building on them. What a brilliant accommodation: graduate school.

"I never knew why life seemed so much harder for me than everyone else. I worked harder than anyone I knew. But things constantly unraveled. Because of FASCETS, I know why now. I'm not a bad person; I'm neurodivergent; I have brain differences."

I was amazed. And full of hope. Julie took her last bite, wiped her mouth, and stood. She thanked Rhonda and squeezed her in a hug. When Rhonda turned to go, she walked to the corner of the room and tried to push a locked door open. She looked up, turned back, and bumped into the table. "Still don't remember where I am in space," she chuckled. *Was her face pink with embarrassment?* She hurried out the open doors she'd entered.

After lunch, Julie touched on secondary and tertiary symptoms of brain-based differences: frustration, anger, sadness, crises, failures. She showed a black-and-white cartoon. A man in a suit sat in a field across from a big oak tree. Leaning forward onto the desk he sat behind, he touched all five fingers of each big hand together. He had a giant nose, a mustache, and a dimple that made it look like he was smiling. In front of him stood a line of animals—scruffy dog, seal, fish in a bowl balanced on a stump, elephant, penguin, chimp, and blackbird. The word bubble over his head said: *For a fair selection, everybody has to take the same exam; please climb that tree.* The room popcorned with "ahs" and "ohs." I shook my head and grimaced.

"Some challenging behaviors of people with brain-based differences are natural responses to the constant stress of a poor fit between a person and their environment. Our one-size-fits-everyone world. They are results. Not primary characteristics," Julie said. "When we understand a person's unique brain function and accommodate differences by building on strengths," she repeated her refrain, "it often diminishes secondary and tertiary symptoms. Those behaviors that meet the criteria for the multiple diagnoses many people end up carrying."

I heard Clare saying she needed to kill herself because she was sad, scared, and embarrassed all the time. Saw her running away. The *pop* and the spider-webbed glass in our front door in Dallas as Anna, flaming red face, held the fist she'd used to break it. I saw their pain and woundedness instead of bad behavior. Grief swelled inside me and burned. *If only we had known all of this sooner. How different would our life have been?* I didn't think I could take much more.

Julie ended by simplifying trying differently rather than harder into nine starter strategies:

Stop fighting

Ask (What does the brain have to do with this?)

Slow down

Think younger

Observe without judgment

Show and repeat

Prevent (match expectations/environment to brain function)

Breathe. Deeply.

Be gentle with yourself

By day three, I was fried. We talked about the hard work of paradigm shifts, what the brain has to do to create new default neural pathways. To implement the Neurobehavioral Model would be a lifelong journey. When the workshop ended at noon, I picked up my social work continuing education certificate, exhausted to the bone. But I knew I couldn't go back to my apartment with my belly swarming with bees again. I had to move. I strapped on my backpack and hat and braved the heat, heading toward the Portland Art Museum, seven long city blocks away. I walked and walked and walked. The buzzing seemed to increase rather than dissipate. Maybe it just surfaced. Eyes on the pavement, I shoved the straps of my pack back on my shoulders as the pounding of my feet jiggled them off. At the museum, I reached for the air conditioning, the art, the smooth, white space to calm me. Beauty and clean lines to give shape and wholeness to the chaos I felt inside.

But it was locked. Closed at noon on Saturdays. I plunked down on the steps and held back tears. Some teenagers skateboarded up and down the wheelchair ramps. They looked homeless: dirty clothes, big backpacks, a skinny dog tied to the handrail. That made me sad. So much pain and brokenness in the world. Too heavy to bear. So I kept moving. Eventually, I turned back north toward my apartment—miles away by then.

Halfway there, I plopped into a downtown plaza folding chair in front of women of all sizes and colors preparing for an aerial acrobatics show. The sun still beat down, but as they performed, my body let go. They twisted, flew, and twirled on silks that hung from scaffolding. Families with small kids picnicked and played. I felt the familiar pang of sadness that our family time never looked like that. Someone was always overwhelmed or unhappy a few minutes in. But the strength and flow of the women acrobats seemed to sink me into a place of strength and stillness myself. My parenting road would not be easy; there were no magic answers, but at least I had the right map now.

I left Portland the next day for a week at home before heading to a Center for Action and Contemplation conference in Albuquerque, New Mexico. I was finding the balance I'd begun searching for twenty years before in Waco.

The first day of school in August brought release for me. A deep inhale, exhale, and letting go into solitude, stillness, and peace. I joined a retreat in September, excited to flesh out what I'd pondered since my first months of centering prayer in Dallas seven years before. *What did I mean when I said* God? *Energy and movement all around us? Creative force and Source we were all part of, connected to and by?* In *The New Spiritual Exercises,* Louis Savary had transposed the Spiritual Exercises of St. Ignatius through the science and cosmology of a Jesuit priest and anthropologist, Pierre Teilhard de Chardin. The creator of HeartPaths translated Savary's work into a nine-month retreat in daily life. We read, journaled, and meditated on the cosmic Christ six days a week and met by Zoom twice a month.

The first meditation asked us to go on an imagined journey to find

God and tell God what we wanted from the Exercises. I ended up in my mind at an adobe house in Taos, New Mexico, where I had gone for a weekend retreat the fall before. My inner self walked the sandstone courtyard and up steps to an arched dark wooden door. Knocking, nervous, I saw a shadow of a person open the door and invite me in. It felt safe and comfortable, entering the coolness of adobe walls and tile floors. I sat across from this God in front of a big stone fireplace. I said I wanted to deepen our relationship and be freed for more intimacy, oneness, feeling embarrassed and vulnerable. But I somehow knew God wanted it, too. The relief made me smile. I also asked for clarity about what my work was each day and how to let it flow out of me. I sensed I would receive it.

One morning the second week, I let Clare's golden retriever, Simba, outside and pushed the button to start the dishwasher. The house was quiet except for its hum. I walked down the white hallway to my bedroom. "Charlie Brown, it's just you and me." The tiny brown poodle had been with us since the summer of the psychiatric hospitals when Clare had to have him, and I'd given in in desperation. At his name, he stood on his hind legs and pawed at me.

"Stay out here, Charlie." He knew my meditation closet—my sanctuary—was off-limits. I'd claimed the second closet in our bedroom as soon as we'd moved in five years before. I had made a small altar on an upside-down, secondhand wicker cube in one corner, covered nail holes in the walls with a tapestry, and told everyone entrance was by invitation only. My bare feet sank into the soft cream carpet as Charlie's toenails *click, clicked* him across the room to my bed. I sat down, moved through a few yoga poses, then pulled my *New Spiritual Exercises* notebook from a brown woven basket. A piece of handmade turquoise-and-navy-veined paper marked my page. Journal and pen in hand, I began my daily practice to Charlie's intermittent barks at people passing by outside my bedroom window.

The meditation for the day was to picture Jesus at any age I wished standing beside me, eager to be with me, lovingly energizing and supporting my prayer. I closed my eyes. In my mind a toddler Jesus snuggled into my lap. I felt the weight of him on my legs and belly and the comfort of his small body in my encompassing arms—like I did with my young friends Zoey, Sid, and Levon. He fell asleep and grew younger. With the infant on my chest, the rise and fall of our breathing synced. Warmth pervaded my core, and my body released into rest and intimacy. His waking startled me. He seemed younger still, a newborn. In my mind I laid him in the crook of my arm, and we gazed at each other. I caressed his face like I had baby Anna's in early mornings. When he began to nurse, I felt my breast respond. The connection was profoundly physical. After a while, he switched sides and kept drinking. An awareness grew: I had enough to offer. The more he drank, the more milk I had. Abundance. My timer chimed to end the meditation, surprising and saddening me.

In my prayers each morning, I asked what my work was. Two mantras emerged: "Say the next true yes" and "I am the best thing I have to offer." *But who am I to offer anything to the world?* Teilhard taught awareness plus response equaled consciousness. I heard *Stay open each day* and *Say yes to one call at a time.* If I remembered that my story, not my expertise, mattered most to people, I would always have all I needed. I wanted to be brilliant at everything, always, but decided that showing up, even not brilliantly, trumped not showing up at all.

Midland Independent School District called me for an FASD training for their counselors, and I said yes with my PowerPoint informed by the FASCETS training in Portland. Jeff came as my personal IT guy because the technology made me shaky. Afterward, a line of people waited to talk to me: *You described a kid on my caseload. Why hasn't anyone ever told me about FASD? It all makes so much sense now.* I felt exhilarated. I'd made a difference for those kids. Those families. Those counselors. And I'd expanded beyond my role as mom back into the bigger world.

I couldn't shake a memory that had surfaced during the MISD training as I sat, trying to work on a sermon for the Unitarian Universalist Church I'd titled "The Power of Silence". Clare sat doing schoolwork in the sun across from me in our vintage yellow armchair from Dallas. I looked up from my laptop and took a deep breath.

"Clare, remember in Dallas when I told you you were broken?" She shook her head.

"Avis asked if Wilson could hang out with us one Friday night. You both must have been ten or eleven." Still no. "You wouldn't come out of your room. He sat in the blue chair in the living room, and I paced between him and your room, wanting you to engage." My back molars clenched. Shame burned from my belly button to my Adam's apple. "But you just read or wrote a story in your bed." She kept her eyes on me, cringing. "You wouldn't be kind or hospitable, put his feelings first, be a 'good friend.' One of my highest values. I was so mad." The lava of self-condemnation rose in me, knowing I'd caused her pain and destruction. She sighed and shook her head, embarrassed.

"Now I know you couldn't, not wouldn't. It was the end of a long week. Last-minute change of plans. You were so tired. I was, too. But it clashed hard with my values. I loomed over you, like I used to. You shrank, cowered. I growled at you, 'You are broken, Clare.' You looked at me, stone-faced. 'Something is broken in you; you need to pray God will heal you,' I said." I cringed, and my eyes burned. "You just disappeared into your covers. And Wilson didn't care. He played his video game. It was about you not performing for me. I'm so sorry." The tears came. So many tears. "You are *not* broken," I choked out. Her face was soft with forgiveness and kindness. "You don't need to be fixed or healed." I paused. "Well, we all need healing. You need it from me." My voice cracked again. The pressure felt like I held a whole ocean in my body. It pushed against my insides. Swelled. Sometimes felt like it would burst me open.

"But look at us now, Mom." Clare smiled at me.

"I'm so grateful for now." And I felt the grace she offered me. Space for my humanity, ignorance, fear, and mistakes. I *knew* it wasn't about not making mistakes; it was about making repair.

I gazed out the door to the orange blossoms on the trumpet vine that climbed the garage. A hummingbird hung there, then darted to the bright red flowers of the Texas Mallow plant, the only two blooms to survive the Texas summer. I heard the slight *whoosh* of its wings and remembered a quote I'd cut from the back of a Papyrus greeting card and propped on my desk against a picture of Clare taken the day after she came home to us in Waco: *Legends say hummingbirds float free of time, carrying our hopes for love, joy, and celebration. The hummingbird's delicate grace reminds us that life is rich, beauty is everywhere, every personal connection has meaning, and that laughter is life's sweetest creation.* I turned back to Clare.

"It's okay, Mom. We're okay."

"Thank you, love. Thank you for listening and forgiving."

Steady-ish

We fell into a rhythm as a family over the fall. Life was full but steady-ish. By our measure. Jeff and I balanced work, home, parenting, and marriage. Clare continued at Midland College and after school at the YMCA. Lucy became a Hillcrest cheerleader; the team was open to all, and she loved it. Anna rode horses and played volleyball. Her games corralled us into one space a couple nights a week.

There was a new coolness in the air, the sun sinking already at just six o'clock—I took a deep breath of relief as Anna jumped out of my front seat at the Hillcrest gym. She went from singing her favorite country song, blaring on my car radio, to banging the door shut without a goodbye or thank you. Her long ponytail swung across the black Libero jersey slung over her arm. She played from the back row, passing and digging to keep the ball in the air for her team.

I turned down the radio as Lucy gathered her things and climbed out. She smoothed her hunter-green cheerleading skirt and pulled the sleeveless top down to cover her belly.

"Thanks, Mom. You're coming, right?"

"I'll just park and come in. Thanks for the 'thank you.'" I looked over my shoulder and smiled. "Have your cheer bag?" Always the reminders. She had everything—green crinkly pompoms, big green bow. As she walked away, I called to her to have one of the Black girls on the team help her with her braids and get her bow on straight.

When I walked in, Anna ran from across the gym. "Mom, do you have my kneepads?"

"Nope. I told you while I was doing dishes to get them from the abyss of your bedroom floor." I felt my left eyebrow raise the way it did in defense or challenge. I *knew* Anna's ADHD knocked her brain off track between the kitchen and her bedroom. And she *couldn't* filter the whole chaotic mess to find what she needed and end up at school with it. But somehow, I had yet to let go of the expectation and help her.

"Coach will let me borrow some." She turned and ran back across the court. *Whew.* Always a relief when she didn't blow up.

The volleyball game started, and one by one my family came in to share the bench with me. First, Jeff in his khakis and brick-red pinstripe button-down walked in. He scanned for me and broke into a smile. *He is so handsome.* Those green eyes and olive skin, almost six feet tall. Sometimes that first glance still got me. He sat down and gave me a kiss. My mom and dad came in, and I waved them over. Mom always looked stylish—white leggings and a flowy, embroidered blue tunic that day. She must've had gray hair, but it had been the same highlighted blond ever since I remembered. Dad followed her, sky-blue eyes twinkling as usual. He smiled at me as they climbed three steps at the handrail and sat down.

"Hey, there. How're the girls?" Mom asked.

"Good. Anna's about to serve." I pointed to the back of the court as Anna smashed the ball over the net. The girl was so strong.

"Yeah, Anna!" Mom cheered. Anna grinned and ducked her head. She'd made me promise not to yell out her name—"That's so embarrassing!"—ever since swim team, but her Mimi could do whatever she wanted. They had a special bond.

During game two, Clare showed up from work to cheer her sisters on. She wiggled onto the bench in between Mom and me, waving at the teachers she knew from her semester at Hillcrest. When I asked about school and work, her face fell.

"I got my test back; I failed again. But I studied. I promise." She defended herself as if I were already yelling at her like in high school.

"I know you did, love. That must be so disappointing. I wonder how you're feeling." She had made the spring dean's list under the support of Hillcrest but opted out over summer and fall. Her grades had plummeted. A different schedule every day threw her off; four syllabi taxed her limited executive function skills. But she had to live it to learn.

I tried to watch Anna *and* talk to Clare, but my brain focused on one thing at a time. I felt Anna's eyes on me and smiled at her. She turned her attention back to the court in time to dive for the ball and catch it on her forearms as she slid on her knees across the floor. It flew over the net, and Hillcrest won game two. We all erupted into cheers, and I turned back to Clare.

"I'm sad. And embarrassed." She mouthed, "Please don't tell Mimi."

I squeezed her hand. "We'll figure it out, love. I know you can do it. We just have to find what works."

Anna and the team ran off the court and scrambled for water bottles and seats on the bench. The cheer coach moved to the first bleacher where she could mime cheer moves as Lucy and her team entered the court: pumping arms; slow motion, wobbly cartwheels; splits. One tiny powerhouse bounded into a cartwheel and back handspring. The team grabbed pompoms, looking proud. They spelled out H.I.L.L.C.R.E.S.T. and cheered. Lucy kicked a leg up. "Woohoo!" They giggled their way off the court. "Go, Eagles!"

Their opponents won game three and the match, but our girls were proud of game two. Anna crossed the court after the line of "good game" hand slaps with the other team.

"Did you bring my jeans and boots, Mom?" Her usual pink cheeks glowed red.

"I did. How about saying hi and thanks for coming to everyone." She looked sheepish and reached out to give Mimi and then Pop a hug.

"Hi. Thanks for coming." She wiped the sweat from her eyes with a tender smile.

"Sure, darling." My mom squeezed her back.

"Good game," Dad echoed Mom.

They waved to Lucy, still piled into a group of kids across the gym and said goodbye.

"Let's go, Dad. We're almost too late to ride." Anna porcupined from friendly and warm to nettled and threatening, quills up as usual with Jeff. He was her need and nemesis, as I had been Clare's; she invited him to heal as Clare invited me.

"Okay. Let's go." Jeff's patience astounded us all. He'd embraced attachment, trauma, and neurodiversity along the way.

Lucy walked up rustling her pompoms, beaming.

"See you later." I brushed Jeff's lips with mine.

"Home for our story before bed, Dad? It's okay if you can't." Lucy acquiesced to Anna's dibs on Jeff.

"I'll try, babe."

"Dad, we gotta go," Anna growled, and he followed her out.

Clare bumped Lucy with her hip; Lucy capsized. She caught herself just before her bottom hit the floor. They both cracked up.

I chuckled. "You two goofballs want to grab tacos on our way home?"

Because I knew the gifts and struggles of parenting kids with brain-based differences and a path to more peace and joy, I said yes to the persistent nudge to offer a support group. My social worker self wanted a central, private location and university occupational therapy students running a concurrent kids' group so parents could come. But that overwhelmed me. Instead, I posted a date for Rosa's Café on all my FASD Facebook groups and invited everyone in West Texas. I arrived early and ordered chips, salsa, and guacamole. My whole plan; my true yes. It was enough to launch Living Well support group: a monthly hour of guided conversation followed by an hour of neuro-behavioral training. My next yes delivered me to Portland's fall foliage and drizzle—making me homesick for Vancouver—immersed in like-minded community and the FASCETS Neurobehavioral Model for the first week-long intensive of FASCETS's Training of Facilitators.

I returned home inspired and energized, and Clare told me she'd added a holiday sales job to her YMCA work to make more money. Then she failed all her classes. She quit the YMCA over winter break, then realized her sales job ended after the holidays. She asked for help. I knew she needed a consistent school and work schedule to give her structure and a lighter school load. No race to graduate. We met with her adviser and chose two classes at the same time on alternate days, and she hunted for a new job.

As my understanding of neurodiversity deepened, I realized the Neurobehavioral Model spoke to all of life. Jeff's and my differences were brain-based, too. I rustled up training gigs and connections where I knew people with FASD ended up: adoption and foster care agencies, speech and occupational therapy offices, counseling centers, at-risk student programs, and mental health collaboratives. Kept Julie, my mentor at FASCETS, on speed dial for consults. I reserved tables at the Autism Walk resource fair and the Kids Mental Health Day at the library, handing out *Trying Differently Rather Than Harder*. And created my first business cards in almost twenty years. All the while, guiding meditation, praying, and trying to show up differently for my kids.

I sidled up to Lucy washing dishes at the kitchen sink one Saturday. Her frown made me check my mental calendar—an imprint of the Flo app that tracked her periods. Man, I wished I'd had one for Clare. No ovulation or menstruation happening, two things that wreaked havoc with Lucy's emotions and energy every couple of weeks.

"You look like a Klingon from Star Trek, your forehead is so wrinkled, Lu. Why are you scowling?" Instead of replying, she deepened the furrows. I should have clued in: she couldn't talk or reason right then. But I started a familiar conversation. "You can't hold the washcloth with two fingers and swipe at the dishes, Lu. You have to scrub."

"Eww." She looked like she wanted to vomit. "I *am* washing them," she groused. She didn't know *why* I used a *dirty*, *nasty* dish cloth to wash dishes. It was *disgusting*.

My defenses raised, I offered her a few minutes to get respectful and calm down. Then we could talk about it. I turned from the sink and focused on my breath as I picked up the quinoa. The tiny grains tumbled into the sieve like yellow sand. Water created valleys and built bumpy hills where it hit as I rinsed them. Breath and attention connected me to my superpower—curiosity. I turned off the faucet.

"Lucy, do you know what I mean when I say, 'get respectful'?"

She shook her head.

"Do you know what a respectful voice and face are like?"

Again, no.

Right, I have to teach her this abstract thing. When we both calm down.

I dumped the quinoa in a stainless steel pot and added four cups of water as she piled the clean-ish dishes on the drying rack. I noticed she *did* put everything upside-down to dry. Something to celebrate. That had taken a year of reminders. Repeat. Repeat. Repeat. She walked away as the *click, click, click* of the igniter lit the gas fire under my quinoa. I lifted the window above my kitchen windowsill collection of rocks, shells, and a succulent, and in floated a cool spring breeze. It spread the nutty aroma wafting from the stove. When I blended chickpeas with garlic, lemon, and olive oil, the fusion of smells grounded me. I walked into the living room.

"Lucy, I want to talk about respectful now."

"Uh-uh." She stood up and walked toward her bedroom.

"Lucia, don't," I warned. "I told you we'd talk about this. I gave you time." She had rounded the corner. Relieved when she walked back, I hoped it wouldn't be an all-out battle. That we both could stay in our wise minds long enough to talk about it.

I asked her to show me what a respectful face looked like. She tried, but the muscles in her face just contorted. I dropped down to basics: happy. She held her blankie up for a sniff to comfort and regulate herself. I waited. Then she smiled. Sad: frown. Mad: scowl. Mean: snarl that turned into a chuckle and grew into her signature giggle. I laughed, too. I scooted closer—game mode instead of fight mode.

I described how our dogs only understood tone of voice, not words. When I asked if she knew what I meant, she said yes, *but* they knew their names, too. I conceded that to her literal truth telling. Then hammered "stop" in a sweet and then a stern voice. To which one did the dogs respond? She got it.

"Say, 'Mom, I like you' in a nice voice."

"Mom, I like you," she said syrupy-sweet.

"Perfect. Now say it mean."

She did just like the kids on the Disney Channel she still loved to watch. Her eyes twinkled from behind her blankie.

"You can always say what you think and feel, Lu. It just matters *how* you say it. Am I making sense?" I checked in again.

"Yeah."

As an afterthought, I asked, "By the way, why do you hate washing dishes?"

She didn't even have to think. "You know how I hate walking through the wet bathroom at the swimming pool? Yucky water and squashy toilet paper on the ground?" She grimaced and I nodded. "It's like that. Putting my hands in dirty water and touching the squishy wash rag with germs all over it." She looked a bit green.

"Hmm. So if you used running water and a clean dish rag, you wouldn't mind?" *Could I really let her waste water like that? Definitely a values clash.*

"I'd still hate washing dishes, but it wouldn't be disgusting."

"That's fair. I hate washing dishes, too. But we can make it better for you."

She looked past me out the window at the familiar woman passing our house with her five dogs. I'd stretched the ten minutes Lucy could focus. And that was if she wasn't hungry, tired, thirsty, or upset. When I thanked her for talking, she jumped up to grab her phone and check her texts. We'd made it to the other side of one of the many confusing conflicts each day held.

Clare landed the front desk position at a local gym after a few failed experiments with other jobs. Her perseverance amazed me. When she broke up with yet another boyfriend and made plans to take Simba and move in with a friend, she asked for more help. She wanted a therapist to work through anxiety and relationships. I asked her and her friend to let me approve an apartment complex and help them plan how to support each other managing Simba, time, money, and health. We agreed.

Traditional counseling required remembering what happened each week and prioritizing what to talk about. Following through on therapeutic homework. I knew Clare's brain couldn't do that. But a counselor named Heather agreed to meet with us together and let me teach her about Clare's FASD. On our first visit, I asked Clare to describe anything in the office environment that distracted her. A humming refrigerator, fluorescent lights, the cold temperature. Heather offered a lamp and blanket. I suggested thirty-minute sessions the same time every Tuesday and Thursday instead of one longer session. Clare might remember to come and be able to stay focused. Heather agreed to check Clare's understanding regularly, not trusting nonverbals. Clare would ask Heather to slow down if she needed. I'd join them once a month to share what Clare had been anxious about that she might have forgotten to mention. Then Heather would remind her each week.

And it worked. I wrote up the process for a support group member: Therapeutic Interviewing and Interventions with a Person with Brain-based Differences.

Clare's computer savvy, friendliness, and extrovert energy propelled her to success at her job. She made A's in both her classes: victory! And had a move-in date for her own apartment just after her nineteenth birthday in June. Memorial Day weekend she stayed in Midland to work while Jeff and I took Anna and Lucy to the family farm.

When she kept her distance the night we got home, I felt the undercurrent of her stress and waited for her to talk to me about it.

"Morning, babe," I said as she bounced from her room the next day. Clearly on her way out the door. Something was off.

"Hi, Mom. I have a session with Heather, but can we talk when I get back?"

My stomach dropped. I said sure and asked if everything was okay. She brushed past me, chirped that it was now, and left. As Clare closed the front door, I sighed, whispered *Thank you for Heather,* and turned back to Anna and Lucy and the pile of kids bounding around.

"Who wants strawberries?" I walked into the kitchen to a chorus of *me, me, me, me*!

When I heard the front door open an hour later, I told Anna and Lucy I'd be unavailable, walked Clare to my bedroom, and shut the door. I led her to the love seat next to my bed. We sat knee to knee on a deep blue, purple, and turquoise rainforest—fabric my mom had splurged on for me. It brought me life. I looked deep into Clare's eyes and saw pain and fear beneath the Happy Clare face.

"What is it, babe? I'm worried."

"Something scary happened this weekend, Mom. But it's okay now." She smiled.

"What?"

"I met this guy at the gym. An older guy. . ."

I tried to listen like in a spiritual direction session—no judgment or interruption. The story confused me, but I didn't attempt to sort the details. That would detour me from the heart of the story; I was following a thread in a tangle of yarn. I sat back and sank into presence instead of inquisition. Clare was trying to tell me something important, and she needed my patience to get there. Her face changed: reddened cheeks, eyes wide, muscles contracted. The kids outside the bedroom ran and laughed. In the bedroom, the click of the spinning ceiling fan dotted the silence. I let Clare find all the pieces in her mind and put them in order.

"I'm trying hard not to confabulate, Mom. I want to tell you like it happened, but it's hard to remember. It's all jumbled up in my mind."

"It's okay, love. You're doing fine." I felt in my gut my worst fear had come true. She was so fucking vulnerable: couldn't predict consequences or plan ahead, didn't know who was friend or foe.

I put my feelings on a shelf in my mind and used all my mindfulness to stay present as she continued. She needed to say every detail. When she finished, I held her and rocked us both back and forth. Back and forth. Back and forth.

And our strength grew.

Walking the Labyrinth

On the last Saturday morning of August, I walked out our front door to join Jeff in the yard. I carried a spade, sand in a silver bucket, a water bottle perched in the sand, level balanced on top, and my phone snug in my back pocket.

"Hi, there." Jeff stood by a sculpture that had found us off Canyon Road in Santa Fe in July. Her creator had introduced her to us as Eleanor. She had a recycled steel train rail for feet, a five-foot silver pipe reached to her shoulders made of a metal smile that held a two-foot silver wheel atop the pipe. A large, upside-down gas cylinder hung as a bell from the top of the wheel into its center. I adored her. Even before I knew *Eleanor* meant "God's light." She would welcome people to enter the twenty-five-foot labyrinth we were building beside her.

A breeze blew past, and Jeff said, "It feels good out here this morning."

"I'm glad it's not too hot yet." I had our red patio umbrella off to the side at the ready for when the heat descended. "So grateful for cool desert mornings. Could you ever imagine I'd say that?" I looked at him in his blue jeans, T-shirt, and boots. *Huh. I'm in love with him again. Wow.* As I found my place in the circle, we talked about how glad we were to be in this day, using our bodies and time for this project, together.

I'd said, "Let's build a labyrinth" one Friday back in April as if it were a weekend project. We'd xeriscape our piece of the desert and offer a contemplative path to the community. Jeff engineered, measured off the biggest circle we could fit in our front yard, and dug it out with a skid steer. We filled it with caliche to keep weeds from growing. He piled the dirt alongside the circle to create a small berm. I had visions of prickly pear cactus; yellow, red-tongued desert birds of paradise; and spring poppies and larkspur growing there one day.

Morning sun glittered off flecks of silver and gray in the pink, crushed granite paths. A few feet of white caliche still showed at the center where I sat on that Saturday morning in August. With Jeff supporting my vision. Working alongside me to make it possible. As usual. I pulled my phone from my pocket.

"What do you want to listen to? Acoustic guitar? Jerry Jeff Walker?"

"Whatever you want. I'll be coming back and forth with the wheelbarrows of granite. Want me to bring over some bricks first?"

"Yes, please." Gray bricks outlined the path of nine circuits that wound around themselves in the pattern of the Chartres labyrinth, my favorite. I picked up a gray brick and measured two feet from the last line I'd laid. I was six rows in from the circumference with only the three smallest circles to go. Slow and steady. Many twists and turns. One brick leveled at a time. Like our life.

Jeff's shovel scraped the granite into the wheelbarrow. I hummed along with the music and rhythmically placed and leveled brick after brick. Anna and Lucy wandered in and out of the house. I stretched my leg out long, took a sip of water, and looked around for Jeff. Sweat wet his shirt, and his biceps bulged under the weight of the full wheelbarrow. It crunched the ground as he pushed it to the spot I'd vacated to continue the path. I'd already brought my umbrella near for shade, but still it was almost time to get out of the heat. After dumping the load, he walked to the shade of a tree between our sidewalk and the street and took a long swig from his water bottle he had balanced on the red slanted roof of our Little Free Library. A green, wrought-iron garden chair invited people to grab a book and have a rest.

I looked down the street as I wiped my forehead with my gloved hand. A pickup headed our way. Lots of people had watched us live our unusual life out loud in our front yard over the months of building the labyrinth. It had taken getting used to. The red truck slowed. Heat coming off the road mixed with the smell of exhaust. The earth beneath me added the tangy scent of minerals to the air. I imagined the driver's view: a middle-aged woman in beat-up overall cutoffs with short-cropped hair and dirt on her face hunched over pale, crossed legs.

The window rolled down. "What y'all doing? Making a maze?"

"Not a maze." I lifted my head. "A labyrinth. A maze has dead ends and tricks, but a labyrinth always leads to the center if you stay on the path. It's a walking prayer or meditation. Just a few more bricks and it's finished. Please come by and walk it soon."

He chuckled and drove on.

The Barefoot Church invited Eleanor to sing and walked the labyrinth together the next morning. When the weather finally cooled, our community served coffee and brunch in the front yard by fire pits for neighbors and friends. An introduction to Eleanor, the library, and the labyrinth.

I had a neurobehavioral training coming up for the Texas Tech Psychiatry medical students and staff. As I sat at my desk preparing, my eyes and mind drifted to the quartz geode sitting there. A cave of white into purple crystals—like mini stalactites and stalagmites—surrounded by rough gray rock. *What's inside is beautiful and sometimes invisible,* I thought. I was distracted. Mostly by Clare and her most recent class at Midland College. She wasn't able to process fast enough or shift quickly between hearing, thinking, and speaking. Her picture sat behind the geode: one year old, just home from Haiti. Her enormous smile, mouth wide open, one eyebrow raised, laughing. The light reflected in both eyes and off her tongue like she was partly made of stars. That passion.

I picked up my phone and looked again at a picture she had sent me of an exchange between her and the professor.

Clare,

I am deeply concerned about your performance and chances of success in this class so far. Yesterday, when I asked you one of the most fundamental questions regarding US government—"How many branches of government are there?"— you could not answer. You tried to say, "I don't know" and "I don't remember," and this caused me great concern. . . . I don't know whether you just froze when I asked you the question, but I did ask you several questions in succession, going from the more complex to simpler and more basic questions. You could answer none of them. I am more than willing to talk to you about this and to work with you. I know that you learn differently than many students, but I am concerned if you are learning anything at all. Please do not take this note as a criticism but as an indication of my desire to help you succeed. On the other hand, I'm not going to give you a passing grade that you did not earn.

Below was her handwritten response:

Professor Brown,

I appreciate you taking the time to write me regarding my performance in your class. Please know that my ability to answer questions on the spot in class has almost nothing to do with my knowledge of the subject, the extent of the content I am retaining, and has everything to do with my learning style and own personal limitations. As per the accommodations Shep sent out at the beginning of the course, instructors are not to individually call on me for questions during class. I know that these are the areas where I struggle the most educationally, and my accommodations are there

*so that my instructors can also understand, and I can be the most
successful in my courses. Please let me know if you need another
copy of my accommodations or if you would like to go over them
together. I appreciate your concern and look forward to a smooth
remainder of this term.*

    Clare

I was so proud of her. I'd posted it on my FASCETS cohort
Facebook page so they could celebrate her self-advocacy with me. But
he continued to shame her, call on her; I felt protective and angry but
honored her desire to take care of it herself. Her first year of college,
she'd asked for help with every email—write something and read it
to me. I'd ask questions to clarify what she meant. Offer words she
couldn't find in her mind. She'd rewrite and read it to me again until
she communicated what she meant. Now she did it on her own. When
he accused her of plagiarism because she wrote more articulately than
she answered in class, she rewrote her work in his presence and got
an even higher grade. By the end of the semester she made an A in
the class.

I finished a heavy schedule of trainings in January and
February and was preparing to offer my first three-day FASCETS
Neurobehavioral Model training in April. I took a break in Clare's
newest home, in view of the duck pond, three blocks from where
Jeff, Anna, Lucy, and I lived. Jeff and I owned the little house and
were about to rent it to Clare and Isaac, her boyfriend of the last nine
months. We really liked him. He was respectful, kind, and kept a copy
of *Trying Differently Rather Than Harder* on his nightstand. We didn't
want them to entwine their lives together so young, but they'd sought
our advice and then made their choice. We wanted to support them.
And help Clare avoid the rent hikes and racism she'd encountered at
the apartment complexes around Midland.

I wore paint-splattered jeans and held a long pole attached to a roller. Spring morning sun glided onto the paper covering the wood floor. My chin tilted up, and the pain lodged in my shoulders from a week's incessant painting twinged as I looked at the ceiling. I dropped the pole, interlaced my fingers behind my back, and opened up my chest. I folded forward and touched my toes. And began again. I pushed the roller to cover the periwinkle blue with eighteen-inch strips of desert white and dusted my hair with paint flecks alongside my many short strands of gray. I paused a few strokes in and took a deep breath of awe: *how the hell had things worked out, again?*

I had been terrified when Clare decided to move out in June. Out from under our roof and my sight. She had unloaded her things into two different apartments since then. Bought and sold a dining room table and washer and dryer. Added two roommates and lost one. She still needed lots of extra time and hands-on experiences to find her way—like she had used red, blue, and yellow plastic bears to count in preschool, she used her body to slowly make sense of things. We'd sorted the bears into neat rows for the moment. We celebrated her grocery shopping, getting to work on time, and paying bills. Her growing executive function skills amazed me.

I meditated and blessed the space as I painted. *May it be a place of love and safety. May Clare and Isaac love each other well here. May she continue on her path of healing and wholeness. May we all.*

I refilled the paint tray and began again. The fresh paint had almost overcome the blue. Only a muted shadow remained. I rolled into the paint and back up the tray, crackled up and down the ridges of the pan to let some loose. Raised the roller to the corner of the wall for two or three strokes, down and up again. Lowered the roller back into the paint tray. This was the last coat for what would be Clare and Isaac's bedroom. *May there be peace.* I tapped my phone to wake it up and touched the purple podcast icon to find *On Being.* Krista Tippett's voice entered the room, beginning a conversation with Lawrence

Kushner on *Kabbalah and Everyday Mysticism*. They talked while I painted.

Krista said to Kushner, "I actually want to quote you to yourself again, because this is so wonderful: 'This is a definition of a mystic. A mystic is anyone who has the gnawing suspicion that the apparent discord, brokenness, contradictions, and discontinuities that assault us every day might conceal a hidden unity.'"

"Yeah, I like that a lot. It's the closest I've come to nailing it down," Kushner said.

I liked it, too.

I thought about how Clare had led me to this mysticism. In a way she'd been my spiritual director all along. I pulled a brush from the Ace Hardware plastic bag where I'd wrapped it to keep it from drying out. One more coat around the edges, and I'd be done. I opened the east window, exchanging paint fumes for fresh air and hopefully not too much dirt gusting around. A line from *The Alchemist* by Paulo Coelho popped in my mind: "Show me where there is life out in the desert. Only those who can see such signs of life are able to find treasure." *He's right. We found it.*

Krista read a story from Rachel Naomi Remen as Remen's grandfather told it to her:

In the beginning there was only the holy darkness, the ein sof, *the source of life. And then, in the course of history, at a moment in time, this world, the world of a thousand, thousand things, emerged from the heart of the holy darkness as a great ray of light. And then, perhaps because this is a Jewish story, there was an accident, and the vessels containing the light of the world, the wholeness of the world, broke. And the wholeness of the world, the light of the world, was scattered into a thousand, thousand fragments of light, and they fell into all events and all people, where they remain deeply hidden until this very day.*

Now, according to my grandfather, the whole human race is a response to this accident. We are here because we are born with the capacity to find the hidden light in all events and all people, to lift it up and make it visible once again and thereby to restore the innate whole- ness of the world. It's a very important story for our times.

And this task is called tikkun olam *in Hebrew. It's the restoration of the world. And this is, of course, a collective task. It involves all people who have ever been born, all people presently alive, all people yet to be born. We are all healers of the world. And that story opens a sense of possibility. It's not about healing the world by making a huge difference. It's about healing the world that touches you, that's around you.*

Finding the hidden light and lifting it up to make it visible again. Healing. That had been my work all these years with Clare, Anna, and Lucy. Their work with me. I felt the heat of the afternoon sun flood the room, bouncing off the white walls. I realized Hillcrest let out in fifteen minutes, so I pulled the plastic bag apart, tucked the roller and brush inside, and squeezed the plastic around them to keep the air out until next time.

I finished the whole house just in time to leave for a FASD confer- ence in my beloved Vancouver—my place of belonging. Jeff, the girls, and Isaac to join me afterward for a holiday.

I got off the sky train at Commercial Drive after the first day of the conference. I needed to walk and walk and walk. I marched down Commercial Drive to Venables, our street from seventeen years before. Twenty-four blocks at a clip the way I had after night class at Regent College. I thought about a session that day that covered FASD as a whole-body condition. It made sense. Everything developing in utero when alcohol was introduced could be affected. That was everything in a human body: eyes, ears, lungs, heart. Allergies, asthma, irregular hearts, and endocrine issues—all possible effects of FASD.

Darkness and rain fell as I passed new restaurants and hipsters. Also, the old community center preschool and favorite coffee shops. I ducked into Sweet Cherubim and grabbed a samosa like little Clare and I had eaten for lunch so many times. Past my old co-op grocery store, I climbed up the hill to our house on Venables. Pausing to look, I felt our life there begin to swirl around me. I imagined Clare at the window on our futon in her rainbow-striped Hannah Anderson pajamas. Jeff coming out in his raincoat with our dog Tress on her leash. I could hear—no see—the echoes of our life.

I turned up Grandview toward Jodi and Michelle's apartment where I was staying. I saw preschool Clare out of the corner of my eye. Down a side street, she sat on the sidewalk where she'd refused to ride her bike any farther. I'd walked away, weary and hoping she'd follow, as she screamed. People had come out of their houses to make sure the abandoned girl was okay. I passed the park where men played bocce ball on summer mornings. Clare swung there with her full-face smile and laughter. On the street where our friends Mary Sue and Dawn had lived, wisps of Clare and Dawn careened through the front yard, screaming like banshees. I pulled my hood closer and held my brown bag at the bottom as rain turned to snow flurries outside our Regent professor's old basement apartment. Inside—overflowing with Regent students—a much younger me was tucked into a nook with Clare snuggled up next to me. I passed our old church, and the echoes stilled as I continued on to Jodi and Michelle's.

I took off my shoes inside the door to their apartment, set down my soggy samosa, and hung up my raincoat. Jodi sat with their gray, lop-eared bunny in her lap waiting for me. Michelle had a late shift at work.

"I saw Clare everywhere just now. Eerie. Like shadows of our life when she was three."

"I remember those days. We marveled at you guys as parents." She stroked the bunny's soft fur.

I looked at the ceiling, transported again to the past. "She is fire, Clare."

"I can't wait to see her."

"It's amazing, Jodi. She's beautiful. Fully alive. Whole. You know, people always say *they are so lucky* about us adopting the girls. Honestly, it offends me, even though I know people mean well. The girls have transformed me into a much better version of myself. I am not a savior; I am a mother. Doing the best I can."

Jodi nodded. She got it. She'd been watching all along from near and far. She put the bunny down and walked into the tiny kitchen. I pulled myself up on the counter as she washed dishes, and we talked theology, justice, peace. I went to bed that night full of gratitude.

By the end of the conference, I was eager for my family. Done hearing about animal experiments and academics. My brain hurt. I planned spacious days with lots of down time; the kids couldn't handle more than one outing a day. After I moved my things into the house we'd rented, I drove to the airport. Outside baggage claim and customs, I craned my neck to glimpse around the corner. Clare's short Afro and bright smile came first. She scanned for me just as I did for her. She quickened her pace and called out, "Mom!" as she neared in her signature black leggings and short T-shirt. Isaac was close behind. I opened my arms wide to them.

"Welcome to Vancouver! It's one of my favorite places on earth. I know you're going to love it, Isaac."

His face glowed. "I know I will, too."

Lucy ran up and joined the hug. "Mommy!" I laughed. I'd only been gone five days. The small braids I'd put in her hair before I left hung past her shoulders and engulfed my face. She was almost as tall as me.

Jeff and Anna rounded the corner together as our pile of four moved off to let other passengers through. Jeff smiled his quiet smile and reached over to hug and kiss me.

"Hi there." He ruffled my short hair.

"Can you believe we're all in Vancouver?" I squealed a bit and bounced on my toes.

"It's so good to be back."

"Hi, Anna."

She slid under my arm to my side and looked up with a small smile. I ran my hands through her ponytail and pressed my cheek against hers flushed pink. "Hi, Mom. It took forever to get here. And Clare and Lucy are so embarrassing in airports." They did like to dance, laugh, and talk to strangers together.

"I'm glad you're here now. Let's head out. I can't wait to show you around."

Over the next three days, we visited all our favorite places. We drove to the UBC campus and parked at St. Andrews Hall. Walking to our old apartment, we told Isaac stories of Clare's running through the courtyard in ladybug boots and watching trash trucks. We wandered to the UBC rose garden overlook onto Howe Sound—the scene that had taken my breath away with Christine eighteen years before. Clare, Isaac, Lucy, and I walked through a grove of thirty-foot evergreens and down the hill to Spanish Banks beach while Anna and Jeff drove down to meet us and take us to Granville Island Market. It buzzed with shoppers, sellers, and diners; sensory overload. Jeff picked something for Lucy when her brain shut down. Anna refused to eat. She loomed over us as we sat by the water with the pigeons joining us for lunch. Definitely time to head home for a rest.

Anna huddled under her covers in the room she and Lucy were sharing. She stared at her phone, watching Heartland—a Canadian series about a young woman with a gift for healing horses. Anna escaped to Heartland anytime she wasn't at school. A few hours later, I went to check on her. The covers jumbled over her like a giant tortoise shell.

"Hey, babe. Thetena just got here, and we're going to walk to the sushi place with her to pick up dinner. Want to come?"

"No. I'm staying here watching my show."

"I wish you'd come."

"I didn't even want to come to stupid Canada."

I sighed. We argued about how long she had been in her room and *we're only here for a few days.* She wouldn't budge. I took a breath and remembered to stop fighting and ask, what if the brain has something to do with this? New places and transitions challenged her; she preferred one circuit between her bedroom, school, and barn where she knew what to expect.

"Okay. You can have a bit longer." I turned to leave, and she disappeared back into Heartland.

"It's just us," I said to Thetena at the bottom of the stairs.

"Anna's not coming?" Thetena asked.

"Better for us to give her some more time alone." *Was it better?* I spent all my time talking about awareness and response to brain-based differences, and I still didn't always know what to do.

"Can I come? I love Vancouver!" Lucy's exuberance cheered me and made Thetena laugh.

"Of course." We walked out the door into the lush green of Vancouver. Lucy skipped along. When we returned, we sat around the table into the night laughing and telling old stories over dark chocolate, wine, and sushi.

Our last day in Vancouver, we slept in and then rode the ferry to Bowen Island with Jodi and Michelle. We walked up to the Snug Cove Café for hot chocolate, coffee, and lunch, almost filling the place with our group of eight. Afterward, we drove the winding road up to Rivendell Retreat Centre.

I leaned over to Jeff. "Remember scrambling up this hill with backpacks on going to Rivendell from the ferry?"

He smiled. "Fondly."

The retreat center grounds flourished, mature and abundant. Much different from the nascent landscaping there when Jeff and I had contemplated becoming retreat hosts at Rivendell's inception fifteen years before. We peeked in a newly built cylindrical chapel. Huge windows invited the evergreens to prayer. Meditation cushions and candles encircled a small altar someone had laid at the center of the room. I wanted to spend the day in the silence and beauty there, but that had to wait for another time.

A small opening led through the trees down the hill behind the chapel; we all entered the forest. Ferns reached out to us. The air was thick with oxygen. Light filtered through tall firs onto the soft, mulchy ground. Lucy and I lagged behind the others. We studied the leaves, tree trunks, and enormous black slugs that pushed themselves across our path. But then even she went on without me as I marveled. I emerged from the trees to find her scrambling down a hill to a labyrinth laid in the grass.

She called up to me, "Can I walk it, Mom?"

I smiled. "Sure." I made my way to a bench overlooking the labyrinth and sat with the yellow flowers there. Farther down, Anna played frisbee with Jodi and Isaac in a field. Clare and Michelle sat in the grass. Jeff lay on a picnic table, shielding his eyes to search for shapes in the clouds. I watched Lucy's slow, deliberate walk through all the turns on the path. When she entered the center of the labyrinth, she dropped to her knees and bowed down. Then she raised herself, spread her arms wide to the sky and looked up with a smile. All instinct and unfettered joy.

That. That was it. What I'd been fighting for all these years: the alchemy of support and freedom that sparked abundance. Transforming us all.

Acknowledgments

Many people vital to my story are missing from the pages of this particular story. I wanted, even tried in the early days, to include everyone, but—as writing teacher extraordinaire Tania Casselle taught me—this story is just one slice of the cake that is my life. It demanded editing again and again to uncover the kernel that fell and sprouted here. Beloveds in Waco, Vancouver, Dallas, and Midland who are not in these pages, please know I hold you in gratitude and love.

Jimmy and Janet Dorrell have lived and worked in Waco, TX for over thirty years now, introducing countless people to a beautiful life of broken barriers, celebration and justice. I eagerly walked through the door they swung wide for everyone—"Black, White, Brown, rich, poor, educated on the streets or in the university" as they say—and grew into a truer, better version of myself. Thanks for introducing me to Haiti and India, forgiving me all my young arrogance and foolishness, and always welcoming me home under the bridge.

My spiritual director, Eunice Cheshire, has accompanied me over the last ten years with grace, wisdom, tears and laughter, helping me keep to the path of Love and reminding me not to take myself too seriously. Miraculously, I've grown to trust Life in her care. The good folks at HeartPaths Centre for Spirituality, where I met Eunice, walked me through the climax of this story and continue to nurture my spiritual life and work. For that I am exceedingly grateful.

FASCETS founder, Diane Malbin, transformed my life through her work on behalf of people affected by Fetal Alcohol Spectrum Disorder. I am deeply honored that she willingly received this book and held my story with compassion and wisdom, offering her reflections and encouraging readers to pick it up. May my work honor hers and contribute to the healing she began.

I am deeply indebted to the extraordinary team at FASCETS—Nathalie Brassard, Stacey Chart, Melissa Elligson, and Suzanne Emery—as well as Diane Malbin, Wendy Temko, Nancy Hall, and Nicole Branson who've moved on. Some stars must have aligned the day I picked up "the little purple book" *Trying Differently Rather Than Harder* in Little Rock, Arkansas; my first trip to Portland confirmed I'd found my people. This community based in respect, mutuality, curiosity, humility, and dedication embraced me, educated me, and invited my own contribution to the beautiful work of celebrating diversity and creating a world where all can thrive.

My Write to the Finish family midwifed this book. So many thanks to our fearless leaders Sean Murphy and Tania Casselle, and my writing partners Kristen Barendsen, Trudy Goodman, and Anahi Russo Garrido. With compassion and candor, you taught me to write and got my butt in the chair to do it. Sean spent two years asking me great questions, scribbling in the margins and making me laugh. All the while weaving a life-long friendship. I'm lucky to have such a teacher of storytelling as well as sensei to follow to the cushion. A deep bow to you and all in our Sage Institute sangha as well.

Early readers who gave generously of their time and feedback include Eileen Devine, reading for adoption and the Neurobehavioral Model, Carrie McKean, offering insight on honoring adopted kids and their stories, and Kristen Barendsen on all things writing. Heather Mason read as Clare's advocate to balance out the power between us a bit and discern what to include and what to leave out—my due diligence as I navigated telling my story that is deeply interwoven with Clare's. I am so grateful. My squad of cheerleaders—Mom and Dad, Kim, Angelle, Deidra, Natalie, Jodi and Michelle—asked for the first draft, celebrated each step and encouraged me to the end.

I feel privileged to have joined the She Writes Press community where publisher Brooke Warner lifts a megaphone for women telling stories that can change our world and holds it with kindness and boldness. She believed my story mattered and offered her expertise to shape it for the marketplace, embodying her call for women to support women so all voices can be heard. Also, my editorial project manager Samantha Strom, along with Krissa Lagos, Julie Metz and Jennifer Caven teamed up to create a finished product far better than one I could have birthed alone. So very many thanks.

This journey and all those I've taken wouldn't have been possible without the support of my parents, Bill and Susan Granberry. My champions. I've taken you places you never would have ventured on your own, and you've stayed right by my side all along. You have taught me generosity, love, and beauty. I am proud to be your daughter and to call you friends. And, truly, no one has a better Mimi and Pop than your very lucky grandkids!

Clare, Anna, and Lucy are the heart of this story—courageous, generous, strong young women with whom I am lucky to walk through life. I pray the fires we start bring light and life to the world and the errant ones get stamped out without too much destruction. Thank you, my loves, for always forgiving me and teaching me how to love; for making me laugh and letting me cry. And thanks for letting me tell our story.

Jeff, you are the beginning and end of every day. You've said a thousand yeses and brought my crazy dreams to life with your steady hand, not to mention IT skills. I still want to waltz across Texas with you. Your curiosity and openness drive me forward; your goofus-on-the-roofus-ness makes me smile. What an extraordinary life we've lived together these thirty years. Thank you for loving me so well and loving our girls with your whole heart.

About the Author

photo credit: Chelsie Hodge

Lynn Alsup is a social worker, spiritual director, and meditation teacher. Her three extraordinary, neurodivergent daughters led her to FASCETS, where she now trains parents and professionals in the Neurobehavioral Model—a paradigm that fosters the celebration and accommodation of neurodiversity. She lives with her family on the edge of the Chihuahuan Desert in Midland, TX, building resilience and joy through writing, yoga, wide-open spaces, and snuggling her four-legged rescuer, Bryn the Bassador.

SELECTED TITLES FROM SHE WRITES PRESS

She Writes Press is an independent publishing company founded to serve women writers everywhere. Visit us at www.shewritespress.com.

Emma's Laugh: The Gift of Second Chances by Diana Kupershmit
$16.95, 978-1-64742-112-0
After Diana's first child, Emma, is born with a rare genetic disorder, Diana relinquishes her to an adoptive family, convinced they will parent and love Emma better than she ever could—but when fate intervenes and the adoption is reversed, bringing Emma back home, Diana experiences the healing and redemptive power of love.

All the Sweeter: Families Share Their Stories of Adopting from Foster Care by Jean Minton. $16.95, 978-1-63152-495-0
The stories of twelve families who have adopted one or more children from the US foster care system, accompanied by topical chapters that explore the common challenges these families face, including the complications that accompany transracial adoptions, helping children understand adoption, relationships with birth parents, and raising a traumatized child.

Fixing the Fates: An Adoptee's Story of Truth and Lies by Diane Dewey
$16.95, 978-163152-577-3
Since being surrendered in a German orphanage forty-seven years ago, Diane Dewey has lived with her adoptive parents near Philadelphia—loved, but deprived of information about her roots. When her Swiss biological father locates her, their reunion becomes an obsession—and ultimately leads her to the answers, and peace, she's been seeking.

Not a Poster Child: Living Well with a Disability—A Memoir by Francine Falk-Allen. $16.95, 978-1631523915
Francine Falk-Allen was only three years old when she contracted polio and temporarily lost the ability to stand and walk. Here, she tells the story of how a toddler learned grown-up lessons too soon; a schoolgirl tried her best to be a "normie," on into young adulthood; and a woman finally found her balance, physically and spiritually.